Risks in the Making

CARE & WELFARE

Care and welfare are changing rapidly in contemporary welfare states. The *Care & Welfare* series publishes studies on changing relationships between citizens and professionals, on care and welfare governance, on identity politics in the context of these welfare state transformations, and on ethical topics. It will inspire the international academic and political debate by developing and reflecting upon theories of (health) care and welfare through detailed national case studies and/or international comparisons. This series will offer new insights into the interdisciplinary theory of care and welfare and its practices.

PREVIOUSLY PUBLISHED

Jan Willem Duyvendak, Trudie Knijn and Monique Kremer (eds.), *Policy, People, and the New Professional. De-professionalisation and Re-professionalisation in Care and Welfare*, 2006 (ISBN 978 90 5356 885 9)

Risks in the Making

Travels in Life Insurance and Genetics

Ine Van Hoyweghen

Amsterdam University Press

Cover design: Sabine Mannel, NEON Design, Amsterdam
Layout: JAPES, Amsterdam

ISBN-13 978 90 5356 927 6
ISBN-10 90 5356 927 8
NUR 741 / 756

Contents

Preface

> *Everybody's a mad scientist, and life is their lab. We're all trying to experiment to find a way to live, to solve problems, to fend off madness and chaos.*
> David Cronenberg

AIDS, gene crops, BSE, stem cells... In an uncertain society like ours we can never demand too much from science to provide conclusive solutions to these issues. Faced with prevailing uncertainties, we need fresh policy perspectives. This book reports on a journey through one of these current issues: the use of genetic testing in insurance. In an effort to find new openings, the book explores this from an empirical sociological angle – by studying the insurance industry *from the inside*. It explores medical underwriting practices and how insurers *make* insurance risks. I highlight the many experiments, oscillations and balancing acts insurers face in order to arrive at "proper" insurability rates, as a matter of *trial and error*. My own methodological approach also capitalises on this experimental character and, as such, the travel metaphor has been used throughout the book. By identifying insurance risk selection as assemblage work, the book creates spaces for negotiation on the insurability of people. From there, I make an appeal for "risk taking" in insurance in dealing with the uncertainties of genetics. Such "risk taking" might take the form of an experimental learning policy *during* the process of risk making. The book provides empirical arguments for this new policy perspective. It is an edited version of my Ph.D. thesis, which was defended at the Catholic University of Leuven (Belgium) in 2004.

Many people supported me during this trip. Special thanks are first and foremost to my thesis advisors, Rita Schepers and Klasien Horstman. They provided the essential moral and intellectual support, listened patiently to my doubts and enthusiasms and helped whenever I momentarily lost track. Many friends and colleagues offered invaluable advice and support over the years. First, I would like to mention my co-travellers of the Department of Sociology at the Catholic University of Leuven: Lesley Hustinx, Anja Declercq, Hans Neefs, Yota Mokos, Jaak Billiet and many others. The NWO-club – Gerard de Vries, Klasien Horstman, Rein Vos, Dick Willems, Ruth Benschop, Marianne Boenink and Myra van Zwieten – offered the kind of learning, disturbing discussions and new insights I sometimes desperately needed. My stay at the SATSU in York was equally stimulating in many respects. I gratefully acknowledge Andrew Webster for acting as my local supervisor there. Special mention goes to Femke Merkx. I greatly benefited from discussions about *our* insurance people. Also thanks to my co-experimenters in the “Ethnography of Genomics” group at the University of Maastricht. It always feels great to return home and reminisce about our travels in genomics world. I am especially grateful to all those I met in the world of insurance. I owe much to many people there, for guiding me through the insurance landscape and for co-exploring it and sharing their valuable insights. My sincere thanks to all the underwriters, medical advisors, actuaries, managers and board members for their cooperation. Furthermore, I could not have even started this journey without the Scientific Fund of Flanders (FWO), which created the financial conditions that helped launch me out into this world. Financial support to publish the book was provided by a number of organisations. Substantial funding was awarded through a grant from the Brocher Foundation (www.brocher.ch). I also received generous support from the Dutch Association of Insurers. This book also received a grant from the Netherlands Organisation for Scientific Research (NWO). I am deeply indebted to all of these organisations for making publication possible. I am grateful to Ton Brouwers who edited the text and improved the original. Most of all, I am grateful to my family, for being the cornerstone of this entire journey. My final and enormous thanks are to them.

Ine Van Hoyweghen
Maastricht, September 2006

1 Risky Business: The Collision of Genetics and Life Insurance

Genetics and Society

Genome mapping, genetic testing, DNA banks, reproductive technologies, pharmacogenetics – all of these reflect scientific breakthroughs and new opportunities in medicine that are both fascinating and disturbing. Over the past decade, the potential of genetics to help us understand and control health and disease in radically new ways has been widely discussed. Some observers view these spectacular advances as part of a larger process they refer to as "Genetic Revolution". Others raise questions as to its ethical, legal and social repercussions, suggesting that this genetic turn will lead to the creation of a genetic underclass.

The fear of genetic discrimination continues to be exacerbated by ongoing developments in genetic research. The Human Genome Project (HGP), a $1.9 billion global program to map and sequence all human genes, has been hailed as spurring a new golden age of medicine, notably with respect to the prevention, diagnosis and treatment of many major diseases. This molecular genetics, or "new genetics", allows us to understand which genes contribute to which diseases. Scientists say that currently there are about four thousand, generally rare diseases – like Huntington's disease, cystic fibrosis, and Duchenne muscular dystrophy – with so-called genetic markers that can identify people who are at risk of contracting them.

Prominent genetic researchers, such as Francis Collins, anticipate that it will soon be possible to test for a variety of susceptibility genes and consider appropriate prevention strategies. This will render medicine more "personalised", in part through the development of new "tailored" drugs (pharmacogenomics), and contribute to an individualised preventive medicine. Similarly, many experts claim that knowledge of genetic predisposition heralds the prospect of shifting medical practice from its emphasis on diagnosis and treatment to an exciting new era of prediction. For example, the European Commission foresees a genetic revolution in health care marked by a move towards prevention rather than cure (Commission of the European Communities, 2001: 6). Others view this recent focus on genetics as part of an already ongoing transformation from a clinical, complaints-bound medicine to a predictive, risk-oriented medicine (Horstman et al. 1999; de Vries and Horstman 2004). Since the 1970s, new disciplines in medicine, like modern epidemiology, prenatal care and the "new" public health care have contributed to a new way of thinking about health and disease, shifting the focus from disease to *health risk* and preventive intervention. In this regard, the genetic turn only contributes to accelerating the transformation towards predictive medicine.

Although there has been much hype about the new genetics, while there are also good reasons to doubt whether its basic promise will ever be fulfilled, new knowledge of the individual genetic make-up is certainly causing a gradual reorganisation of health care and the integration of genetic knowledge into daily clinical practice (Ling 2000; Kumar et al. 1999). Increased accuracy of genetic risk calculation combined with cheaper and faster genetic detection will also provide a major incentive to apply predictive genetic testing beyond the medical field, for instance, in insurance, employment, migration issues and forensic issues. In this regard, genetic technologies raise fundamental legal, ethical and political questions, as well as basic questions about the elementary units of our social order. The shift towards a predictive style in medicine is likely to affect social values and relationships and redistribute responsibilities of individuals, professional bodies and government with regard to both public and personal health. This book aims to contribute to the analysis of the social shaping of genetics and its effects on the social order by focusing on a specific institutional practice in which the issue of genetics is hotly debated: the insurance industry.

The role of medicine in life insurance

The development of the modern life insurance industry is commonly traced back to the opening of Edward Lloyd's coffee house on Tower Street, London in 1687 (Bernstein 1998). Many of the insurance principles developed to cope with the vagaries of seventeenth-century maritime trade continue to underpin today's life insurance industry. In essence, insurance is a way of protecting against risk. Risk exists when people are exposed to the possibility of a future loss, the occurrence and/or extent of which they do not know with certainty. The insurance mechanism or "insurance logic" then basically involves the reduction of risk through pooling. Using the "law of large numbers", uncertainty decreases when many similar but independent risks are brought together. If it is possible to sufficiently reduce risk in this way, an insurer can successfully offer to take over individual risks against a premium covering the expected loss and the remaining risk. Private insurance thus serves the public interest of diversifying risk and expected loss across large segments of the population for commercial gain.

While private insurers provide for the pooling of risks and mutual aid among policyholders, at the same time, they also select their policyholders in advance, group them and price them according to market considerations. To this end, they rely on the principle of risk selection. It holds that premium rates should be differentiated so that each person will pay in accordance with his or her risk quality ("actuarial fairness"). Underwriting is precisely the method to assess this "risk quality" and to classify people according to their risk. In order to build these risk ratings and classifications, actuaries are first of all deployed to calculate excess mortality risks based on the insurance company portfolio. Based on these medico-actuarial statistics then, underwriters can make a risk assessment of individual applicants. Technical underwriting involves the calculation of the standard rate based on technical characteristics (e.g., capital sum insured). Medical underwriting is accountable for the medical risk assessment, that is, the extra mortality risk the applicant represents. Usually medical underwriting leads to the classification of three groups: standard, substandard and uninsurable.[1] In this way, medicine serves the objectives of the insurance business.

According to insurance logic, underwriting is essential to the workings of private life insurance because the insurance relationship takes the form of a private contract, and, as such, it fulfils the requirement regarding the validity of consent. Insurance contracts must be made *uberrimae fides* – in the utmost good faith – with full disclosure from the applicant. This is particularly important because applicants' knowledge regarding their risk status may also affect their insurance behaviour. In insurance terms, this is the principle of "moral hazard". This moral hazard arises when applicants misrepresent information while applying for insurance, and it results in increased costs (claims) for the insurance company (or other policyholders). But above all, the rule of truthfulness in the disclosure of risk is considered a prerequisite for the optimal functioning of the insurance market. If information is withheld, insurers face financial risks from adverse selection. They argue that applicants are likely to take out more insurance, which in turn negatively affects the whole insurance pool and results in an unbalanced portfolio. After all, it means more claims than expected, which will force the company to increase its rates. This means that it will lose its *good* risks, which over time will result in a pool of only *bad* risks. This, in turn, may cause the company to go bankrupt. It is particularly the task of the company's medical underwriting department to put together a well-balanced portfolio.

When life insurance companies were established at the end of the nineteenth century, the practice of medical risk selection became a subject of public debate (Porter 2000; Horstman 2001). Since then, however, the issue has basically disappeared from the public agenda. The practice of risk selection has generally been accepted as a standard step in the application procedure for insurance, while the gatekeeper role of medicine in insurance has rarely been criticised. The legitimacy of this practice rested on the scientific medico-actuarial dealing with risks via the development of actuarial science, life tables, medical expertise and technology. The rise of DNA technology, however, has prompted new debate of the issue of risk selection while also bringing the relationship between medicine and private insurance back into the foreground. Over the past fifteen years, the refusal of insurance companies to insure HIV patients caused a major outcry, but it was largely seen as a problem limited to a specific group. Genetic testing, on the other hand, may indeed transform medical risk selection into a major public policy issue again. In this regard, genetics can be expected to play a prominent role in the design of risk profiles of applicants and in the risk categorisation of high and low risk applicants.

Black-and-white: Public policy debates on genetics and insurance

The use of genetic testing by insurers has met with considerable public opposition. It has triggered public policy debates in many countries, whereby different interest groups and experts were invited to participate, such as the insurance industry, geneticists, lawyers, bio-ethicists, consumer or patients groups, and the public at large. In these debates, the fear is that the increased knowledge of genetic mutations will render individuals uninsurable, leading to a "genetic underclass". For example, in reports on such debates in the UK one reads:

> Consumer interest groups were worried about the possibility of a two-tier system of insurance, and the possibility of discrimination against a genetic underclass of people who have or are carriers of serious genetic conditions. (Human Genetics Advisory Committee Sub Group on insurance, HGAC 1997)

> There is also clear public concern about the risk of creating a 'genetic underclass': a group of people for whom, owing to their genetic make-up, insurance will either be too expensive or actually unobtainable. (British House of Commons Committee on Science and Technology 2001)

Apart from genetic discrimination, ethical arguments against letting insurers demand and use genetic information are also identified, including confidentiality doubts, the non-reliability of genetic tests, testing deterrence and genetic privacy. Regarding the respect for privacy, it is argued that genetic information is too private to be dealt with by third parties. In some European countries these public concerns have led to legislation aimed at prohibiting insurers from demanding that applicants undergo genetic tests as well as restricting access to existing genetic information.[2] The world's first insurance law prohibiting genetic information was enacted in Belgium via art. 5 and 95 of the Law on Insurance Contracts (LVO) in 1992.

The insurance industry argues that if it is denied access to genetic information at the time of underwriting, the consumer will use genetic information to abuse the insurance system, taking advantage of the private knowledge of the risks they submit for coverage ("adverse selection"). There should be no exception for genetics on the general insurance principles, the business claims; high risk applicants (or:

"burning houses") should be given a premium consistent with their risk in order to protect the collective risk group and the company's portfolio. For example, the medical advisor Lowden (1998a) argues: "When your house is a flame, it is time to call the fire department, not the insurance broker." And, in a similar vein, this insurer suggests:

> While it is a truism in our industry that it is not possible to insure a house that's already on fire, equally important is the corollary that a prudent consumer will not do business with a company that would actually insure such a building (Nowlan 2000).

By and large, however, these debates tend to be rather speculative and abstract, while metaphorical notions such as "the threat of a genetic underclass" and "burning houses" hardly seem productive. By pitting the economic against the ethical, or the "free market" against "regulation", these discussions frequently end up in a deadlock. Kaufert (2000: 827) has labelled such debates a "literary construct", put together by multiple uni-disciplined experts, each relying on their specific knowledge and assumptions about the new genetics. In light of the many unknowns and in the absence of data for scientific evidence, Kaufert argues, this barely comes as a surprise. Such black-and-white thinking, though, is all but productive, especially given the complex and conflicting larger realities involved. Moreover, what is striking is that many elements – varying from the so-called "insurance logic" and "market laws" to the "law of the large numbers" – are presented as "givens", as inevitable facts to deal with. Both insurers and their critics invoke insurance-technical principles as invariable facts, uniformly valid for each underwriting practice and governed by abstract and irreversible economic and statistical laws. This abstractness implies that the space for finding solutions to the many dilemmas elicited by the issue of genetics in insurance is rather limited indeed.

On a more general plane, the genetics and insurance debate can be seen as an example of today's "socio-technical controversies" (Callon et al. 2001) in risk society. Since Beck's pioneering work, it has become an academic common-place to argue that the nature of risk in today's risk society is distinct from that of any other era. The primary reason for this is that a globalised, knowledge-based society "manufactures" new risks in its attempt to resolve the very problems it seeks to address. In addressing these new techno-risks (e.g., genetics), policymakers struggle with the intricate question by trying to adapt the political-normative frameworks to these new technological developments and their related *uncertainties*. In the same line, organisations or economic firms face trust issues in the context of increasing uncertainty. This can foster negative perceptions of "organisation irresponisibility" (Beck 1999) towards companies.

Towards experimental learning

In general, two policy approaches for dealing with these issues can be distinguished: a technocratic strategy and, as we may call it, an experimental learning approach. The first one can be described as our traditional response to controversial issues of science and politics. It refers to the Enlightenment ideals and implies that dilemmas and political differences can be settled with "a double delegation" (Callon et al. 2001), at the heart of representative democracy. This is the delegation of technical and scientific issues to experts and of political discussion to elected representatives. In this configuration there is a separation between science and political power, and there is a divide between lay people and specialists, on the one hand, and ordinary individual citizens and professional representatives, on the other. This configuration has become a cornerstone of our Western democratic order. The basic idea is that scientific, value-free and politically neutral facts can serve as the foundation for compromises and consensus in political conflicts. This technocratic approach often takes the form of statistics (Porter 1995; Alonso and Starr 1987) and, as such, it has become quite dominant in western political culture.

However, the new technological risks in today's knowledge economy indicate serious problems with this approach. In this regard, the state and its expert class often betray differences of opinion that reveal the *uncertainty* of expertise itself. Policy debates on biomedical issues for example are pervaded by disagreement not just between scientists and non-scientists, but also within the scientific community. From there, social philosophers have argued for another strategy that acknowledges the inherent normative character of public issues. From this perspective, it is questionable whether scientific results are considered legitimate enough to solve the issue, and, as such, to reward trust from the public. The political philosopher Van Gunsteren (1998) argues that in a complex society, in which diversity, plurality and lack of predictability are the rule, technocratic strategies for addressing public problems will necessarily come up against their own limits because such strategies neglect the main characteristic of *uncertainty* of that society. In this kind of society a deliberative approach that acknowledges normative differences is called for. So while the technocratic strategy expects much of statistics, the second one defines the dilemmas of genetics and insurance as normative dilemmas that have to be dealt with by public deliberation and collective learning. What is at play is not a logic of representation but one of *intervention*. This implies a broadening of terms of expertise, which is inclusive of a wider range of understandings of the world. Some authors speak of "hybrid fora" to stress the fact that these learning processes are often organised beyond the traditional political arena and contribute to the invention of "new politics" (Callon 1998).

There have been some proposals to open up the debate on genetics and insurance that coincide with this policy approach of experimental learning. From a pragmatic perspective, the French insurance expert Ewald, for example, suggested that reference is often made to genetics and insurance in general, "but there is no such thing as insurance in general. There are only insurance companies who are in competition with one another" (1999: 21). And: "Before getting embroiled in overtly abstract speculation, it would be useful to consider insurers' actual strategies for obtaining information" (1999: 19). Seen from this angle, medical underwriting is not a given mechanism, but a concrete practical process shaped in a localised context. For similar reasons, the medical sociologist Kaufert (2000) argued for sociological research of the private insurance world.

This book is an attempt to commence with this. It explores the issue of genetics in insurance from an empirical sociological angle – from *within* the insurance world. As such, it should be seen as an effort to open up the black box of medical underwriting and the insurance-technical principles it relies on. The challenging slogans involved in the debate on the issue of genetics in insurance deserve, I believe, a more careful consideration, notably from the angle of *underwriting-in-action* itself. The sociological perspective of constructivism informs my journey through the insurance world. This means that insurance companies, medical technologies, insurance-technical principles and insurance risks are not considered as self-evident and conclusive facts. Instead, this approach stresses the various acts of assemblage – of things, people and interests – involved in the *making* of insurance risks. Below I will discuss this theoretical perspective in more detail.

Reconstructing Risky Business

In order to gain insight into the assemblage work invested in medical underwriting, I rely on notions from different sociological fields, like medical sociology, science and technology studies (STS), Actor Network Theory (ANT) and economic sociology. The label "constructivism" may well serve as a common denominator of these fields. In different ways, they contribute to the formulation of an alternative to the modernist discourse on risk, which emphasises the rational scientific control and management of risks via quantitative calculation as in practices tied to actuarialism, epidemiology and statistics.[3] By contrast, a constructivist approach emphasises the assemblage work involved in the measures of risk. This approach allows us to clarify some important "givens" in medical underwriting and to analyse the mobility of these "givens". Below I will briefly introduce these perspectives by "following" the "givens" of risks, technologies, insurance markets and social order.

Risks

The first area of consideration that has focused on the construction of risks is medical sociology. Medical sociology has made a huge contribution towards our understanding of the meaning of health, doctor-patient relations, the social and economic rationing of health care, health policy and practice and so on. The constructivist paradigm developed in this field stresses that health, disease and risks are constructive categories, rather than objective truths (Lupton 1994; Petersen and Lupton 1996). For example, since the emergence of biomedicine, some medical conditions have basically disappeared and are no longer accepted as *real*, while others have emerged because of changes in the ways of seeing that are inextricably linked to the social world. Conditions like hysteria and chlorosis, commonly diagnosed in privileged women in the nineteenth century, are no longer deemed physical illnesses. Similarly, we have recently seen the emergence of "new" diseases like stress-related disorders (e.g., chronic fatigue syndrome). These changes are not simply an outcome of new discoveries of medical knowledge, but are tied to broader social, cultural and political changes that shape what kinds of knowledge are considered to be important. So while the "burning houses" metaphor in insurance suggests that individuals more or less *embody* a specific insurance risk, this approach conceptualises an insurance risk not as a discovery, a fixed or stable reality one encounters in the human body, but as a fabrication or an invention (cf. Bury 1986). While the notion of "discovery" implies that the insurance risk existed all along and that it was just sitting there, waiting to be assessed, the notion of "fabrication", by contrast, implies that the risk was established as risk by means of a specific investigative effort that confirmed its reality.

Another theme in the sociological approaches to risk concerns the different types of knowledge that inform the making of a risk. For example, Gifford (1986) studied the different meanings of breast cancer risk in epidemiology, clinical medicine and women's lay experience. She refers to two dimensions of conceptualising risk: the "objective" and "scientific" approach, which emerges from epidemiology, and the "lived" or socially experienced dimension. Although epidemiologists define risks as de-individualised, based as they are on statistical patterns within and between groups, Gifford argues that clinicians and women themselves redefine this risk based on their individual context. Risks can thus have different meanings according to the "frames" or "knowledge practices" or "ways of seeing" in which they are couched. According to this perspective, the frames with which different social groupings or "knowledge communities" operate in consideration of risks are politically negotiated and constructed (Wynne 1996). The use of such frames can result in profound discontinuities between, for example, expert assessments of risks and those of lay people. From a constructivist perspective, all knowledge about risk is thus bound to or a product of a specific way of seeing, whether in relation to scientists' and other experts' knowledge or lay people's knowledge. A risk, then, is anything but a static phenomenon; it is constructed and negotiated as part of the network of social interaction and the formation of meaning. As Ewald puts this, in relation to insurance risk: "Nothing is a risk in itself; there is no risk in reality. But, on the other hand, anything can be a risk, it all depends on how one analyses the danger and considers the event" (1991: 199).

Technologies

If work in medical sociology has regarded the body as the principal site for investigation, science and technology studies (STS) has sought to explore technology in a wide range of fields. Over the past two decades, the multidisciplinary field of STS has grown rapidly. In different ways, they all stress that scientific knowledge is not so much discovered as *constructed*. This specific position bears much resemblance to medical sociology's argument on risks as the result of fabrication or assemblage work. By foregrounding science's disordered practices through fieldwork in, for example, laboratories (e.g., Latour and Woolgar 1979), STS strips away the public image of science, its stable façade and its imposed coherence or sense of order. Latour (1987) refers to the Janus-faced world of science, the public-reassuring world of hard facts and certainty, and the much messier, uncertain, hidden and provisional world of the lab with its experiments, disagreements and conflict. This closure by scientists of a relatively stable set of devices and practices is a result of negotiation and often conflict between the interests of a variety of actors in an extensive network – not just scientists but also sponsors, academic gatekeepers, regulatory authorities, advocacy groups and so on.

In addition to science's embeddedness and the demand for socio-cultural competence, STS also pays attention to the technical objects or materialities as requirements in the *making* of science. For some, this means that science and technology are "socially constructed", a perspective in STS that became known as SCOT (social construction of technology) and has its roots in the work of Bijker et al. (1987). They proposed the notion of a "seamless web" to indicate how technological processes, organisational practices and social practices are routinely meshed together. At the heart of this approach is the belief that the meaning of a technical artefact does not reside in the technology itself, but is determined by the meanings – problems and solutions – attributed to it by those participating in its development. Bijker's analysis of the development of the bicycle is illustrative. During the long process that led to the bicycle's stabilisation, some social groups described it as having a safety problem that required the front wheel to be made smaller. However, others viewed it as a machine for producing speed, and this was better achieved with a larger front wheel. For this social group, falling was part of riding a bicycle and thus not a problem (Bijker 1995). This "social shaping" of science and technology requires us to accept that there is no inherent logic to their development.

In contrast to the SCOT perspective, actor network theory (ANT) – developed by Callon (1986a, 1986b), Latour (1987), Law (1991a) and others – argues that the view of the social construction of technology is problematic because it is impossible to give a purely social explanation of technical change. After all, technical objects (facts, artefacts, devices) are themselves a critical part of what the social is. Derived from semiotics and post-structuralism, ANT theorists show how central actors enrol others to build networks of different parts, as "heterogeneous engineers", bringing together a range of human *and* non-human actors. Such networks are the "mechanism by which the social and natural worlds progressively take form" (Callon 1986b: 224). ANT thus describes the constitution of a reality from heterogeneous elements (materials, texts, bodies, skills, interests) all of which are *performing* to produce relations which give them their shape, style, or mode of ordering. It is not the solidity of the resulting construct that is in question, but rather the many heterogeneous ingredients, the long process, the various forms of expertise, and the subtle coordination necessary to achieve such a result. This so-called "realistic constructivism" highlights the collective process of mobilising heterogeneous crafts, ingredients and coordinative efforts that leads to solid constructs (Latour 2005).

Despite differences, the STS approaches all highlight the fact that technologies, statistics or other deployed objects in practices are not "givens". On the contrary, they have to be activated or "translated" along the particular concerns of actors and the practices involved. Genetic technology, for one, has no singular, essential meaning that defines how artefacts are used, how they are seen to be fitting the concerns of the actors. Technologies need to be translated into specific localised needs: the social and technical are in this sense mutually constitutive. In this respect Nelkin and Tancredi (1989: 75) argue that social organisations (such as insurance institutions) can be particularly interested in deploying genetic technologies because the latter respond to particular needs or concerns of such social organisations towards both further preserving control and enhancing efficiency:

> For those found to be at risk, diagnostic categories may themselves have a social meaning shaped by the needs of social institutions. Medical conceptions of behavior and disease pervade ... . as these diverse institutions embrace the power of diagnostic prediction. They are placing a new emphasis on objective and predictive information about the individuals within their domain, and they are interpreting such information to meet their immediate social and economic needs.

At the same time, STS stresses that these technologies or devices, once they are "encapsulated", are not merely passive tools; together with the user, they also *act* to produce effects. Devices are "inscribed" (Akrich and Latour 1992) with the network relations of which they are a part, thereby contributing to a particular performance. That means that, besides the language or accounts of insurers, medical technologies, statistics, risk classification tables and questionnaires are also used in the underwriting practice and can be observed for their normative acts, or performativity. The subject of these devices then co-constructs the final insurance risk result – how normal and abnormal risks are defined and who is excluded or not in insurance.

Markets

In public debates on the organisation of welfare and health care, the "state" is often offset against the "free market", while recently we have seen an increasing turn to marketisation or privatisation. The insurance market is extending its reach and at the same time claiming its universal applicability. But is there something that can be called "the insurance market"? Notably Callon has written on this topic. In *The Laws of the Markets* (1998), he argues that markets are constructed rather than given. Consider, for example, the purchase of an automobile. This transaction is possible because rigorous framing has been performed, whereby the three protagonists – buyer, seller and car – clearly have to be distinct in order to allow a particular "framing" (1998: 16-19) or "qualification" (Callon et al. 2002).[4] This involves a controversial process through which the car's qualities are attributed and objectified by the involved actors. For example, a particular buyer may have clear ideas about the car he/she wants, based on the aesthetics, its price or the image of the make. Likewise, the local car dealer has his own concerns, such as competition with other dealers in the same niche market. Moreover, at a much earlier stage, car designers have invested in the "imagining" of this car as a product with a potential buyer. These economic suppliers jointly take into account and balance out all kinds of considerations in order to reach acceptable *compromises* on the value of the car (Callon and Muniesa 2002). Supply and demand are not discerned here because consumers actively co-construct in the making of the car.[5] This process of qualification or framing then aims to establish a constellation of characteristics that are attached to the car and transform it into a tradable good, if only for the time being. After all, cars can be "re-qualified" or "re-framed" or have their characteristics adjusted. Consider, for example, urban pollution caused by automobiles. Frequently, this effect is not taken into account when a car is purchased, which means it exists outside the framework of economic calculation. However, this situation may change once local authorities begin to install pollution monitoring devices near roadways, and drivers are fined for driving a car with high levels of polluting exhaust. The possibility of being fined may begin to affect the drivers' calculations regarding the car they drive. They may choose to buy a car that uses cleaner fuel. Likewise, the environmental costs of driving may also enter into the manufacturers' calculations. Or the current attention to health and safety measures may prompt suppliers to re-qualify the car by investing in ergonomic seats, larger airbags or innovative ABS systems. Callon argues that qualification is an unfinished process of *trial and error*: testing one's positioning in the market, observing consumers' evaluations, trying to clarify their judgements and taking them into account when reframing or requalifying the product (2002: 204).

As such, a dual process of "complexification" and "simplification" always takes place in economic markets (Callon 2002). In order to satisfy consumer demands, a company regularly has to allow complexity to proliferate, by balancing out diverging considerations, or to facilitate negotiations that lead to compromises ("process of qualification"). But this growing complexity also has to be controlled, reduced or simplified if the company is to maintain its hold over the process (2002: 192). This "simplification" is performed by a company's writing devices, management tools or "calibrated measuring instruments", like statistics. These enable the "framing" of the market transaction, while at the same time they can again be re-written, resulting in a re-framing.

This suggests that insurance markets and principles are *multiple* and have to be performed in specific historically, culturally and materially located practices. But also within an insurance company, *multiple* considerations have to balanced out towards a specific underwriting policy or framing. With this focus on the multiplicity of considerations, Callon (along with other economic sociologists) offers us a possibility to pay attention to societal considerations *within* economic framings. Each market or economic policy is constitutive of a host of considerations, be it profit making, administrative, social, ethical, aesthetical or price elasticity concerns. Whereas in public policy debates on genetics and insurance, the "economic" is often weighed against the "ethical", the above suggests that the underwriting policy of an insurance company might involve (mixtures of) both. Insurance companies only differ *to what extent* their economic policies are directed towards such social dimensions, as part of their overall business strategies. And of course, these economic policies may result in diverse insurability ratings.

Social order

"Premiums fatten on weight rules" read the headlines in a July 2005 *Daily Mail*. Are overweight people discriminated against when it comes to insurance coverage? Are we prepared to pay for them? Implicit within these debates are broader questions about the distribution of individual and collective responsibility and different arrangements of solidarity. How much risk segmentation in insurance do we justify? Which risks do we subsidise? And when do we decide that these individuals need to "take their own risk"? Where insurance markets differ, they in turn also shape different insurability results. As I will demonstrate in this book, some underwriting policies enact better insurability for people than others, or enact better insurability for only a particular *category* of people, and so on. For example, an insurance company may choose to insure a large group, in which the bad risks can easily be spread across this group. Or it may choose to cover one particular niche, e.g., healthy young whites, and exclude others. In this way, insurance reflects broader imageries on solidarity between those included in risk groups, or differentiation tendencies – and an emphasis on difference – between people. Insurance thus contributes to the creation of *difference* in people, for instance, who is part of the member group and who not. On a wider front, it contributes to the making of the social order. That is, insurance as a social organisation co-defines the boundaries between normal and abnormal in society and, therefore, can be considered a co-producer of social order. As Nelkin and Tancredi (1989) for example argue in the introduction of *Dangerous Diagnostics. The Social Power of Biological Information*:

> In examining the use of tests in specific tests in specific organization settings, we will suggest how diagnostic advances and their underlying scientific assumptions affect the boundaries of what is viewed as acceptable behaviour; how they delineate and define classes of what is or is not 'deviant' or diseased. (18-19)

The issue of insurance as a co-producer of our social order is particularly addressed in the "sociology of insurance" literature (Baker and Simon, 2002; Ericson et al. 2003; Ericson and Doyle 2003; Ewald 1986, 1991; Castel 1991; Dean 1998, 1999). From a neo-Foucauldian perspective, these authors consider insurance a social and normative technology.[6] Insurance is not only a passive reflection of a pre-existing social and economic reality, but also involves the *production* of social realities, modes of classification and governance. Seen in this way, insurance institutions cease to play a passive, loss-spreading role and, instead, actively construct the world they inhabit. By making statistical distinctions and risk categories, insurance distributes ideas on who we include or exclude in our society. Private insurance is a method of organising mutual aid by deciding which citizens qualify or disqualify as members. It thus contributes to the development of the ideals and competencies linked up with citizenship.

It will be clear from this outline that my specific interest in underwriting concerns the ways in which insurance assemblage work leads to the creation of insurance risks and which effects this embraces regarding insurability. This highlights that categorising individuals is not a 'natural' given, but the result of hard, productive work reflecting socio-political, technical, economic and other considerations. That way, insurance arrangements stop playing the straightforward, somewhat boring character they may have in the public eye. Instead, this book stresses the *uncertain* (and often exciting) character of "doing underwriting". In a globalising insurance context where highly competitive market pressures ask for relentless flexibility, where new technologies come into play, where actuaries lose their authority and where consumers ask for increasing participation, underwriting can indeed be seen as puzzling and bewildering work. The book's "behind-the-scenes" look will display insurance as a never-ending story of *trial and error*, that is, as an *experimental* adventure or an "*uncertain* business" (Ericson and Doyle 2004). But in order to study uncertain institutions, we needed uncertain methodologies as well. This will be explored hereafter.

Risky Travels

While my focus was on risks "in the making", it was not sufficient to study the end products – premium rates, insurability rates – to assess insurance policy making. To get insight on the experimental character of insurance practices, I needed an ethnographic qualitative study. Ethnographic inquiry can be attentive to the internal messiness of any organisation; to the mix-up of all kinds of considerations; to the ways in which institutions contain elements which are not always part of their external conceptions; in short, it can be alert to the specificity of the institution. In keeping with this expeditionary orientation, I started from the version of "ethnography" which is theoretically aligned with Actor Network Theory (ANT). The point of this approach is to "follow the actors" and to unravel the complex chains of connection of actors that constitute the "thing" one is studying (Latour 2005). In line with this literature, I rely on *travel* as an extended metaphor for framing my insurance expedition account. The travel metaphor, I believe, nicely reflects the *processing* character that is part and parcel of all serious research efforts. In line with the assemblage work of insurers in coming to terms with insurance risks, the travel metaphor is used here to stress my own assemblage work in experimenting with a sociology of insurance.

Travelling the fields

The first location I focused on were the insurance industry's written sources on genetics in Europe and the United States since 1988.[7] Although it is impossible to totally separate internal developments from positions in public policy debates (Best, 1995), my reconstruction was based on specific insurance sources, including academic and non-academic underwriting journals, actuarial insurance journals, medical insurance journals; reports, statements, papers and proceedings of insurance associations; policy statements of insurance companies; and proceedings of seminars and workshops in the insurance world. In this manner, I considered a total of 400 written insurance sources for further analysis.

The second leg of my journey involved a careful consideration of the Belgian insurance landscape. More specifically, I did fieldwork in the medical underwriting departments of two Belgian insurance companies.[8] I started with some introductory interviews with each company's department head, the medical advisors and some underwriters in order to get a first-hand look at the process of underwriting. After a while, I moved on to observation. By following the underwriters, observing their activities and asking them about their present activities, I primarily focused on investigating what underwriters *do*.[9] This implied looking at the "devices" (Latour and Woolgar 1986) they use in making reference to insurance risks and that help them in coming to closure, such as medical questionnaires, handbooks, computers and guidelines. Another major strategy I relied on was following an insurance risk "trajectory", from the initial application to the final risk assessment.[10] Besides talking, interviewing and observation, I also analysed the devices I observed from another, *dis*-connected angle. I studied the reinsurance manuals that were used (comparing "older" and "newer" versions); the medical questionnaires filled out by the applicants; the protocols sent to the medical experts for medical information and the guidelines provided by the company management. I also opted to study interests and relevant connections within the whole company, all having one or another link with underwriting, such as the claims, actuarial and marketing departments and corporate management.

Finally, I explored the significance of the various sites linked to medical underwriting. I collected written sources and held in-depth interviews with several key informants from the national and international insurance fields. This allowed me to elucidate various relevant issues, including the regulative context of medical underwriting (national and international), the general details of the Belgian insurance market, the background of the actors involved in medical underwriting (professional organisations of actuaries, medical advisors and insurers), and the institutional context in which private insurance operates. These kinds of data offered me an additional tool for exploring the process of medical risk selection in my case. Throughout this expedition, I analysed these sites with the help of the software program Nvivo.[11]

In sum, I considered it helpful to capitalise on the experimental character of my own research in coming to terms with insurance *produceries* of insurability. Just as insurers invest in tryouts and balancing acts, I did not have a Lego kit in stock that could provide me with detailed maps of the building site, and so I went on expeditions, as a process of trial and error. A major advantage of this approach, then, is that it exploits the *riskiness* involved in doing such travel. As Haraway puts it: "Ethnography is a method of being at risk.... [I]t is about risks, purposes and hopes – one's own and others' – embedded in knowledge projects" (1997: 190-191). How should these various risks be understood? The first risk factor involves the selection of the type of journey. Instead of striking a deal with a tour operator, I designed my own "adventure", camped out in the wilds and hiked in the woods without the help of detailed maps. By discarding the stereotypical pictures from the tour operator's package, the challenge became: How and in what ways is my account just as reliable, "objective" and generalisable? After all, my final account is the immediate *effect* of my journey, including all the various choices made along the way. Secondly, precisely by putting myself at risk by doing this research, the issue emerges whether the object of my study is at risk as well? Because these questions mainly apply to the effects of my account on the object of study, they will only be taken up towards the end of the book.

Making Risk, Enacting the Social

If anything, my argument in this book demonstrates that the *language of risk* cloaks a whole range of practices in the creation of insurance risks. It is not my intention, however, to lift the lid on insurance techniques, principles or medico-actuarial science, and thus merely deconstruct these practices. On the contrary, along with other STS analysts, I am interested in seeing how underwriting in insurance might be made more accountable by making it more "socially robust" (Nowotny 2003). This may involve a broadening of the terms on which the underwriting process is built, as a way to move towards a more accountable insurance market that reflects a wider range of understandings of the world. Paraphrasing Latour (2005), as a "compositionist", I engage in the task of nurturing the fragile habitation of insurance underwriting.

In this manner, I hope to provide some relevant building blocks in order to develop an experimental learning policy for the genetics and insurance issue. Identifying risk selection as construction work means creating space for negotiation, change, opening or, in short, the stimulation of *learning processes*. By opening the black box of insurance, this book will reveal all kinds of *locations* within the underwriting process where such learning can take place. In this regard, my travel is an attempt to enlarge mental and practical space: It demonstrates the possibilities of bridging the apparent gap between insurance economic realities and social needs. On a more general level, my case may give insight on the transformations in the public sphere that deal with today's uncertainties that involve risks. That is because insurance can be seen as the institution *par excellence* of risk society (Ericson and Doyle 2003). It is one of the great modern institutions of science and technology, indeed, insurance was central to the development of the sciences of risk and probability thinking (Hacking 1990). Thus, by studying this case, I hope to say more about how to deal with uncertainty and public distrust as issues that confront our risk society.

In chapter II, the first leg of my journey, I will discuss the insurance literature on genetics in order to gain insight into insurance accounts on genetics. In particular, I look at the way the insurance business frames and reframes genetic risks in light of ongoing public policy debates. It becomes clear that insurance is not a uniform world and that underwriting itself is imbued with internal complexities. These internal soundings echo the two aforementioned policy approaches: the technocratic strategy and the experimental learning strategy. From there I extend my analysis on the issue of risk calculability in today's risk society.

In the subsequent chapters, I further explore this framing of insurance risks by zooming in on the next stage of my journey: my fieldwork in two Belgian insurance companies. To demonstrate the various acts of assemblage, chapters III, IV and V focus on the specific risk trajectory of an applicant, fictitiously called Karen, from the initial application to the final insurance risk determination. Accordingly, chapter III focuses on the way Karen enters the underwriting practice. Before any medical data on Karen has been established, several considerations and strategies already frame her insurance risk outcome. This framing is a result of the company's specific underwriting policy, its general economic policy and the confines of the Belgian insurance market. Chapter IV goes on to explore Karen's risk trajectory by focusing on the medical risk assessment. The chapter concentrates on medico-actuarial statistics, risk classification factors and the medical tools used to put Karen into a particular risk category. In chapter V our attention shifts to the underwriters and their articulation of Karen's final risk assessment. I discuss the relevance of judgement in their dealing with the available tools and data. For each of these stages in the risk trajectory, I will locate the different spots where negotiation or the co-construction of consumers is possible in the making of insurance risks.

Having analysed the assemblage work throughout the risk trajectory, chapter VI focuses on the particular issue of predictive medicine in insurance. It becomes clear that the introduction of a prohibition on genetics by the Belgian Law on Insurance Contracts (LVO 1992) contributes to a fault-based approach in underwriting. While collective responsibility is attributed to genetic *risk carriers*, lifestyle *risk takers* have to bear individual responsibility. Thus the chapter illustrates how regulation can perform the underwriting practice as well and have particular effects on insurability and the way we *imagine* the distribution of responsibilities. I argue that such regulation (resulting from a genetic essentialism) may generate relevant side effects for the insurance industry as well as society in general. In this regard, I illustrate the shortcomings of legislative policy approaches in coming to terms with the controversy of genetics and insurance.

Finally, in chapter VII, I again draw attention to the book's central theme by presenting a travelogue of my journey in order to demonstrate what we can learn from such travels. This chapter explores the philosophical and policy questions that arise from the journey. Hirschman's framework of "exit, voice and loyalty" is used to reformulate the controversies that are involved and to offer a different approach to accountability, in a way that may facilitate *social learning*. I use this framework to discuss its potential in life insurance with regard to medical underwriting. Having traced the "black boxes" of the various "givens" involved in public policy debates on genetics and insurance, some locations for redefining the issue will be identified as a way of cooperating with the actors involved in a policy of experimentation and learning in dealing with the dilemmas of insurability.

II "Genetics Is Not The Issue": Insurers on Genetics and Life Insurance

Introduction

In the wake of my general research chronicle, this chapter focuses specifically on the insurance industry's concerns regarding the issue of genetics. In particular I am interested in the ways in which insurers frame the issue of genetics and articulate their understandings for their business.[12] In the first sections, I will sketch how the insurance world originally conceived of genetics. Next I will show how ideas with respect to this developed beyond the policy debates. Although it is hard to discern a strictly linear trend, the initial position of most professional associations in insurance differs from their more recent position. As to their current views, I discuss the various conflicting voices in the insurance industry regarding the framing of genetics, including the proposed scientific, actuarial solutions. In the last section, then, I build on Callon's (1998, 1999, 2001, 2002) insights to elaborate this analysis. Using the data that focuses on the controversy of genetics in insurance, I will address some key changes in present-day policy making regarding technological risks.

A Public Relations Problem

When, in the early 1990s, genetics and insurance became a public concern, medical director experts warned the insurance floor to take this issue very seriously. In 1993, for example, Chairman of the Genetic Task Force of the American Council of Life Insurance (ACLI) Chambers announced in the *Reinsurance Reporter*: "Insurers unite! Genetic testing is coming of age". Insurers followed this advice, but in a very specific way.

During the first phase of the public policy debates on genetics and insurance, the insurance industry largely saw itself as a victim. Insurers felt that others – the general public, the medical profession and the biotechnology industry – were overly worried about the potential role of genetics in insurance. There seemed to be the widespread fear among the public that increased knowledge of genetic mutations might render individuals uninsurable, thus leading to a "genetic underclass". What also alarmed some was the notion that insurers might seek to identify a genetic "superclass" with positive genetic characteristics, and offer them preferential terms, with a consequent worsening of the terms for everyone else. In addition, the public thought genetic information was too private to be dealt with by third parties and that the "right not to know" would be harmed. Because genetic code changes are passed on through families, some considered genetic information different from other types of medical information. Finally, as genetic information is immutable or inherited, it was seen as unfair to penalise affected individuals with higher premiums. Moreover, some interpretations of what constitutes fairness in insurance resulted in the idea that life insurance is a basic necessity and, therefore, the possibility of access must be ensured for everyone.

The insurance industry also regretted the unrest in the medical and scientific community concerning the use of genetics in insurance. Geneticists argued that the risk of being refused insurance, plus the fact that testing might be detrimental to their health, would deter patients from participating in genetics-related research projects (Chambers 1999: 28). Insurers referred to cases in medical journals where physicians openly recommended their patients not to communicate genetic results to insurance companies. They also identified the biotechnology industry as an opponent. After all, people's fear of losing insurance could squelch the booming commercial opportunities in testing technology (Hall 1996).

In response to these various concerns, the insurance industry countered by arguing that it was not fair that it was being singled out as a "trouble spot". It asserted that the industry was only reacting to external influences for which it could not be held responsible. For one thing, insurers emphasised, they were not the driving force behind the genetics revolution. They claimed to have no interest in genetic technology because it was simply not their business. As one American actuary put it: "Insurers are not in the business of pushing the technology frontiers – we are in the business of assessing risk in a cost-effective way" (Holmes 1999: 30). Apparently, the financially and economically powerful insurance world considered itself disinterested if not impotent with respect to genetics. But of course insurers were forced to deal with it: "Life offices are loathe to initiate social change, but they have to respond to it" (Leigh 1999: 22). Basically, insurers reasoned that they would pursue genetic testing as part of risk selection only if such testing was introduced into medical practice: "We are not proactively pushing the bounds of genetics science. All we're saying is, we need to know what people know when they apply for insurance" (Smee cited in: Howard 1996). These reactions demonstrate that insurance companies felt that they were being forced to respond to developments in genetic technology, rather than that they themselves could be held responsible for encouraging such developments.

Secondly, insurers claimed they were not responsible for the public's "gene fright". They argued that people's expectations regarding the genetic revolution – with many ascribing almost magical predictive accuracy to genetic tests – were misguided. In this respect, one European reinsurance spokesman referred to the "rather emotional public perception of genetics, exacerbated by ignorance, erroneous opinions and unfavourable prejudices. Unfortunately, there is very little insurance companies can do to educate the public in genetics" (Chuffart 1997: 20). If the popular media exercised very little restraint in capitalising on the horrific potential of genetics, insurers sought to detach their industry from such alarming stories as much as possible:

> The insurance industry is entangled in this heavily emotional discussion on genetics. Although we have no relationship to gene manipulation or even cloning experiments, we get mixed into this confusion and as a consequence one wants to refuse us the right to benefit from the predictive value of genetic testing. (Akerman 1999: 8)

The insurance industry considered the dominant public perception of genetics as a real constraint on both its business and its public image. The emerging concept of a "genetic underclass" was certainly not going to help the insurance industry.

Finally, the public was not just misinformed about genetics, according to the insurance industry, but it also had little understanding of private insurance principles and techniques. Insurers felt that the distinction between private and social insurance was not at all clear to the public, while the difference between solidarity and mutuality was essentially misunderstood. In this context, some insurers referred to the recent transformations of the welfare state, where private insurance has increasingly taken over the insurance functions of the social insurance system. As a consequence, "it should not come as a surprise that private insurance is increasingly perceived as a right, or to use a fashionable expression, as an entitlement" (Chuffart 1997: 21). According to insurers, these developments gave rise to false expectations with respect to private insurance.

The insurance industry, then, when it first addressed the issue of genetics, perceived itself as merely responding to specific social and technological developments. Moreover, it saw itself as the victim of an ignorant public. Insurers had no problem; it was the public that had created problems that did not really exist. This caused the industry to frame genetics as a public relations problem, rather than as an insurance problem. Insurers thought they had a clear message in the debate. If only the public would listen to and properly understand their message.

A defensive approach

The industry took a defensive approach by resorting to the general private insurance principles and techniques. In this way, the individual and social advantages of the risk classification system were recapitulated.

Overall, it was stressed that private insurance had no desire to alienate potential customers from its business and that its rates were both fair and financially adequate. As to genetic information, it was argued that it was in no way different from other medical information. Insurers argued that genetic tests, much like other forms of medical information, might also help individuals actually obtain insurance. The example was frequently given of a person with a family medical history in which the Huntington's gene was prominent. A negative genetic test result would simply help approve these people for insurance policies. In the event of a positive result, their situation would merely remain the same, at least with regard to their eligibility for insurance. Moreover, insurers argued that competition between insurance companies would help people who had had genetic tests to obtain insurance. Someone with a genetic disease may represent too large a risk for one company, while another company – given the competitive insurance climate – would possibly still be willing to sell this person a policy at normal rates. In other words, the free market would take care of the issue. But above all, the risk classification principle or "actuarial fairness" (each paying according to their risk) was emphasised as a way of being fair to all policyholders. An exception made for genetics would be unfair to those individuals who bring an equivalent level of risk arising from non-genetic sources and who have to pay for it in full or are denied coverage. Moreover, making an exception for genetic information, as was originally done in the case of AIDS in the 1980s, would result in adverse selection and financial disasters for the business. This, in turn, would force the industry to raise its rates to offset the increased risk.

The industry's defensive approach was a direct result of framing the problem of genetics and insurance as a result of public fears and ignorance. Accordingly, the industry looked for a solution primarily in the education of both the public and the policymakers. Earlier efforts by the American Council of Life Insurance (ACLI) to offer public information and education about insurance principles were cited as an example: "The ACLI made a good attempt in 1986 during the AIDS test debates with a promotional campaign entitled the lower your risk, the lower your premium" (Krinik 1999: 79). In the same way, campaigns arose that promoted a better image of the insurance industry. Furthermore, insurers also decided in favour of a lobby. This "classic" strategy that had been fairly effective during the AIDS debate of the 1980s (Subramanian, Lemaire et al. 1999: 534) was to be used again by the industry as a way to tackle the issue of genetics. The lobbyists were to "educate lawmakers on the ramifications of adverse selection and to prove the need for full disclosure by insurance applicants, including the disclosure of test results" (ACLI-HIAA 1991).

By educating the public, insurers meant explaining the ins and outs of overall insurance principles and not reflecting on the meaning of predictive genetic technology. While public fears concentrated on genetic tests in particular, the insurers' public relations effort focused on denying the special significance of genetics. According to them, genetics did not bring any new issues to the fore.[13] The same insurance principles that had worked in the past should therefore be applied to genetics as well. The "freedom to underwrite" had to be maintained and no exceptions should be made for genetic information. In this respect, the Deputy Director General of the Association of British Insurers (ABI) claimed that genetics is "a natural extension of the use of medical information" (Sklaroff 2001: 6). This meant that insurers wanted to have a full disclosure of the results of tests done prior to a person's application for life insurance.

The fear of legislation

The framing of genetics and insurance as a public relations problem by insurers implied that they were not aware of the specific meaning of genetic technology. Essentially, they dealt with genetics as just another prognostic technology. If insurance principles were relaxed in the area of genetic information, it would result in "a slippery slope" (Pokorski 1997), or even the industry's demise. The opposite, however, seemed a more likely reality. As an outcome of the 1990s public policy debates, restrictive legislation on genetic information was prepared or introduced in several countries. Insurers viewed this development with great concern because the definitions of genetics were so broad and vague that many other prognostic instruments ran the risk of being banned as well. For instance, US laws being prepared at the time relied on such a broad definition of genetic testing that commonly performed tests, such as those for cholesterol, would end up being prohibited (Zimmerman and Meyer 1998; Lowden 1998a). In Europe, the first bills did not even offer a definition of what a genetic test or genetic information was (Chuffart 1997:16). Medical director Engman (1998) warned the Society of Actuaries about the possible consequences of a US law passed in 1998 by indicating that virtually "all underwriting tests institutionalised over the last 50 years are suddenly not permissible. Underwriting, in effect, has become illegal." Pokorski further stated:

> Underwriting is the main reason why insurers react so heavily [to the genetics issue]... The issue is not 'will premiums increase a little or a lot'; rather, it is that prohibiting use of predictive information – genetic or non-genetic – represents a frontal assault on a fundamental business practice. (1997: 116)

From the perspective of the insurers, these legislative procedures clearly put both the risk classification processes and the continuation of the system of private life insurance to the test.

However, the international trend towards legislative crosshairs stimulated some authors to reflect critically on the insurance industry's defensive approach towards genetics and insurance. For instance, the British underwriter O'Leary (1998: 23) recognised that "the two main pillars of our arguments had fatal flaws". First, the insurers' argument that there was no difference between genetic and other medical information was not perceived as valid by the public, the media or the legislators. Second, the public did not agree with the argument of actuarial fairness. These views were also denounced by other insurers (e.g., Chuffart 1999) and were backed up by results of the annual (public) surveys of the ACLI, *Monitoring Attitudes of the Public* (MAP). Within this context, the industry acknowledged that public relations work and education were ineffective ways of silencing the debate:

> Once educated, members of (discussion) groups understood and agreed with the industry's need for full disclosure of medical information, but they still felt that genetic information should be private and unobtainable. This issue is highly emotional, very political, and extremely resistant to logical argument. (Jones 1999: 62)

Confronted by these crosscurrents, the industry acknowledged that the arguments they had made in the past had very little sway: "We were right and fair in our approach and this would hold us in good stead. This issue should not and would not be a problem to us in the future – how innocent we were!" (O'Leary 1998: 23).

The insurers' lobbying strategy in the political arena became the object of critical internal reflection as well. In Europe, the industry was constrained by "a professional associations' general lack of strength and experience in timely identifying, analysing and reporting issues, as well as in lobbying" (Chuffart 1997:21). Thereby, the American Council of Life Insurance (ACLI) in the US was applauded for its efforts and was taken as an example for the European industry (e.g., Chiche 1995). At the same time however, in the US, criticism was also aimed at the ACLI's efforts in dealing with the issue because its defensive industrial lobbying had not succeeded in stopping the cascade of restrictive legislation. As medical director Engman said at the Society of Actuaries' spring meeting in 1997:

> The National Breast Cancer Coalition and its allies made the case effectively that insurers had their opportunity to develop reasonable policy positions throughout the 1990s, but failed to do so (...) I doubt that many here would think that America's life insurance industry has been doing all that it needs to do to revert this sort of legislative holocaust.

The insurance world had not taken advantage of the generous head start it had in 1989, when the issue was first put on the agenda by the ACLI:

> If the ACLI holds with its position that genetic information is no different than all other medical information and continues down a pathway that relies primarily on traditional reactionary methods to deal with the genetic testing legislative initiatives, it is the considered opinion of many who are close to this scene that insurers will ultimately be overwhelmed with adverse legislation. (Chambers 1999: 24)

Reflections on the ways insurers had dealt with public policy debates on genetics and insurance resulted in the acknowledgement that the main insurance argument against restrictive legislation, namely that genetic information is not essentially different from other medical information, was used by policymakers to formulate a broad definition of genetics and to restrict many tests that were already in common use. So, the debating strategy of the insurance world resulted in exactly the opposite of the goals that were aimed at. Therefore, the genetics issue was considered a reason to depart from the traditional approach towards public policy issues (Pokorski 1995; 1997). Slowly insurers acknowledged that their historical defensive arguments were beginning to fail them, and consequently, that "it may be time to consider a change in tactics" (Jones 1999: 62).

From Playing Defence to a Proactive Approach

Debates as well as legislative measures on genetics and insurance had confronted insurers with the limits of their power and stimulated a change in self-image and strategy. At least part of the insurance world felt the need to show their intention to find socially acceptable solutions. As an American actuary articulated:

> The insurance industry has two strategic choices: play defence or begin a proactive search for solutions that are both workable and acceptable to the public. Playing defence is in our nature. We have many times faced 'ill-conceived and emotional legislation' and have usually succeeded in salvaging at least a liveable result ... However, we might also try to find potential approaches that could enable the insurance industry to take on at least some of the risks associated with genetic testing that are worrying the public. (Dicke 1999b: 65)

This change in approach to the dilemmas of genetics was understood by the American Council of Life Insurance (ACLI). As Campbell, the President of the ACLI, explained to the annual ACLI meeting:

> The days when we could sit and watch the skirmishes on the Hill are over. We have to be proactive, and we need to look from the broadest possible perspective. (cited in Friedman 1997).

And this change was launched in Europe as well:

> Many European private insurance companies are beginning to understand that Society's demands and expectations have evolved and, consequently, that their response to the advances in genetics cannot follow the 'traditional pattern'. (Chuffart 1997: 22)

Now the industry explicitly strove to present itself as a constructive party in public policy debates and policy processes. They reasoned that as insurers "[we need] to transpose our industry from being seen as part of the problem to being, in fact, a part of the solution" (Chambers 1999: 21).

The strategy of denigrating the opposing parties because of their misunderstandings and irrational fears and ideas was replaced by the importance of dialogue.

> It was once said that it is better to debate a question without settling it than to settle a question without debating it. Dialogue may not resolve certain differences, but in the absence of dialogue insurers run the very real risk that damaging legislation will be passed. (Chambers 1999: 25)

In line with the rise of this proactive approach, the industry took initiatives to deal with insurance and genetics by endorsing "forward looking management strategies" (Bergstrom in: *Society of Actuaries* 1997), aspiring to prevent further legislation that way. Proposals towards the development of a code of practices, self-regulation, moratoria and technology assessment committees were launched (e.g., Chambers 1999; Pokorski 1997; Braun 2000).

One of the consequences of the change in strategy was that the central message of the public relations approach, or the idea that genetic information is the same as non-genetic information, had to be abandoned:

> Given that 'perception is reality', those who attempt to argue that genetic information is not special, but rather that it is like all other medical information, are swimming up a swiftly moving stream. (Chambers 1999: 24)

However, acknowledging the difference between genetic and non-genetic information did not mean that the actuarial logic, that was the calculative base of risk selection, had become unimportant. On the contrary, if exceptions were to be made for genetic information in the insurance industry, these should be based on actuarial evidence. Although some insurers acknowledged to some extent the political claim of acceptability to private insurance, they held that an acceptable insurance system must be workable in an actuarial sense. As the British actuary MacDonald argued:

> The objective is therefore to find sufficient common ground between what is acceptable and workable, but if you want to have an insurance industry at all, you must have some regard for what is workable. (MacDonald 2001)

That way, insurers (still) wanted to look at the genetics issue "as a risk problem, instead of an emotional infringement issue" (Lowden 1999: 45). In their move towards negotiations with the other parties, insurers thus resorted to their (internal) scientific actuarial bases, like the actuarial quantitative modelling of the genetics issue. This was because insurers considered such research as a vehicle to the possible removal of tensions in the public policy debates. Yet it was soon acknowledged that the industry had almost no empirical actuarial data on the actuarial impact of genetics. Consequently, academic actuaries were called upon to invest in this type of actuarial research. As MacDonald (1999a) commented: "Little quantitative research into this has yet been done and that seems to be one of the main sources of heat rather than light in the debate".

Exactly what were the expectations from the actuarial approach? First of all, actuarial research might be able to provide insight into the financial implications for insurers (prevalence of adverse selection) if insurers were prohibited from using genetic information. If that insight turned out to be minimal, the industry could comply with a ban on genetic information. For instance, actuarial research resulted in identifying modes of purchasing that indicated a heightened risk of moral hazard (and adverse selection) above certain well-defined financial ceiling limits. Consequently, below this financial limit, a ban on genetic information would not result in adverse selection. Secondly, regarding the financial implications for individuals, actuarial research could supply evidence on the effects of the use of genetic information of people with adverse genetic test results. In this regard, research was also recommended in order to offer people with genetic risks substandard coverage instead of simply denying them access (Lowden and Roberts 1998; Lowden 1999a; Chuffart 1996a, 1996b; Smith 1998). This approach was called "forward underwriting" (Lowden 1998b, 1999a; MacNamara 2001). That way, they hoped public aversion towards genetic testing in the insurance industry could be alleviated and legislation forestalled. As the medical advisor Lowden (1998b) advocated:

> Lobbying of legislators is one means to delay or remove this risk but I believe that approach has serious limitations. It must be accompanied by positive demonstrations by insurers to allay fears of the concerned groups who assume we plan to threat their clients unfairly. We must learn to underwrite genetic disease. (1998b: 11)

Furthermore, ideas were initiated regarding the design of new products, such as endowment life insurance (Pokorski 1997; American Academy of Actuaries 1998). The main idea was to offer a standard risk classification to persons who engage in healthy behaviour that is shown to mitigate the higher risk of their genetic predisposition to disease. Finally, there was a demand for research to investigate constructions that might distribute financial consequences of genetic risks among the private industry, taxpayers, policyholders and the state. For example, Tabarrok's (1994) idea of a "genetic insurance" has received much attention in insurance literature. This is a mandatory genetic insurance for everybody who takes a genetic test that would insure against the possibility of a positive test result. Another model that has been suggested by a number of commentators is that of using a pooling mechanism as a way of encouraging cooperation among the insurance companies and/or the state to insure those revealed to be at an increased risk as a consequence of a genetic test (e.g., Johansen 1999). A detailed model for such a reinsurance pool has been developed by Professor Wilkie (UK).

The insurance industry expected the actuarial approach to provide a way, instead of placing an emphasis on the equality of genetic and non-genetic information in an abstract and monolithic way, they would handle the issue on a case-by-case base. Through actuarial research, the issue of genetics and insurance could be reconstructed into bits and pieces: The implications of genetic testing on insurance need not be dealt with in a general way. Instead it could depend on a whole range of conditions varying from the type of the insurance product to the predictive value of a specific genetic test, the specific genetic disorder and the amount of insured capitals and the term of the insurance product (see, for example, Braun 1999; Ewald 1999; MacDonald 1999b). So the industry expected that exceptions to the general insurance principles for genetic information could be dealt with in a technical actuarial way.

In some cases this appeared to be the case. This was, for example, the way the issue was dealt with in the UK's policy on genetics and insurance. In this regard, the 1997 Human Genetics Advisory Commission (HGAC), in their report *The Implications of Genetic Testing for Insurance,* introduced technical actuarial conditions for the use of genetic testing in the insurance industry. They argued that a requirement by insurers that prospective policyholders disclose the results of particular genetic tests would only be acceptable when a quantifiable association had been established between a given pattern of test results and events "actuarially relevant" for a specific insurance product (HGAC 1997). In November 1998, the British Government agreed with the HGAC that an effective mechanism should be established to evaluate the reliability and actuarial evidence relating to the use of specific genetic tests by insurers (Department of Trade and Industry 1998). In this regard, it welcomed the then recently published Genetic Testing Code of Practice of the Association of British Insurers (ABI) (ABI 1997 and revised in 1999), which committed insurers to not require genetic tests for insurance purposes, and imposed a limited moratorium on the use by insurers of pre-existing genetic test results for mortgage-related life insurance policies for sums insured up to £ 100,000. This Code of Practice also suggested that the use of genetic tests should be limited by their reliability. As a response, the Government established the Genetics and Insurance Committee (GAIC) in April 1999, as a non-statutory advisory body to inform policy at the UK's Department of Health. GAIC was given the role of developing evaluation mechanisms for assessing genetic tests and the use of their results in setting insurance premiums. The criteria on which the GAIC would evaluate a submission from the insurance industry whether a test was suitable for insurance purposes should meet the conditions of "technical, clinical and actuarial relevance" (GAIC 2000).[14] The GAIC was approved by the ABI, with a spokesman commenting in the *Insurance Day*: "Such an initiative may well provide the industry with a much-needed route map if it is to negotiate its way through the minefield of public opinion." ("UK treads carefully on issue of genetic testing" 1998)

In October 2000, the GAIC announced that the genetic test for Huntington's disease was sufficiently reliable to be used for life insurance purposes. Furthermore, in response to a report *Whose Hands on Your Genes?* and recommendations from the Human Genetics Commission (HGC 2000, 2001a), the ABI negotiated a revised moratorium on the use of predictive genetic test results with the Government. For two years, beginning in October 2001, UK insurers continued to *not* require any genetic test results concerning *all* applications for life insurance products with sums insured for less than £ 300,000 (ABI 2001).[15]

This UK policy approach of dealing with the issue of genetics and insurance in a technical actuarial manner is currently considered by the rest of the insurance industry as the example to follow. For example, an American reinsurance spokesman notes that: "The United Kingdom is clearly ahead of the United States in terms of its government's response to the genetic testing issue" (cited in: Hiatt 1999: 65). In addition, current European policy on genetics and insurance also seems to take the technical, actuarial way of dealing with genetics as the prime model for finding solutions, even if not everyone shares this view.[16]

Fairness is not an actuarial issue

In discussing the actuarial solutions to the dilemmas of genetics and insurance, the insurance world appeared to be anything but an homogeneous community. Above all, it was the actuarial profession in reality that found it problematic being profiled as the "problem solver" in these dilemmas.

First of all, in the UK, there were actuarial profession comments on the "sound actuarial evidence" criteria of the GAIC to use genetic information in insurance situations. As indicated above, the actuarial sections of the submission to GAIC required evidence that demonstrated the "actuarial relevance" or significance of the genetic test to the type of insurance covered by the application. However, "actuarial relevance" was not formally defined. Moreover, in a reaction to the application requirements of the GAIC, the actuarial profession[17] commented that "there is no unique criterion (or set of criteria) for saying whether a test is significant" (Institute and Faculty of Actuaries 2001). In fact, the concept of "actuarial relevancy" and its definition appear to be a blurred concept. In actuarial training programs, for example, it is not mentioned or discussed at all and there are no univocal definitions in actuarial academic publications. Therefore, actuaries criticised the "woolly term" of "actuarial significance", as found, for example, in an editorial in the official publication of the UK Actuarial Profession, *The Actuary* (Dolan 2001).[18]

Secondly, UK actuaries commented on the shortcomings of the model and the data used in the submission results of the GAIC. Among others, they included the paucity of data in the research; the use of non-UK data; the choice of subjects for the studies (focusing on families with very strong family medical histories); and no standard published actuarial tables for some insurance products. For example, given that there was no precedent for the GAIC process for approval of test results anywhere in the world and that the industry had never been required to publish papers or statistical evidence to justify medical underwriting, there was little formally published actuarial material available describing any recognised methodology for this type of work. In addition, there were no statistics available which would directly indicate the probability that a person with an adverse genetic test result of any kind would make a claim on a particular type of insurance policy, since there was no existing research in this area. Therefore, it was necessary to use a combination of the most relevant published data from medical and epidemiological research together with expert opinions and results were sometimes used for a purpose which differed from that for which the studies had been established. The volume of data was also quite small and actuarial tables from non-UK countries were applied to the UK situation. In addition, it was regretted that the actuarial resource for the GAIC submissions was provided by a number of reinsurers and insurers, "whereby no attempt was made to obtain academic input" (Daykin et al. 2003: 20). Though the GAIC required a review of the submissions afterwards by relevant experts, it did not appear to demand that the work be carried out to the full peer-reviewed standards required for publication in scientific journals. Yet, there are still many problems regarding the academic peer-reviewed actuarial research in the area of genetics and insurance. For example, there is the lack of genetic data available to the insurance industry (actuaries depend on genetic epidemiology results) and problems regarding assumptions involved that affect insurance behaviour (cf. MacDonald 2001; 2003a).

Thirdly, and most importantly, actuaries noted that the burden of proof should not be solely based on sound actuarial principles and that actuarial criteria alone were not sufficient to deal with the genetics issue.

For example, the actuaries Moultrie and Thomas argued that "the actuarial profession has no monopoly on wisdom when society comes to decide between competing interpretations of fairness" (1996: 5). The authors did not claim that the actuarial approach was wrong, but that it was incomplete: besides actuarial principles, social acceptability underwriting criteria should be recognised. Consequently, the authors urged the insurance industry to recognise that they are not the only arbiters of fairness:

> The acceptability of underwriting procedures is societally determined and a profession which fails to recognise and make allowances for this may find itself ostracised and increasingly ignored. (1996: 11)

A broader social policy debate is necessary to deal with the genetics issue:

> A choice between alternative views of fairness is essentially a question of social philosophy. It is not an actuarial question, and actuarial science is of little assistance in thinking about it (1996: 4).

In the same way, the UK Actuarial Profession (2001) commented on the GAIC policy:

> ... in formulating UK policy in regard to insurers and genetic testing, it has to be recognised that the use of genetic tests results for underwriting purposes constitutes only a microcosm of the much broader issue of judgement about what constitutes 'fairness' in relation to differentiating between different policyholders in a free insurance market. There are social policy issues at stake here, which involve what are undeniably political decisions – how the interests of minority or potentially disadvantaged groups are to be protected and to what extent the majority can or will volunteer to 'pay' for that protection, or be required to do so by legislation (UK Actuarial Profession 2001).

Again here, the call was made for a political debate on the role of private insurance in society:

> The concept of 'common social good' has not been debated as fully as it might have been. What constitutes the common social good is a political issue and not, in the final analysis, the property of insurers, interest groups or actuaries (UK Actuarial Profession 2001).

Similarly, the ABI's voluntary abstention of genetic tests for normal-sized mortgage-related life insurance policies and/or the moratorium were evaluated by the UK actuarial profession[19] as examples of "lightweight social obligations" (2001). The GAIC has also been assessed for these reasons (Daykin 2001).

In the context of this, actuaries, for example, point to the commercial policy decisions of insurance companies. The private insurance market can be managed in different ways and insurance companies make commercial choices regarding their own underwriting "models". Consequently, although a particular risk factor can be made "actuarially relevant", it does not necessarily mean it is always taken into account by insurance companies:

> An insurance market segment may operate on 'actuarial equivalency' with a highly detailed risk classification but it could work equally well from an actuarial point of view if a less detailed classification were adopted, provided that there is a stable mix of risks within the class. This sort of variety exists between market segments, and any particular segment may also see change in this attribute over time (Daykin et al. 2003: 8-9).[20]

It is also not the case that a simple requirement that information be actuarially relevant is sufficient for society to consider it appropriate that the information be taken into account. Therefore, although the UK actuarial profession still acknowledges the actuarial-scientific approval of the GAIC as a necessary condition before genetic tests can be used for insurance purposes, they question whether this might also be a sufficient condition to resolve the issue. Along the same lines, Moseley and Allen stress:

> Suffice it to say, that an adequate concept of fairness has not sprung and will not spring automatically from actuarial calculations. They are a necessary condition for fairness in insurance, but they are hardly a sufficient condition (1999: 114).

In this regard, the use of a specific model of underwriting – "preferred underwriting" – is particularly criticised (e.g., Johansen 1999; Krinik 1999: 80). Whereas private insurance is theoretically based on mutuality, marketing practices and financial interests push (particularly American) insurers more and more into this model of underwriting. Instead of "rough", large sub-classifications (dividing the insurance population into some small subdivisions), this preferred underwriting strategy aims to sub-categorise the population into many categories as possible.[21] In that way, marketing can be directed to attract the healthy segment of the population by giving them cheaper rates and discourage the unhealthy individuals from joining the insurance risk group. The use of genetic testing thus "fits" perfectly into this fine-tuned actuarial rating approach of preferred underwriting. Yet, if the emphasis changes to a broader risk pooling approach in economic policy, the use of genetics is considered less relevant (Engman 1998; Institute and Faculty of Actuaries 2001).[22]

Some actuaries, therefore, feel the need to articulate a separate, professional perspective on the issue of genetics.

> The actuarial profession needs to be clear that, although actuaries are involved in the process of establishing the statistical justification for particular underwriting processes, the decision as to whether to implement them is not an actuarial one, but is a commercial decision taken by the life offices, modified by other social forces. This distinction between the role of the actuary as a professional and that of the industry is crucial if national associations wish to be regarded as professions, as opposed to trade unions of life insurance company employees or technicians (Moultrie and Thomas 1996: 9).

Although insurers prefer professional actuaries to provide scientific-based solutions to dilemmas of insurance and genetics, these experts take their professional role and scientific approach so seriously that they deny their ability to do so. They argue that the issues at stake demand political and not scientific solutions. They believe that the industry should not rely on statistics, but should instead reflect on its values.

Besides the actuarial profession, similar criticism came from some actual economic agents themselves. Again here, the different stances regarding genetics and insurance were due to the different economic policy visions of the companies and those operating within the various markets. For example, after the approval of the Huntington's disease test by the GAIC in the UK, some UK market players acknowledged they needed genetic information for profit and competitive reasons, while other insurance companies insisted that they did not want to use these test results at all, even when scientific-actuarially "approved" by the GAIC. Mr. Brady, a spokesman of the Co-operative Insurance Society (CIS), for example, noted that his company would not request that potential life insurance customers disclose the results of any genetic tests because "we simply do not feel it is right for CIS and our 4.5 million customers who support the co-operative ethos which underpins our business" (cited in *Insurance Day News* 2000). For these insurance companies, a total ban on genetic information is preferred to maintain general public trust in life insurance by not adding more hurdles for the customers.[23]

The Politics of Waiting

Confronted with internal and external discussions, the insurance professional associations have recently adopted a holding position towards the issue of genetics in the policy arena because there are still so many intangibles and unknowns surrounding genetic testing:

> Most agents did not seem to be overly anxious to become actively involved in evaluating applicants for genetic suitability. Instead the insurance industry is more likely to take a wait-and-see approach on the introduction of genetic testing for insurance purposes rather than take the lead in the debate (Zimmerman[24] cited in: West 1997).

These compromises are not merely publicly motivated, but must also be seen as reflective of the divisions within the insurance world. For example, the introduction of a broad moratorium by the ABI in the UK was evaluated as follows: "the policy statement could only ever be a compromise within the insurance industry" ("Genetic Deal" 2001). In the same way, umbrella organisations like the Comité Européen des Assurances (CEA) currently experience difficulties in coming to a uniform European insurance stance on the genetics issue due to internally divided opinions in insurance companies and national professional associations.

Actually, this move towards a wait-and-see approach seems to depend on the national regulatory and policy contexts in which professional associations have to manage the issue. In this respect, solutions vary from the introduction of temporary industry moratoria on the use of all genetic testing and on the use of genetic information within certain parameters or for some products or codes of practices to compromises being made within the regulatory legislation framework. In several European countries, including Germany, France and the Netherlands, moratoria are common in the genetics and insurance debates.[25] The insurance industry merely considers this a temporary situation and wants to reserve the right to use genetic information in the future because they fear the possible impact of widespread genetic testing for common diseases and its potential for adverse selection.[26] However, this reasoning cannot hide the fact that they remain worried about being forced to give up their routine underwriting methods. As the British actuary Daykin expressed in his lecture to the Royal Institution:

> The nervousness displayed by the insurance industry on this issue [of genetics] is most probably the product of more general concern about the serious erosion of the right to underwrite (2001).

In the same line, the CEA's note to Europe's national trade organisations indicated:

> Insurers do have to take action as otherwise restrictive legislation will be put in place. What is really at stake, however, is not only the right to have access to the genetic information available for insurer's risk assessments, but more generally the right and duty which insurers have to assess fairly the risks offered to them (Comité Européen des Assurances 2000: 2).

By contrast, the strategy of self-regulation in the United States was less enthusiastically received by the industry. Lowden and Roberts (1998) note that a lack of consensus between American insurers on the genetics issue obstructed the development of a voluntary agreement by the insurance industry. As a result, the ACLI is taking a "safe harbour" approach (Campbell 1998) by supporting legislation under the conditions that legislation should preserve insurers' access to medical information and by deploying an "exclusionary definition of genetic testing" (American Academy of Actuaries 2001).

Although insurers define these compromises as temporary, they substantially value them as a vehicle for the (re-)creation of public trust. According to Breyer of Cologne Re, the temporary moratorium in Germany is

> an effort to prevent restriction (by legislation) that insurers are considering their PR-effective declaration of intent ... At present, insurers are struggling to retain their status quo by showing goodwill (cited in: Fromme and Klager 2001).

The CEA memo of 2000 also considers codes of practices as a means for public trust:

> [This] code of practices may not be sufficient to prevent the enactment of restrictive legislation as world-wide there is a trend to legislate. Such a code would however contribute to significantly enhancing the insurers' image in the public eye and also show legislators their goodwill and desire to find a socially acceptable solution (CEA 2000: 2).

The holding approach, such as the British moratorium, is also a way "to take the heat out of the debate" (Tarling cited in: Hanney 2001). Thus insurers hope that within a couple of years, when genetics will become a common practice in clinical medicine, that the public's gene phobia will have abated, if not disappeared altogether, and that there will be a radically different public stance on the use of genetics in insurance. Pokorski, for one, suggests that there is "some hope for the future that unfavourable press will fade when testing spreads to the general population" (1997: 118). Or as the ABI's Francis argued after the introduction of a broad moratorium in the UK, it is important to show that the industry is concerned with "ethical issues" ("UK insurers grapple with an expected genetic moratorium" 2001), and that they "now have the breathing space to get this policy right and achieve agreement on the best way forward" (cited in: *BBC News* 2001). By negotiating temporary compromises that make an exception for genetic information, insurers try to maintain the status quo and to prevent worse scenarios. As such, these compromises function as a strategy to save their right to underwrite.

Conclusion

In line with Callon (1998), one could say that insurers, while originally viewing the genetics issue as a public relations problem, considered the genetics topic as an "externality". Callon's use of this concept should be situated within his theory of the "framing" of economic markets (see chapter I). "Genetics was not an issue", because it did not differ from other medical information and, as such, from the general insurance workings and principles. The business failed to frame ethical issues like privacy as relevant and therefore ignored them.

Yet, this framing of genetics has prompted regulative initiatives that have intervened in the insurance market. This changed the insurance industry's relationship, having a negative effect on the insurance business itself. Again, "genetics was not the issue" but insurers realised that their underwriting principles in general were at stake now. Confronted with these new externalities, insurers reflected on their original defensive approach and decided to *reframe* the externalities. Callon stresses that, in order to be reframed, such "externalities" or "overflowings" must be made measurable to allow incorporation in the insurance frame, via "calibrated measuring instruments" (1998: 268). This, then, is exactly what the insurance industry did. They returned to their actuarial devices in order to calculate the effects of genetics.

However, as we have seen, many difficulties arise with these actuarial solutions. First, these solutions are not immediately straightforward because of the shortcomings of the available models (too simplified), the lack of genetic data in insurance, in short, the uncertainties related to genetics as a science-in-the-making. Although Callon's emphasis is on the necessity of the calculativeness of the overflows, he also refers to the situations in which calculations are hard to establish, calling them "hot" situations.

> In 'hot' situations, everything becomes controversial... the controversy lurches first one way, then the other – because nothing is certain, neither the knowledge base nor the methods of measurement" (1998: 260-261).

The mitigating mechanisms of calculative measurements are hard to find here. In our case, this means that insurers, when confronted with the uncertainties of genetics, revert to temporary compromises and holding positions. To some extent, these provisional solutions can be considered ways of "taking the heat off" genetics (cf. quote Tarling supra).

But apart from this, the "calculators" themselves and other economic agents were not always enthusiastic about this actuarial approach as a way of solving the issue. Moreover, they considered it to be incomplete. They argued that within this actuarial approach, several kinds of political choices were involved, which involve the economic policies of insurance companies and the types of insurance markets. This is why they were in favour of political debates as a way to resolve the issue. How are we to account for this? Again, Callon's insights may help us. He argues that the current "hot" situations in society indicate serious transformations for our traditional technocratic policy-making. According to him, new forms of technology-science-society interactions have begun to appear. The rise of the service economy, or what he terms the "economy of qualities" [27] (Callon et al. 2002), leads to consumers becoming increasingly involved. This "economy of qualities" favours talkative, or "voicy" consumers. Because it creates more and more externalities, it increasingly affects consumer groups that can be a source of "overflowing" as well. These groups collectively formulate and express demands, that call for certain actions to be undertaken. The groups involved must then, in some way or another, be taken into account in the *making* of the product.

In this regard, Callon argues that there is a growing sense of the plurality of market forms and the need to open up the question of the particular form that markets take: "The organisation of markets becomes a collective issue and the economy becomes (again) political" (Callon et al. 2002: 197). He warns that it would be mistake for the actors involved in these complex "hot" situations to be simply opposed to markets or to marketisation. The issue is to develop new institutional arrangements that make it possible to debate how markets should be organised, calling them "hybrid forums". Forums because they are public spaces or arenas. Hybrid for two reasons. The first one applies to the variety and heterogeneity of the actors involved. Besides experts (e.g., economists, actuaries, medical directors), these hot issues should also be discussed by the economic agents themselves (e.g., CEO's of insurance companies, insurance trade organisations, consumer associations), as well as by researchers in the life or natural sciences. Secondly, these institutions are hybrid because the questions raised concern economy, politics, ethics, laws and science. Such processes are needed so that all of the actors *learn* about the qualification of the product. So where the limits of delegation become clear, *ex ante* participation is required in the *making* of the market, by means of "economic experiments".

Callon's analysis approximates our own when he proposes debating the plurality of markets forms, thus recognising the normative aspects involved in insurance companies' economic policy. As such, advocating hybrid forums as public spaces for debating "hot" situations implies the recognition of dimensions, such as the relevance of larger social effects in economic markets. Callon writes that in these hybrid forums

> it is impossible to separate or dissociate the different components of the issues, even for the sake of simplifying the analysis. The forms of organisation of markets defended by the actors engaged in the controversy vary, depending on those actors' political or ethical points of view or the way in which they evaluate the reliability of scientific facts or the efficacy of avail-

able technology. Isolating problems and solutions that could be considered purely economic would lead to socially illegitimate solutions. (Callon et al. 2002: 195)

These public debates can enhance "the emergence of new forms of competition" and a new form of organisation of markets (Callon et al. 2002: 196).

On a more general plane, then, the issue of genetics in insurance hooks up with current policy concerns around the uncertainty of scientific risks. As we have seen in chapter I, two approaches can be distinguished here: a technocratic strategy and an experimental learning strategy. At the end of the nineteenth century, when life insurance emerged as a commercial practice, technical and political strategies were largely interwoven into the public debates, so as to win public trust in this fairly new large-scale business (Porter 2000; Horstman 2001). As I have shown in this chapter, both strategies are represented in today's insurance world as well. While many authors expect much from the technocratic approach (the actuarial piecemeal engineering) – others call for a political approach that acknowledges that the definition of the main issues (risk, fairness, solidarity, responsibility) – and the way underwriting and the market are set up are matters involving normative acts.

As such, two modes of reflexivity seem to be involved. While acknowledging that insurers have to take genetics seriously as a way to enhance their business, one mode focuses on a type of accountability whereby more calculative measures, actuarial tables, audits and actuarial "evidence" are required from the insurance industry. The second mode emphasises the relevance of also involving the views of non-experts by means of political debates, "where facts become pliable and beyond the control of science" (Webster 2002: 453; cf. "post-normal science" in Funtowitz and Ravetz, 1993). Instead of delegation (to science), this approach focuses on the politics *of* economic markets, that is, *within* the process of knowledge production, or "the market as a public space" (Latour and Weibel 2005). The two approaches also require different kinds of actors and institutional work as a way to arrive at legitimate solutions. While the actuarial approach expects much from expert authorities, like actuaries or geneticists, the experimental learning approach expects more from the negotiations between the actors involved, meaning insurance professionals, consumer groups, ethicists, sociologists and economic agents. Such arrangements might entail inclusive debates on the organisation of the insurance market, the underwriting criteria to be used and the value of insurance.

Which one of these two strategies will dominate in the future debates on insurance and genetics? It is questionable whether technocratic solutions will be considered legitimate enough to build an economic practice on, and, as such, to reward trust from the public. This is exactly what voices from within the insurance business maintain when reflecting on the issue of genetics. The actuarial approach might be fruitful, but only in the context of a wider, political approach.

The insights into the world of insurers covered in this chapter offer a first illustration of the controvertibility of insurance principles, which are often denounced in public policy debates (cf. chapter I). By looking more in depth at the insurers' own accounts, it has become clear that the insurance world itself is divided and that, significantly enough, insiders themselves comment on the "givens" of insurance practice. In particular, I stressed the internal complexities of underwriting and the larger insurance markets. In the next chapters I will further explore these ideas by zooming in on the underwriting practices of insurance companies as another way to shed light on the "givens" of the insurance industry, including its actuarial principles, mortality statistics, and so on. At the same time, this will provide us with more insights into the genetics and insurance issue.

III Risky Bodies Stage 1: Constituting the Underwriting Practice

Introduction

The study of the process of risk assessment serves the broader purpose of offering more insight into the everyday practices of medical underwriting. This chapter is the first of three in which I address the risk trajectory of Karen, from her initial application to her final insurability result. As such, these chapters have a linear organisation: they trace the process by which Karen is gradually transformed from an *unknown* entity into a *known* insurability risk. In so doing, a host of actors is introduced, including underwriters, actuaries, medical advisors, questionnaires, lab tests, statistics and many others who have a role in risk assessment.

This first chapter focuses on the very beginning of this trajectory and I will start by looking at the way Karen "enters" the underwriting practice. What are the first indications that underwriters have of her? In other words, how is Karen caught in the web of underwriting and what machinery is set in motion? At first sight it might seem that this process acts like the assessment of an *unknown* applicant, via the request for medical information and "hints", towards a final *known* risk result. Yet, already from the start it will become clear that actually the reverse occurs: The way Karen is caught in the web is already pre-shaped and reflectively thought out *a priori*. An insurance company's underwriting practice is based on a wide array of economic, political, social and technical considerations. These are incorporated in the general policy of the firm and as such they pre-shape the process of medical underwriting. This character will be demonstrated here through a discussion of two major *entry devices*: the table and the medical questionnaire. This is how the chapter develops how the economic policy of an insurance company and its related underwriting strategies constitute underwriting as a practice. I highlight that policy considerations are woven as a fine thread through the broad tapestry of activities and embedded routines that together make up the underwriting practice of an insurance company.

The Non-Medical Appetiser of the Table

Flash 1: 20 April 2002:
John and Karen got married last year. With a loan from bank X they just bought a house in the centre of Leuven. Because the bank also sells insurance products, the bank representative informs the young couple about their mortgage products and offers them an information leaflet titled "General Conditions". After some deliberation the couple decides to apply for a mortgage insurance with the other person as beneficiary. They each sign the insurance application form, with the amount of capital insured (143,000 euros), their age (John 27, Karen 25), their income, the interest rate and the type of insurance contract.

Flash 2: 14 May 2002 - Case 1, medical underwriting department: Observation underwriter E:

E [*grabs a new file*]: Well, what have we got here? This is a young girl, with over 125,000 euros capital. So, apart from the medical questionnaire, they've also asked her to go in for a lab test. Let's see if the results have come back...
IvH: Huh? Hang on... I don't get it. Aren't you the one who decides what medical information is necessary to assess medical risk?
E: No, that has already been done at the bank. The bank officer has already stored the application form's data in the computer, like here, "mortgage insurance, for 143,000 euros capital, 25 years" ... And then the system says: "Well, 143,000 euros, that means we need a questionnaire filled in, a PV[28] and lab tests."
IvH: Ah, so they've already calculated that beforehand? The *system* decides?
E: Yes, that happens via the system, based on the computer program. So all applicants have to fill out a medical questionnaire... and it is the system that decides whether *extra* medical information is needed, such as a PV, which is required for capital above 75,000 euros. The system automatically shows this; we don't have to do anything.

As outlined in chapter I, based on the applicant's technical data (e.g., sum assured, age, gender), the ordinary rate (OR) or standard premium is calculated by the technical underwriting department. Meanwhile, the medical underwriting department is responsible for the medical risk assessment, that is, the extra mortality risk the applicant represents. However, as the above fragment illustrates, *before* the medical underwriting department actually comes into play, various technical facts are already taken into account as a way to pre-structure the medical risk assessment. Although all of the applicants need to fill out a medical questionnaire, depending on the technical data supplied, additional medical information may also be required, ranging from a medical examination by an appointed expert to several more or less specialised types of lab testing. The tool that is essential in this respect is the insurance *table*. From the outset of the underwriting process, this tool already provides a classification of applicants along non-medical characteristics. This enables the company to do a preliminary risk selection of applicants. In other words, this non-medical information functions as a *filter* for detecting Karen's proper way into the medical underwriting process.

Typecasting clients

In this first table-based classification of applicants, underwriters work with different norms of accuracy. A closer look at the table suggests that the accuracy of the medical information, rather than its content, serves as a primary selection criterion. Insurers need accuracy to control possible moral hazard or adverse selection, but depending on an applicant's non-medical data, they use different accuracy standards. For clients with large insured amounts of capital they immediately want to have detailed insight into their health status through extensive testing, but for others they are satisfied with a less detailed medical profile. This indicates that underwriters are not merely interested in *all* of the medical information supplied by *all* of the applicants. The level of information needed depends on the preconceived categories to which they belong. In this way, some clients are constructed *a priori* as higher risk than others, and, accordingly, stricter accuracy norms apply. An underwriter explains that he first looks at the amount of insured capital, because a large amount

> is of course a higher risk to us. The more capital, the higher the risk will be ... Well, no, not exactly the risk, of course that remains the same, regardless of the amount of capital. But I mean if somebody dies, the claim will be much higher in case of a large amount of capital, so we certainly need to... fix our rates correctly. With a smaller amount of capital, it is already less dangerous to overlook something, because the claims will be smaller as well (C2, K, 2).

The norms on what is *accurate* or *enough* information for medical risk assessment already colour Karen's further risk assessment trajectory and, as such, her final risk result as well. And this first colouring is above all based on technical characteristics. At this early stage of the underwriting process, Karen is still mainly considered as a collection of abstract technical details, rather than a *body* with her own medical profile.

Balancing acts: Constructing underwriting norms on accuracy

The initial selection via the table, based on the type of client, and its associated norms on accuracy indicate that insurers do not pursue detailed knowledge about every client's risk. This suggests that the insurance company, apart from accuracy, also takes into account *other* considerations. Where do these considerations come from? To answer this, let us go back to the first fragment above in which the underwriter explained that it was the "system" that calculated the required information. This system, a computer program, is grounded in statistical studies and underwriting policy considerations. Statistical studies offer information on how margins can be delineated and types of clients can be classified. This allows the company's management[29] to determine the accuracy norms that ultimately fix insurability results. In other words, accuracy norms are the outcome of the management's balancing acts involving a variety of considerations that all play a role in the underwriting policy. Several considerations are relevant here. First, the level of accuracy needed is balanced against cost-efficiency considerations. Consider this fragment, for example:

> When do you decide to send an applicant to a medical expert? It's hard to say... Is it necessary because he wants insurance for 50,000, 75,000, 100,000 or 125,000 euros or because he is 20, 30 or 40 years of age?... For large amounts of capital we ask expert information to protect ourselves. Imagine that you haven't been able to trace anything on the medical questionnaire and we insure him for 300,000 euros and then, the next day, there it is: we'll have to pay this 300,000 euros! So it is precisely because we want to protect our portfolio that we're sending him to the medical expert. Of course... we cannot send someone to a medical expert for an insured sum of a mere 12,500 euros. After all, where would our profit be, you see. Because these medical examinations cost us money! So... it's always more or less a balancing act, a weighing of things... (C2, J, 2).

Given that sending *all* applicants to a medical expert would imply too large a cost for the company, the management has built in a first selection criterion at the start of the process. It is aimed at selecting only those clients for whom the expenses of tests and examinations outweigh the risk of large claims afterwards. Insurers thus have to balance the promise of cost-efficiency against the risk of potentially large claims.

Secondly, the need for a certain degree of accuracy may also conflict with customer-friendly concerns. This consideration mainly applies to the marketability of insurance products. As a manager explained:

> These tables are imposed in a certain way, so that we cannot push it too far, you know. I mean, if we immediately send an applicant who has applied for 50,000 euros to a medical expert, this applicant might say: "Hey, if this is

the case, then I'm off to the competition because *they* won't ask me to do this." So that's really something we have to take into account as an important factor, the commercial battle. But of course, we also have to keep up a solid portfolio. Imagine the situation where we have to pay out 250,000 euros to a client and the claims department says: "Okay, but was the medical underwriting done correctly at the time of application?" Then we have to prove we did our job, isn't that right. It would be hard to say: "Well, okay, it's true, we didn't ask this information, but you know, she was such a good-looking woman. ... So all these things matter" (C2, I, 2).

Another marketing consideration involves customer relations: the company may opt for making an extra profit by selling multiple insurance products to the same applicant at the expense of medical accuracy. For example, if an applicant is already a loyal client with large sums insured for other insurance products, it is possible to attach less value to the dictates of the table:

I think that beyond the medical aspect – 'Is the applicant medically acceptable or not?' – you should also take into account other aspects. For example, there is the aspect of whether he is already a good client of our company. This is something we are changing right now in our underwriting policy because I think we've been rather too strict with that. Someone with a very large amount of capital insured in life insurance who applies for a small extra capital insurance for, let's say some 12,500 euros, because he needs some credit or something extra for a very restricted period, let's say some 3 to 5 years. In these cases, I think we have to work with more flexible criteria than the usual ones (C1, J, 2).

In other words, having a well-balanced portfolio is one thing, but procuring new clients or working on customer relations may be just as essential for the company's profits.

Underwriting, then, is based on a balance of a variety of considerations. Accuracy, though very relevant to the company's earnings, is just one aspect of the business. In fact, the underwriting leadership addresses a wide array of objectives and considerations, ranging from short-term production targets to long-term solutions. All these considerations contribute to a particular company's performance in the insurance market. The difficult task of finding the right balance between these considerations is a responsibility of corporate management. To some extent, their work is like building a house of cards and keeping it standing. Adding one extra card may undermine the structure's stability and cause it to collapse. Playing the card of accuracy, for example, may disturb the balance with the risk of low returns or losses due to excessive spending on medical examinations. Therefore, sound underwriting policy depends on an ongoing process of carefully balancing all of the relevant considerations and available strategies. This often entails a precarious balance. First, how does one define a high-risk group? And second, what if new or unforeseen elements influence the established risk involved? How should one take this into account and readjust one's assessment? Managing an underwriting department can be likened to walking a tightrope.

Reflective managers: Assessing the risk of risk assessment

The management has several tools for predicting or re-assessing a properly balanced underwriting policy. First, it may rely on statistical studies, like cost benefit studies performed at the actuarial department, which compare the costs of tools for obtaining and processing medical information with the value of the mortality savings that would result from using these instruments. Such studies, then, may give rise to insurance table adjustments. Consider the following excerpts:

> Sending an applicant to a medical expert costs us some money and the question is whether this outweighs the benefits. Q [the chief actuary] is in charge of this task. In the long term, we would like to raise the table's limits because these days, well, you have to take into account that the insured amount of loans is increasing, given that properties and homes continue to become more expensive. For us this means that at some point we realise that all these people in fact belong to a higher bracket; I mean the amount of capital has continued to increase while we continue to work with tables based on old figures. Therefore, we would like to raise our current capital limit in the tables and study how far we can go. We have to of course ask ourselves: Can we afford being more lenient by requesting less medical information from that group? And if we were to work with a new limitation, how much would we save annually? (C1, K, 2).

> We're always updating the statistics of medical costs. And I suppose everything is currently well balanced. But of course, it's quite possible that it will turn out later that we spent too much on medical examinations in a given year, and that they [the management] will probably react by saying: 'We're going to have to lower the cut-off point in the tables because we've noticed that these medical procedures did not yield us much additional evidence' (C2, I, 2).

In response to new situations or while trying out new underwriting strategies, the management may benefit from actuarial models and studies, from "calibrated measuring instruments" (Callon 1998: 268). Such tools may confirm that changes in the underwriting policy are urgently needed.

The quotations above also demonstrate that a particular underwriting policy can only be evaluated properly *a posteriori*. Based on specific actuarial models, the management may choose to implement a new underwriting strategy, but there is always a chance of bias in these actuarial models. After all, the statistical models are based on *previous* underwriting results and clients' behaviour. In a way, the management thus has to rely on predictions of the insurance market in the future as well as on the *expectations* or *perceptions* of prospective clients' behaviour in the market. The statistics, then, have to be complemented with specific expectations. In the first quotation, for example, the management anticipated the future clients' behaviour by taking into account the current trend toward rising real estate values. This external influence may necessitate that risk categories be adjusted because more insured capital is at stake, which in turn, means that more testing or more stringent medical examinations are called for. That more stringent procedures come with the risk of losing potential clients, however, is also a management concern. In this instance, this is all the more relevant because the particular group of young people buying homes is considered quite interesting from an insurance angle. In other words, the company anticipates this group's future market behaviour. By upgrading the table's statistical limits they attempt to attract this group of insurance buyers. In a "re-framing" or "re-qualification" (Callon 1998), the pros and cons of marketability and accuracy are weighed. The above fragments also shows that insurers closely monitor changes and developments in society because of their potential relevance to their business. Because the social norms on property values have changed, the norms for insurability will have to be changed accordingly.

Finally, underwriters also tend to monitor the activities of their market competitors and this may even cause them to revise their own underwriting strategies. For example, I noticed that my informants were quite well informed about their competitors:

> We are one of the most stringent underwriting firms in the Belgian market. For example, we already sent an applicant who requested a 70,000 euro's loan to a medical expert. Yet in company Y, as I happen to know, they only do so beginning at 100,000 euros and in company Z they only request examinations beginning at 150,000 euros (C1, R, 2).

This information about other companies also contributes to decisions regarding underwriting strategies, as a way to "keep up with the Joneses". So besides calculating their own underwriting policy (with statistical studies), insurers also calculate in the other market players' policies. In this respect, Callon (1998: 50) argues that "once a market is organised, economic agents could include, by construction, in its calculations the calculations of the other agencies."

The underwriting management, then, in re-framing or re-qualifying its policy, may rely on actuarial tools, expectations about clients' behaviour and assessments of their competitors' actions. Its calculations, however, can also be wrong. Depending on how clients or the market reacts, a new underwriting policy succeeds or needs to be re-adjusted along the way. In this regard, a company's underwriting policy is always subject to a process of "trial and error". Despite its mathematical models, underwriting remains to some extent *uncertain or guesswork*: insurers have to *take risks*. In this sense, deploying underwriting strategies is a matter of "assessing the risk of risk assessment".

Risk categories have wheels: The mobility of the table

The above suggests that risk assessment involves a variety of underwriting considerations regarding accuracy, cost-efficiency or marketing. They are reflected in the insurance table, which serves as a first filtering mechanism for selecting the appropriate medical procedures for particular types of applicants. Economic considerations around the distribution of available sources thus come first, pre-structuring the medical risk assessment. But insurance companies can select different margins for their tables, or depending on underwriting policy reforms, rearrange the table's margins. In our example with Karen, it turns out that changes in underwriting policy affect the medical procedures she will be required to undergo. After all, underwriting strategies may change the boundaries of the risk category to which she belongs and this may alter her final insurance risk result. In other words, risk categories have wheels (Prior 2001). Underwriting considerations shape the nature of the risk category Karen belongs to and determine her future risk trajectory. But these considerations not only serve as a first filtering mechanism; they also play an important role in Karen's *medical* risk assessment. By exploring the device of the medical questionnaire, I elaborate this aspect below.

Positioning the Product: The Medical Questionnaire

Luring clients

The medical questionnaire is the general device deployed to all applicants as part of risk assessment. For one thing, the questionnaire is crucial in obtaining medical information from Karen. After all, such information is vital to acquiring medical accuracy and, as such, safeguarding the company's portfolio. At the same time, the questionnaire also offers Karen the first inside glimpse of the company's workings. For this reason, management considers it a relevant instrument in the deployment of marketability strategies. Advertising is one way to attract future clients, but the medical questionnaire may have a similar function. To some extent, the medical questionnaire then functions as the company's display window. As such, it helps to draw in clients and to "position the product" (Callon et al. 2002) and this is why management is constantly looking for ways to make it as attractive as possible to future customers.

This relevance of marketability can be situated within the overall economic policy of the company. How does it want to make or raise profits? Choosing for a solid portfolio by means of accurate underwriting is just one option. A company may also be after higher sales by offering more flexible underwriting guidelines, or it may target young affluent clients by not requiring any underwriting at all in order to lure them into purchasing its other products as well. Or it may attract customers via other strategies, such as favourable interest rates or offering profit sharing. Medical accuracy can thus be relevant, more or less, depending on the company's overall economic policy.[30] Such policy choices are in turn related to the company's specific local characteristics, for example the type of insurance company it is. Companies may work with brokers or – as is currently the trend – merge with banks. My case 1 was this type of bank insurance company, so it had to take into account the profit interests of the bank as well. This meant that if the insurance company was too strict in its underwriting policies, it might put the clients' commitment to the company at risk, including its banking products. A less stringent questionnaire thus may raise the company's sales figures.

However, as my informants stressed, it is essential to bear in mind that the crucial role of the questionnaire is acquiring accurate medical information, which in turn may prevent having to reward excessive claims afterwards. Maximising sales, then, can be a risky strategy in the end. In this regard, Belgian insurance companies are also monitored by the Insurance Supervisory Authority (ISA), installed by Belgian legislation.[31] Each year the ISA examines the overall financial situation to ascertain whether a firm is able to meet its commitments. Notwithstanding these regulative mechanisms, Belgian insurance companies can still compete for higher profits *within* these collective confines:

> So we all are bound by statutory margins ... There are of course some competitive opportunities we can exploit, such as cost-cutting measures or trying to sell products with more flexible underwriting ... I think there is a tendency that the market is becoming more divergent. I think that right now there are already companies that pursue more flexible underwriting, thereby accepting applicants more easily than companies that hold on to traditional politics ... All of the companies are trying to find the best market niche and then, well, they say: 'We're going after ... that type of client, that's ours', or 'Well, from now on it will be young people we focus on', to try and lure them in. Each company has its own analysis, doesn't it? (BVVO, M, 2).

In this regard, my informants noted that currently several foreign players have swept through the Belgian market, focusing on marketability and profit-making rather than on a solid portfolio, even though this may have major consequences for their stability in the long run. In addition, some foreign players attract clients through lenient underwriting, but when it comes to rewarding claims they refuse to uphold their responsibilities. In other words, being lenient in the beginning and then more stringent later is just another marketing strategy. My Belgian informants all expressed their discomfort with these types of business strategies, referring to these companies as "cut-price shops" or "under-cutters" (C2, D, 2).

The above again illustrates that different considerations need to be balanced in the a company's own underwriting policy. The medical questionnaire is one of the "outputs" of these *a priori* balancing acts. But the insurance company may also re-evaluate its strategies, as a way to requalify its products. In fact, during my fieldwork in case 1, it turned out that the company already had plans to reform its underwriting policy, including the design of the medical questionnaire, reducing it to a list of ten items. I discuss these planned reforms in more detail below.

Balancing acts: Reforms in the making

The management plans to reform the questionnaire were mainly tied to product marketability and sales figures because of its recent merging with a bank. One manager favoured working with a more abbreviated questionnaire because the product "first of all needs to be sold", adding that the company in general could use a better "sales mentality" (C1, J, 2). In supporting this sales-oriented approach, the management argued that clients have a dislike of medical underwriting:

> The public doesn't understand the principles of medical selection and its advantages... So clients shy away from medical underwriting ... From the moment you say 'You'll have to go in for a medical examination or a medical test', then, oh dear ... ' (C1, J, 2).

This marketability argument ("What the client most wants") used by the management was also emphasised by the underwriters in the department in support of medical accuracy. For the underwriters stressed accuracy as the most expedient way to be fair to clients, assuming that clients want insurance rates that are tailored to their specific insurance risks, whereas a more sales-oriented approach might result in problems concerning claims afterwards. As an underwriter explained:

> Yeah, that's, hmm, that's more a choice they want to make now in underwriting policy. But I think we'll gain more legitimacy in the public's eye if we do our underwriting on an accurate basis After all, if *they* [management] introduce more simplified questionnaires, *we* run the risk of not having established certain medical facts, which may turn out to be a problem in the end. Afterwards, if there is a death, the claims department will tell the client's relatives: 'Yes, but you didn't declare it at the time of underwriting so you weren't bona fide.' And that's when the dust starts flying because the

client's relatives will say: 'Okay, but *you* didn't ask for it on your medical questionnaire (C1, K, 2).

In other words, the underwriters assumed the clients' preferences to be just the other way around, suggesting that clients *do* want medical underwriting.

This example again illustrates that *assumptions* on a client's future buying behaviour were taken into account. So clients, or rather, assumptions about clients, indirectly contribute to (or "co-construct") future risk assessment (Callon et al. 2002). The above also demonstrates that these assumptions might vary. Tellingly, both management and underwriters applied the same maxim: "The customer is always right".

In light of these conflicting views between management and the underwriters, it is instructive to have a look at each of their particular competencies within the company. Apart from rivalling views regarding *external* marketability ("what does the client want"), their differences may be related to their *internal* roles, relations and interests. First, corporate management's preference towards productivity and sales figures seems to be closely related to the general economic policy of the firm and the history of its recent merger with a bank. This puts into perspective the view of one of the managers, as quoted above, that the company was in need of a better "sales mentality". The company's insurance division, which used to be independent before the merger, had always been concerned with the company's portfolio rather than with maximising sales, and hence with prioritising "restricted access" and "conditionality" in selling insurance products. In our fictitious case of Karen who applied for mortgage insurance, the company runs the risk of losing her as a client for both insurance *and* loans if she considers the company's medical underwriting practice too stringent. In the same way, a manager in case 2 commented on bank insurance:

> But you also have to consider the difference between a bank-insurer and a normal insurance company. For bank-assurers, the loan is most important, isn't it ... So I think these underwriters receive the order for these mortgage products from their management accompanied with a phrase like 'not too much drivel here, or else we risk losing money!' So I think, as these cases illustrate, medical underwriting really is of less relevance ... (C2, I, 2).[32]

A closer consideration of the underwriters' concern for accuracy reveals a direct link with their competencies within the company. Because it is the medical underwriting department which is responsible in the company when the number of claims or their amounts are excessive. As discussed above, medical underwriting is vital to avoiding excessive claims afterwards. In this regard, the medical underwriting department is closely associated with the claims department. The quality of the underwriters' work is always formally checked by the claims department. In the case of a relaxation of the underwriting standards, therefore, the underwriters fear they will be the ones held accountable when things don't go according to plan. Consider the following comment on another product (group insurance) sold under more flexible conditions:

> We already have, for instance, this X product, with its simplified questionnaire ... Afterwards, it is the claims department that gets into trouble and they come back to us asking: 'Why haven't you asked for this particular condition?' And all we can say is: 'Well, because it wasn't mentioned on the medical questionnaire' ... So these simplified statements give us a lot of trouble these days ... Well, hmm, you see, if we only have this bit of information to build our decisions on ... it's not very easy, is it? And afterwards we're the bad guys (C1, P, 3).

This, in part, explains the underwriters' focus on accuracy. In order to win internal credibility, underwriters feel they need the information that allows them to create an accurate risk profile.

Notwithstanding this, it should be noted that in the end, *all* of the actors serve the company's collective goals, and this certainly includes the task of creating a solid portfolio. However, given this bottom line, there are margins, of course, different priorities or considerations, alternative strategies. Even though managers favour flexible underwriting, this does not mean they completely ignore the solidity of their business.

> We would never relax the underwriting rules just like that, at random, solely for the sake of pleasing customers. But that doesn't mean we're not doing our utmost to make underwriting as efficient and client-friendly as possible (C1, J, 2).

Again we see that diverging considerations reflect different norms on "having enough information". The balancing of these considerations is centred around the *right* construction of accuracy. In other words, the central question for management is: "When is enough 'enough'?" Obviously, accuracy, or actuarial fairness, is a *fluid* concept, largely depending on how a company establishes its standards of what constitutes "enough information". And this is, as we have seen, the result of a balancing of countless considerations, interests and priorities. Again here, the actuarial tools are essential in assessing this "right" balance between these considerations. In the period of my fieldwork, the different stances seemed to be smoothed out through the company's actuarial expertise. In other words, actuaries were called upon to find expiatory solutions for the management's final decision.

Actuaries: Assessing the risk of risk assessment

Some months before my fieldwork started, an actuary had been appointed to the head of the underwriting department. From management I learned that he was meant to serve as a bridge between the actuarial and the medical underwriting department, a role mainly inspired by the reform plans. So, this actuary engaged in statistical research of the risk assessment aspects of the reform plans. As such, he conducted cost benefit studies of the medical tools used in underwriting, analysed to what extent a more flexible approach could "co-exist with" accuracy considerations by using the ISA statistics and compared the firm's strategies with other market players by doing a comparative study of their competitors' questionnaires.

As actuary, he felt that reform, however, was not a straightforward matter. This became clear in a presentation he gave to management. Being aware of the reform plans, he prepared a rather defensive paper with an overview of the theoretical necessity of medical underwriting. This actuary's views suggested that management's effort to deploy actuarial expertise in support of its reform plans involved a complicated matter. Generally speaking, it seems that actuaries to some extent need to bend their views and standards with the company's specific economic plans and policies. In this respect, an informant at the Royal Association of Belgian Actuaries (KVBA-ARAB) explained:

> The actuary has to adapt to the firm's economic policy and indeed develop his strategies accordingly ... One can only really learn such matters on the job because there is no time during one's academic education ... and also, of course, because it differs so much from one company to the next, given that such things largely depend on the company's culture. I mean, from the moment an actuary begins working for a company and grows familiar with its *culture*, he'll be able to deploy his technical expertise. But first he has to wait and see, doesn't he, until he has become actively involved in the company. So there is in fact a difference between theory and practice. You can imagine the most beautiful actuarial theories, but in the end, when you join the insurance industry, you always end up having to go along with the company's own economic policy and guidelines (ARAB, A, 2).

Actuaries at insurance companies must *translate* their actuarial know-how and considerations into the company's economic policy, or, inversely, the company's economic goals are translated into actuarial know-how. Thus the actuary takes on the role of "intermediary" between the economic ordering and the actuarial ordering in the company (Callon 1991).[33] As such, the above is a further illustration of the fact that insurance principles are *made* to fit the specific localised objectives of a particular insurance company:

> Because, well, if an actuary works at a particular insurance company and he starts to calculate the actuarial reserves ... Well, then you might say that the calculation of the actuarial reserves can only be done in one way. However, you always offer an interpretation; there is always some latitude. So if you ask two actuaries from different companies to calculate the same case, you will probably end up with two different results (ARAB, A, 2).

To some extent, therefore, actuaries perform a double role while working at a particular insurance company. This seems particularly true for the appointed actuary who monitors the company's actuarial-technical orthodoxy in matters like the marketing of a new product, the technical provisions and profit-sharing. In this regard, he is responsible for the annual accounts to the Insurance Supervisory Authority (ISA) (cf. supra). This actuary has to reconcile the company's economic policy strategies with the ISA standards. As a vital link in the company's decision making and risk management, he is considered a kind of internal watchdog, often labelled "conservative" by the more liberal, business-minded actors involved. On their double role as actuary and employee, an Association of Belgian Actuaries (ARAB) informant explained:

> Sometimes the actuarial advice may end up slightly contrary to management's ideas. This may be a rather tricky situation for the actuary at an insurance company. Because sometimes he has to oppose economic management. And, well, he can't say too much of course, for he is also an employee, you see. But this is often a rather difficult situation for actuaries. I mean they are in fact wearing two hats, isn't it? (ARAB, A, 2).[34]

It is not surprising that actuaries ultimately tend to conform to policy strategies and reform plans initiated by the company's management:

> Anyway, the actuary attempts to realise his technical expertise, while the company may support a more cost-efficient approach, but when the chips are down, the actuary will probably have to conform to the company's will. I mean, in the end ... you end up having to obey the company rules imposed, even if they prove counterproductive. These are the times when you feel you are in a rather weak position as an employee (ARAB, A, 2).

Ultimately the corporate managers not only benefit from actuarial studies when planning these reforms; they also compare their strategies with those of other players in the same market. In this regard, the company where I performed my fieldwork did a comparative study of the medical questionnaire used by competitors in terms of its layout, phrasing and contents. This was just another strategy in setting out the new business strategy – in an effort to assess the risk of reforming risk assessment. By comparing their standards with those of others, insurers trace out their own business strategies and this allows them to position their product as effectively as possible.

Risk categories have wheels: The mobility of the medical questionnaire

As a result of the reforms in the company, the medical questionnaire was indeed *rewritten*. This shows that the questionnaire is indeed a "script" (Akrich and Latour 1992). First of all, a script *inscribes* a particular program of actions. As we have seen, the questionnaire can be considered a (temporarily) "outbalanced" outcome of different considerations on underwriting circulating in the department. In other words, the questionnaire is important in establishing order or enabling the framing of the market transaction. To some extent, it is the crystallisation of a variety of considerations, values and priorities of the different actors (e.g., underwriters, corporate management, echelon managers and clients). Secondly, while deploying these considerations in the questionnaire, it also *pre-scribes* the positions and tasks of the involved actors. Consequently, it also *pre-scribes* Karen's risk trajectory. In other words, the questionnaire is rewritten in such a way as to direct or pre-structure Karen's answers. The company *pre-scribes a priori* (based on its studies) how much medical information Karen should give and which applicants should be attracted.

Such writing devices often operate on a method of "successive adjustments" (Callon 2002: 192). That is, they are only temporarily crystallised. As we have seen, the insurance company can re-adjust its policy towards new clients' expectations, shifts in balances between several considerations or newly enacted regulations. Moreover, applicants themselves seem to indirectly participate in this rewriting act because, as we have seen, they co-construct the underwriting policy. This happens first of all through the data provided by previous clients as found on the questionnaires, which, after being processed into statistics, offer managers specific insights for their future underwriting policy. Secondly, this occurs through the insurers' perceptions on clients' behaviour, which are also taken into account in efforts aimed at reforming underwriting policy. In this regard, the actuaries (in statistical studies), the underwriters (in their evaluations of the underwriting department) and other managers (as in reports from the claims department) are also involved in rewriting the questionnaires. As Callon (2002: 205) playfully comments: "Just as spokespersons exist, so do "wrote-persons", or more simply, scribes." Who, then, is ultimately the questionnaire's author? This is corporate management, because only they have the authority to oversee the entire set of statistics, measurable results and collected writings. All the data and writings, in other words, converge in a manager's office. Although all of the other actors may have valuable insights, interesting strategies, or good foresight, they all lack the management's overview of the operations.

A web of considerations, then, seems to pre-structure the risk assessment process, while its particular framing is written in the medical questionnaire. This influences the risk status of applicants and this is also why medical questionnaires may differ from one company to the next. Moreover, medical questionnaires are subject to revision. In line with our previous argument on the insurance table, the malleability of the medical questionnaire demonstrates the flexibility of risk categories.

Conclusion

To conclude this chapter, I would like to single out some observations that further illuminate how this assemblage work pertains to public policy debates on genetics and insurance. First, the considerations mentioned above not only deal with underwriting policy but also with the broader issue of the relevance of underwriting in the company's general business strategy. Throughout the chapter, I have generally referred to this web of considerations as "the economic policy" of the company. The adjective "economic", however, should not be understood narrowly here. As we have seen, underwriting, though based on economic goals, has to take into account many considerations, such as the assumed preferences of clients, social acceptability concerns, regulative issues, or the public image of insurance. In other words, the realm of the "economic" in this context also implies a variety of social, legal, and ethical considerations. Whereas in public policy debates on genetics and insurance, the "economic" is often weighed against the "ethical", the above suggests that the company's economic policy might involve both. Of course, it is up to each individual company to decide *to what extent* its economic policy is directed towards or reflective of such considerations as part of their business strategies.

Secondly, the technical criteria in the table (e.g., sum insured) pre-structure the medical risk assessment trajectory of the applicants, and this has particular relevancy in light of the genetics and insurance debate. To some extent, these policy debates tend to have a narrow focus on the *medical* aspects of risk selection, while the proposed solutions seem to be primarily directed towards medico-actuarial aspects of genetics. However, the above demonstrates that there is a major preliminary side to underwriting that is based on *non*-medical characteristics and that pre-shapes, pre-selects or filters the medical risk assessment. This suggests that the debate on genetics and insurance commences at the *wrong* stage of the applicants' risk trajectory. After all, the preliminary work determines the route the applicant will take in later stages of the risk assessment process, and, as such, this work already influences the final risk result.

Next, the fieldwork material revealed the various interactions between the company's economic policy and its statistical know-how. Thus I argued that insurance principles, such as actuarial fairness, are *flexible* concepts, linked to the company's underwriting standards on the amount of medical information needed and fashioned to fit its particular economic policy. Unlike staged in debates on genetics and insurance, insurance principles are not static or "given", but produced and performed in variable, configured and particular localised underwriting practices. As suggested in chapter II, it is exactly within the actuarial professional group that doubts have been raised on actuarial solutions to the problem of genetics in insurance. They acknowledged that in this context it was not possible simply to construe actuarial fairness or actuarial relevancy on the basis of actuarial devices alone because these concepts reflect political *choices* in underwriting policy.

Fourthly, in sorting out the various considerations, it is also possible to take into account the clients. Although they are not physically present in the underwriting process, indirectly they may co-construct or co-write underwriting policy (e.g., via assumptions on clients' expectations, via statistics based on answers supplied by previous applicants). This also echoes the argument, addressed in the previous chapter by some insurers, that the insurance industry should take into account clients' concerns about genetics, notably the ethical dimension, as a way of maintaining public trust in insurance. Yet, it appears that this taking into account of clients in insurance is mainly done *indirectly*. In this regard, no direct surveys or other feedback mechanisms are available in a particular insurance company (as in contrast to other service organisations such as telecommunications, informatics, or tour operators). As a result, views about clients' expectations are often largely based on *assumptions*. But it is difficult to establish whether these assumptions actually correspond to reality. This indirectness increases the chance of "noise" in the translation of clients' expectations into underwriting policies and into the making of insurance risks.

Finally, it should be noted that this idea of deploying underwriting strategies or *choices* in the company's policy does not imply some kind of "voluntarism". After all, I have argued that such choices are (also) embedded in the particular local regularities of the company or the general insurance market. As such, these policy choices can be confined by the particular history of a company or by a particular insurance industry regulation the company abides by. The latter may lead to certain local insurance industry traditions or even some kind of uniformity in the market. However, *within* these regulative confines, innovating profit-making strategies (aimed at more cost-efficiency, automation, marketability and so on) still might prove possible. Insurance companies innovate their policies by comparing their economic strategies with those of their competitors. But, of course, this "carefully watching each other" may in turn create a rather uniform insurance market. It is a question, in other words, if the *free workings* of the insurance market place specific confines on a company's policy. Thus, even in the absence of regulative confines, the policy choices of insurance companies may dissolve in the particular localities and shared understandings of the insurance market. To some extent, this can be considered a kind of self-regulation of the "free" insurance market.

These observations again raise two other concerns about the public policy debate on genetics and insurance. First, these self-regulative confines between companies in the insurance market may question the free-market principle as proclaimed by insurers in the genetics and insurance debate. As we have seen, it was argued that the free market itself would solve the issue of genetics. Where one company refuses to take a genetic risk, other companies, as a competitive strategy, might still take that same risk ("You can always go to another company"). But the above raises doubts about whether consumers are really *free* to go somewhere else. It suggests that the free market is an artefact because companies tend to always be interrelated through their collective history and their comparisons of competitive strategies. Secondly, when I asked informants about self-regulative initiatives in regard to insurability issues, it was often claimed this was not possible because of the fear that such measures were legally sanctioned due to cartel formation. In other words, cartel regulation pre-formats the Belgian insurance market in a particular way: it restricts insurers from making inter-company agreements on this matter. Or should we read this as a case where insurers are not *ready* to take inter-company initiatives when it comes to these kinds of concerns? As illustrated in chapter II, ethical issues might affect insurance, if only by contributing to a negative public image of the industry. In other words, it is the *collective* insurance industry that suffers major setbacks from these kinds of issues. This might explain why it is primarily the insurance industry's professional organisations who appear to be concerned.

IV Risky Bodies Stage 2: Governing by Numbers

"Father, I have often thought that life is very short."
"It is short, no doubt, my dear. Still, the average duration of human life is proved to have increased of late years. The calculation of various life assurance and annuities offices, among other figures which cannot go wrong, have established the fact."
"I speak of my own life, father."
"O indeed? Still," said Mr. Gradgrind, "I need not point out to you, Louisa, that it is governed by the laws which govern lives in the aggregate"
Charles Dickens, *Hard Times*, 1990

Introduction

In this chapter, I will follow another step in Karen's risk trajectory by focusing on the medical risk assessment itself. If the previous chapter demonstrated how insurance companies *a priori* select specific medical information from the applicants, this chapter deals with how they use this information for establishing risk categories and final decisions on insurability. Before moving on, let us first return to Karen and see how she is faring at this particular stage of the risk trajectory.

Flash 1: Leuven, 21 April 2002, at home – Fictional prologue:
Karen is filling out her medical questionnaire.

Flash 2: Leuven, 2 May 2002, medical expert's office:
Because of the sum insured for the mortgage, Karen was required to have a medical examination. After seeing Karen, the medical expert sends the medical examination report ("protocol") to the underwriting department of insurance company X in Brussels.

Flash 3 Brussels, 14 May 2002, case 1, medical underwriting department: Observation of underwriter E
"What have we got here? [*reads from Karen's questionnaire*] 'Young woman of twenty-five, works at university, 143,000 euros.' For this in-

sured sum they required a questionnaire and a medical examination. [*reads on*] 'Diseases: 'asthma'. But the last occurrence dates back twelve years, she writes. Hang on, let me check the black cover [= internal guidelines]: [*reads*] 'asthma longer than five years ago', which means I don't have to ask the GP for extra information. Further there are no major problems, she does not smoke, no weight problems. Oh, well, here she writes she's taking medication... [*checks medical dictionary*] well, that's a product for hypertension ... Let's first have a look now at the protocol from the medical expert. [*reads*] Well, so this is her blood pressure, systolic and diastolic [*reads the numbers*]. Now we can look. [*opens to a table in the reinsurance manual*] This table here is established to calculate the 'degrees' of hypertension: 'borderline, slight, moderate or serious hypertension'. So she's in the category of '88-92' mm Hg for diastolic and '148-162' mm Hg for systolic. This suggests slight hypertension. But she was already taking medication. Well, I think it's best to ask for additional information on this hypertension. Let's have a look in the guidelines. [*reads*] For this insured sum, we are required to ask for additional information on 'arterial hypertension' from the GP. That will give us some more detailed information. What else do we have here in the protocol? [*reads on*] 'slight swelling of the thyroid glands', with the expert adding at the end of the report: 'possibly check thyroid gland'. I'll thus need to ask for an additional lab test on the thyroid gland, again according to the guidelines here [*points to the black cover*]. So, I'll enter in the computer that we need to send an additional questionnaire to the GP and do an extra lab test for the thyroid gland."

Flash 4: Brussels, 24 May 2002, Case 1, medical underwriting department: Observation chief underwriter

"[*reads from the questionnaire*]: 25 years, 143,000 euros, ... [*checks protocol*] Here we have the protocol from the medical expert. [*reads results*], Hmm, that's hypertension and the thyroid gland... What else did they [*underwriters*] ask? I see, they ordered lab tests for the thyroid gland. Well, let's go on, here we have the lab results for the thyroid gland. [*reads*] Here are all her results and here are the reference values, and as you can see, the results all fit in perfectly within the limits. So she is in the normal zone; that's okay with me. What else have we got? The additional GP questionnaire regarding her hypertension: [*reads*] Oh, I see, she's currently under treatment ... [*reads measurements*] Well, she's doing fine here. '130, 6+3= 9' ... So that's 101 ... Adding them up, divided by 3 ... gives '86'. Next, I check the relevant table in the reinsurance manual: '139, 86', that's range '138-147' for systolic and range '51-87' for diastolic, which falls into the category of 'borderline hypertension'. Now it's 'borderline hypertension', but in the medical expert's protocol it showed up as 'slight hypertension'. Well, normally [*looks in the reinsurance manual*] we don't have to give a substandard rate for 'borderline', that is defined here as 'standard rate'. So starting from 'slight hypertension', the substandard average rate is 50 per cent. But depending on additional factors like, for example, a recent normal ECG, the average rate can also be reduced to 25 per cent. Well, actually I don't feel like rating her for this hypertension. Let's first look to see whether the rest of the questionnaire is fine. I mean, if she was a smoker, for instance, that would change my opinion. [*checks questionnaire*] Okay, fine, she's not a smoker. [*reads*] So, the GP also sent the ECG results, and these are okay, too. 'No over-exertion', and 'no grounds for pulmonary hypertension'. Apparently she reacts well to her medication. Hmm, the medical advisor here suggests a substandard rate of 25 per cent ... Well, I think I'll just accept her at standard rate because everything looks quite okay to me. She's in between 'borderline' and 'slight' hypertension, but her ECG results are fine, and that's also a determining factor for reducing the substandard rate from 50 per cent to 25 per cent. And if you consider the different tests over time, she's improving, which means she's responding well to the medication. So I think she qualifies as standard risk."

As the above example illustrates, the underwriter did not consider Karen's file "clean". Because it contained a few "abnormalities", additional information was required. This involved the introduction of a whole range of new actors, from lab tests, statistics, a GP to the reinsurance manual. As I will demonstrate, their deployment serves only one goal: to transform an unknown Karen into a known insurance risk. Yet, as with chapter III, actually the reverse seems to be the case. The way Karen is caught in the web of underwriting is pre-configured by underwriting policy inscribed in these very devices. The chapter will also shed some light on how the underwriting process frames Karen's health in a particular statistical way. As a person, "Karen" will basically disappear behind the questionnaire and its strictly delimited categories, the statistical numbers of *her* blood pressure, and the statistical risk categories of *her* hypertension figures. All these factors contribute to her categorisation as an *individual* insurance risk. But what is the origin of this desire for statistics in insurance? Where do these medico-actuarial instruments and numbers come from? In order to develop a basic understanding of their deployment, let us first briefly return to the historical roots of the medical risk selection process.

The numerical rating system: "Sometimes you need an objective partner"

At the beginnings of the insurance industry, life tables were developed by actuaries to help establish rates for annuities and insurance contracts. A life table defines, for some category of people, the number per one hundred thousand that can be expected to be alive at each birthday up to the age of one hundred. Stable mortality rates were widely advertised in the nineteenth century as evidence that even human life is subject to statistical laws. Yet, the validity of these mortality tables depended on careful selection of so-called "quality lives" (Porter 2000: 227). It was universally understood among actuaries that without careful selection, life insurance was purchased by people who feared they were in poor health and who would thus die at higher rates than the tables predicted ("adverse selection"). Life insurance was in fact the first insurance product based on medical selection of people's lives. At first, this type of insurance was sold to people who passed a medical examination performed by the company's medical advisor (Jureidini and White 2000). This examination determined a candidate's insurability. At the beginning of the twentieth century, however, the life insurance industry increasingly met with public criticism and distrust (Porter 2000; Horstman 2001). The public saw medical examinations as suspect because they were dependent on the medical advisor's judgement. The insurance industry itself wasn't entirely happy either with this selection procedure because of dissimulation, moral hazard and fraud. The latter in particular could adversely affect the company's solvency, which in turn could influence the public's perception of the business. But above all, the public increasingly demanded the insurability of people who did not meet the business standards for insurance policies, but who still represented very low risks of dying young.

Several authors have argued that in order to counter this problem of distrust, the insurance industry began to develop a more *objective*, science-based approach. As such, this is one illustration of the argument that professionals turn to numbers, not when they are strong, but when they are weak. In *Trust in Numbers: The Pursuit of Objectivity in Science and Public Life*, Porter (1995) notes how the transition from expert judgement to the "language of quantity" did not grow out of the attempts of powerful insiders to make better decisions, but rather emerged as a strategy of impersonality in response to exposure to pressures from outside. Along those same lines, Rose (2002a: 223) has argued:

> Strong professionals, who are invested with public trust, have no need to justify their judgments in the supposed objectivity of numbers. Yet when under threat – when their powers and capacities are disputed by a distrustful alliance of politicians, professional rivals, academics, and public opinion – the lure of the number, the 'power of the single figure', is hard to resist.

In the early years of the twentieth century, then, in response to the industry's declining reputation, insurers resorted to an assortment of scientific entities and measurements. Refined actuarial methods, statistics and instrument readings were developed to (re-)establish their credibility and the public's acknowledgement of the necessity for insurance. As Porter (2000: 239) notes:

> On this account, nothing was more necessary for insurance examination than simple, reliable instruments, that did not depend on refined skills or subtle judgment on the part of medical examiners and that got around the habitual reticence of applicants. The companies needed objects to measure and tools to measure them.

In addition, the insurers' reliance on testing instruments can be related to the growing success of the sector in that period, because these instruments contributed to a more efficient way of doing business. Instead of submitting every applicant to a complete examination (performed by the medical advisor), "rapid, accurate methods of lab testing" (Dupree 1997: 101) and diagnostic tools could be deployed as a more efficient way of doing business. Moreover, these historical examples demonstrate that it was the insurance business itself that could push the frontiers of medical technology. Besides bringing medical tools into the insurance business, some insurers were the actual inventors of these instruments.

This overall development resulted in the establishment of a specific measurement and classification scheme, called "the numerical rating system". This method, designed for calculating premium rates for people who normally would not qualify for life insurance, was first described in 1919 by a physician, Dr. Oscar Rodgers, and an actuary, Arthur Hunter. It relied on tools aimed at detecting medical information (e.g., lab tests, height and weight tables), which allow one to assign debits and credits to applicants and put them into statistical risk categories. Via underwriting manuals, a detailed list of mortality risks and diagnostic tests was established; it explained how insurance companies should assess the various medical data of their applicants. Over the years, this numerical rating method has become the standard in life insurance underwriting. The development of this system, including the extensive mortality investigations prompted by it, facilitated a vast expansion of substandard underwriting, thus enlarging the business's potential clientele. But its most significant effect was that insurers were no longer dependent on the judgement of medical advisors alone. The insurability of applicants was no longer exclusively based on an examination of their body, but on abstract numbers, statistical techniques, and diagnostic tools. The deployment of abstract mathematical numbers and tools, then, was considered to be a boon for technical certainty and objectivity in the insurance business, as a way to enhance both public trust and efficiency.

The numerical rating system is still the central mechanism insurers use for translating individuals into insurance risks. As our Karen example illustrates, the reinsurance manual used by the underwriters played a crucial role. It provides a detailed list of mortality risks (derived from mortality statistics) and related guidelines on measurement readings, cut-off points and numbers. The manual also suggests how the insurance company should interpret Karen's medical data and which additional information should be requested. Based on this information, Karen's final insurance rating can be determined. This chapter then concentrates on how these medico-actuarial devices are embedded in underwriting practices. We trace this by first focusing on how mortality statistics and risk classification factors are constructed, after which the attention will be on the measuring tools to detect Karen's medical information and to inscribe her into the "right" statistics.

Categorising Risky Bodies

First, the statistics and risk categories trigger a number of obvious questions. On what are these devices based? Which considerations are used in their establishment? As discussed in chapter II, the insurance industry views the devices as a technical, scientific and objective activity. For example, a European reinsurance company study claims that

> Entrance into a cohort of insured lives is controlled by the insurer, who must see to it that each new entrant pays a fair and adequate premium. This is not determined according to socio-political criteria, but rather according to the principle of causality, whereby persons who are expected to cause higher costs need to pay a higher entry price (Swiss Re 1991: 4).

The "principle of causality" refers here to actuarial-scientific mechanisms revealing the extra mortality risk for a particular risk category, such as smokers, for example. It is possible to address the assemblage work involved in these insurance statistics with the help of several key insights from studies on the construction of statistics. In this literature, the concept of "ethnostatistics" is used to describe the constructed character of statistical data, as well as to refer to the socio-cultural and political practices that label statistical data as "objective" and "scientific" phenomena (Bloor et al. 1991: 131). It is argued that in the construction of "quantification accounts" several considerations reflect *a priori* on what should be counted and how it should be counted. For example, in applying these insights to epidemiology, Petersen and Lupton (1996: 39) argue:

> The very choice of what phenomena require measurement and surveillance is a product of socio-cultural processes, related to such factors as the research interests of the epidemiologists involved, current knowledge systems

> about the links between human behaviours or embodied characteristics and illness and disease, access to resources to fund research and surveillance strategies, the interests of the organisations in which epidemiologists are located, feasibility of measurement, and ethical and political considerations.

What then are the considerations embedded in choosing a risk classification factor in insurance? To demonstrate this assemblage work of insurance statistics, I first reconstruct the introduction of smoking into the insurance industry. This case sheds some light on the web of concerns involved in the deployment of risk categories in insurance.

Case: The insurance making of the smoking risk

After World War Two, the rise of modern epidemiology contributed to the development of a predictive style of reasoning in public health.[35] In this context, several studies were done on the link between smoking and lung cancer as well. In 1950, for example, Doll and Hill published their now famous study speculating on the linkage between smoking and lung cancer (Hennekens 1998). Although this research has been applied in clinical medicine since the seventies, it took the European insurance industry some more decades before it began to differentiate between smokers and non-smokers. Why did insurers not use this information on smoking at the time when it became known?

Of course, insurers closely watched developments in epidemiology pertaining to smoking as a new means of differentiation in their business. However, in order to use this new risk factor, the insurance business needed to transform epidemiological data into insurance data. That is, in order to study the actuarial relevancy of smoking, actuaries needed to collect data on the mortality risk of smoking throughout the insurable population. But to do so, actuaries were dependent upon the underwriting *practices* of insurance companies. Insurance statistics are usually based on the medical information supplied by applicants at the time of underwriting. It turned out, however, that data on smoking behaviour had neither been collected systematically, nor did companies request such information from their applicants. For a long time, insurance companies believed that society would not be prepared to tolerate differentiations based on smoking (McGleenan 2001: 60). In the 1960s, as one life insurance handbook suggests, life insurance companies were nevertheless "well-aware that smoking had deleterious effects on health and longevity but *intentionally* chose not to include it as a rating factor" (Huebner and Black 1969: 477). As long as the public did not consider smoking as related to unhealthy behaviour or an irresponsible lifestyle, insurers felt it could not be applied as a standard for risk classification in underwriting. Apparently, insurance companies, when pondering the introduction of a new risk classification factor, carefully take into account its level of social acceptability.

After some time, however, innovators in the insurance business, in pursuit of market incentives, began to develop alternative ways of introducing smoking behaviour into the insurance industry. In 1969, for instance, an American insurer, State Mutual Life Assurance company, started collecting data on smoking behaviour, motivated by marketing concerns aimed at attracting healthy, non-smoking clients and indirectly acting on the Surgeon General's 1964 report on smoking and health (Brackenridge and Elder 1992: 902, 906). To some extent, these innovators were thus constructing the smoking population. Since the late 1980s, the American life insurance industry has gradually adapted this risk rating approach for smoking, followed in the 1990s by the European life insurance market. Still today, however, it remains difficult to collect the right literature on smoking, given the out-of-date nature of the available statistics. In other words, current underwriting policies on smoking still bear the consequences of social preferences previously embedded in underwriting practices. A recent study of a European reinsurance company indicates that data on smoking habits are lacking because companies failed to ask for smoking information or because confirmed smoking was not always reliably coded. In some countries, the "recording of smoking habits was for a long time very patchy, and this is reflected in small exposures for smokers" (Swiss Re 2002: 11), as well as limited opportunities for insurance companies to take smoking rates into account.

The smoking example illustrates that insurers take various considerations into account when faced with the acceptance of a new risk classification factor. First, they weighed concerns tied to social acceptability. Insurance statistics were, to some extent, dependent on whether information on smoking was actually available. This in turn was related, in part, to social images of smoking as an unhealthy habit. The implication is that insurance company clients themselves are, to some extent, co-constructors or producers of underwriting practices (Callon et al. 2002). We see that along the lines of chapter III a new underwriting policy may depend on available statistical data and on information provided by the responses of previous policyholders. The constructed nature of insurance then becomes evident here in the way that the statistical data are collected and analysed. Socio-cultural processes determine the adoption of smoking as a risk factor. Insurance mortality risks are thus subject to negotiation and revision and are not merely static or unambiguous facts.

At the same time, market innovators, inspired by profit-making concerns, attempted to bypass the acceptance of smoking as a risk factor. Because they began to consider smoking as very useful in further differentiating between the insured, they started to collect data on smoking habits and, as such, to construct a smoking population. Based on these new statistical data, they established the actuarial relevancy of smoking, while establishing relationships between smoking and mortality. Again, this further illustrates the construction work involved in insurance statistics. The ways in which the smoking risk category was defined and measured in insurance was subject here to particular profit-making concerns. By collecting data on smoking habits, insurers were now able to *produce* the actuarial relevancy of smoking.

In this regard, some authors have criticised the "simplifications" used in the causal models between the observed correlations in insurance in the deployment of the "actuarial relevancy" criterion. They argue that much of insurance knowledge consists only of observed statistical correlations between risk variables and future losses, but that causality is never proven. Brockett and Tankersley (1997) use the example of smoking to illustrate this point. While it seems widely accepted that smoking "causes" certain types of cancer, the actual causal link has never been proven, they argue. In the same line, Wils (1994: 457) notes that observed correlations between smoking and mortality "can be understood as reflecting a causal relationship. But they normally indicate only one among many causes, and explain only part of the risk or loss occurrence." More generally, the risk classification process is not based on causality, but on empirically observed statistical increases in the probability of loss. "If a causality test were required there would be no classification system which would be acceptable" (Brockett and Tankersley 1997: 1667). In the same vein, McGleenan argues that many of the classification factors used to set insurance premiums "are not causally related to future loss in the sense that there is a direct link between gender, for example, and motor accidents" (2001: 43). In other words, the factors insurers often choose in their classifications happen to show a statistical correlation with the risk concerned, thereby probably hiding some real causes with which they correlate imperfectly. Though these risk factors only indicate one cause among many, while they explain only part of the mortality risk, they often receive a taken-for-granted status as a major insurance mortality risk.[36] In this regard, the choice of whether to adopt a risk classification factor in insurance is often related to the cost-efficiency and practical concerns of insurers. Wils (1994: 457) comments that the obvious reason is practical: "insurers will choose risk factors according to how difficult (costly) it is to gather the necessary information and administer the classification." As an example, Wils adds the preference of insurers to use gender classifications over more sophisticated classifications based on (partly underlying) real causal factors "because gender can be observed at virtually no cost." A private insurance market, then, seems interested in adopting just a few correlations in risk classification. The risk factors they use are mostly selected on economic and practical grounds, according to their utility, efficiency, or availability (McGleenan 2001: 40).

The smoking example then serves as an early illustration of the web of concerns that determines how specific health characteristics are turned into risk classification factors in insurance. Below I will return to my fieldwork material to further establish this.

Balancing acts in deploying statistics

If we return to Karen's case once again, we may observe that the underwriters used the risk categories and related insurance ratings from the reinsurance manual. In general, the role of the reinsurance company is to take on the share of large risks that the insurance company cannot carry alone. The reinsurer restores the balance by spreading risks globally and over longer time periods. In other words, whereas the insurance company is the direct insurer of an individual, the company itself can spread its risks by transferring all or part of those risks to one or more reinsurance companies. At the beginning of each year, an insurance company enters into an agreement with one or more reinsurance companies, in which the terms under which the risks covered by the agreement are ceded and accepted. To some extent, the reinsurance company is thus the insurer of the insurance company. As the website of a European reinsurer puts it:

> If the role of our clients, life and health insurers, can be summarised as protecting the lifestyle and meeting the future financial needs of their customers, then the role of Swiss Re might be described in similar terms. Our purpose is to protect the balance sheets of our clients and to help them meet their future capital requirements.[37]

Most of these reinsurance companies are internationally oriented, have offices in many countries, and have a large portfolio.[38] Examples for Europe are Cologne Re, Münich Re, Swiss Re or Gerling Re.

It is precisely these reinsurance companies that provide most to the establishment of insurance mortality statistics and the risk categories. This is not so surprising because the reinsurance business is most often confronted with "special risks". Hence its interest in managing medico-actuarial knowledge and its (financial) input in medico-actuarial research. Reinsurance companies have a separate department at their headquarters dedicated to medico-actuarial statistics and studies. In order to build their ratings and risk classifications, the medical directors and actuaries from this department are provided with the reinsurance portfolio. This is a statistical database of all of the information on the policies received.[39] Based on these reinsurance mortality statistics, excess mortality for particular mortality risks can be calculated. The key task thereby is to find variables that group similar risks in such a manner that there are statistically significant loss differences ("excess mortality") as compared to the standard rate class. Based on these studies, reinsurance manuals are provided to the ceding insurance companies, including risk categories, guidelines, tables and insurance ratings.

By and large, reinsurance companies are relevant innovators when it comes to medico-actuarial research in insurance. First, they have the know-how to do these studies, plus they have a large international database of insurance policies at their disposal. Secondly, the relevance of doing such studies and investments is directly related to their profits (and those of the insurance companies). Moreover, and perhaps as a consequence of this more than average interest in medical innovation and knowledge, reinsurance companies can sometimes be innovators in medical scholarship. For instance, it is telling that a document of a European reinsurance company suggests its mortality studies are "not only used for a commensurate risk assessment in life assurance. They have also provided much valuable impetus in general medicine, e.g., the knowledge gained from life assurance studies on the prognostic importance of overweight" (Swiss Re 1991: 11).

Thanks to these medico-actuarial studies, reinsurance companies are capable of rearranging risk categories, and, as such, influence the insurability results of applicants. In other words, reinsurance companies constitute another level in which the manoeuvrability of risk categories and statistics becomes visible. This rearranging of risk categories is motivated by several considerations. Besides the need for risk classification factors as a new means of differentiating between applicants (profit-making), as in the case of smoking, reinsurance companies may rearrange their ratings to arrive at more accuracy for the insurance companies so as to avoid excessive claims. In addition, reinsurance companies can readjust their ratings because the pattern of diseases changes over time. A medical advisor of an American reinsurance company indicated that the definitions and exclusion criteria used by the insurance companies it works with "vary widely and change over time, largely because the incidence of chronic disease is not static" (Ivanovic 1999: 25). Yet, modifications in the conceptualisation of disease in society or clinical medicine might prove difficult to apply in insurance because the older statistics do not yet reflect this new knowledge. In the case of a "new" disease, reinsurers have no insurance statistics on which to build their ratings. In this regard, the chief underwriter of case 1 referred to chronic fatigue syndrome (CFS). While this condition is increasingly conceptualised as a physical disorder in clinical medicine, the company still lacks any insurance data on CFS for rating these people:

> Consider for example this new chronic fatigue syndrome. It is only known in parts of Western Europe and the US. But if you go to Italy or Spain, they have just never heard of this condition ... So these are things I can't find anything on in my reinsurance manual, you see. But I also can't deny this thing exists. We have these reports from GP's stating they have diagnosed this person with this condition, and then I feel we also have to do something for the insurance rating. (C1, K, 2) [40]

Such time lags between insurance and clinical medicine have also been reported in the case of the insurability for patients who now have an increased life expectancy thanks to new treatments (e.g., diabetes, HIV).

Because the old insurance statistics are still based on the mortality rates of the previous policyholders, the insurance ratings present excessive mortality that does not reflect the current mortality rate. In other words, because of this time lag, these patients are currently over-rated in insurance. Yet, to comply with such innovations or modifications, reinsurance companies also may opt to revert to clinical or epidemiological data. These medical data then are translated for particular insurance interests. In this regard, recent studies from reinsurance companies resulted for instance in better insurability ratings for hypercholesterolemia patients (by taking into account recent treatments), Hepatitis C (HCV) patients and (kidney) organ transplants patients, sometimes as the result of negotiation with these patient groups themselves.[41]

On the basis of these innovative medico-actuarial studies, then, reinsurance companies may invest in the adoption or rearrangement of risk categories. The incentive to invest in such research can be related to quite different concerns, resulting in quite a variety of effects on insurability. As the smoking case illustrates, investments in new statistics and risk categories can be motivated first of all by profit concerns. The "discovery" of a new disease in clinical medicine is translated into increased ratings for these people because insurers consider these applicants an increased risk for their portfolio. In other words, an aspect's medicalisation is translated into a substandard rating in insurance.[41] At the same time, we have also seen that the investment in this medico-actuarial research could result in *better* insurability for people, as in the case of taking into account new treatments for specific disorders. The manoeuvrability of reinsurance statistics can thus be played out against quite opposite concerns or benefits, and, consequently, highly variable insurability results for applicants.

The actuarial research effort of reinsurance companies, then, demonstrates again that statistical risk categories are flexible rather than static. During my fieldwork, for instance, the reinsurance manual used in underwriting was periodically replaced by a newly updated version. As an underwriter explained:

> Our reinsurance company provides us with the underwriting manual that lists the substandard rates for the different risks. But the reinsurance company also revises it periodically. Right now, for example, a new manual from our reinsurer will be coming out soon (C1, R, 3).

Given the revision of the reinsurance statistics then, insurability ratings in this insurance company have been changed. Along these same lines, insurability results may differ because there are several reinsurance company players on the market, resulting in inter-company differences in insurability ratings. In addition, as we have seen, an insurance company has to negotiate with a reinsurance company on the contract conditions. Based on the mutual evaluation of this contract, in some cases an insurance company may decide to discontinue the contract with one reinsurance company and switch to another. In case 2, for example, corporate management recently decided to enter into a contract with a new reinsurance company (Re2). But occasionally the underwriters still compared the risk ratings of Re2 with those of the reinsurance company they used to work with (Re1). The difference in insurability results among reinsurance companies was an issue:

> I clearly see some rating differences between [Re1] and [Re2]. That was really awkward for me. Like take some diseases, for example, this 'Chronic Fatigue Syndrome', at [Re1] it just was not rated at all, except when it also involved a psychic disorder, like depression or something. But now, I had this file, I thought, I'm gonna send that to [Re2] and [Re1] to compare their ratings, and indeed, they are really two different companies because at [Re1] it was accepted and at [Re2] they advised a substandard rate of 50%. And then I think like: 50%, that's really something. Normally we only give that to people who already have a really serious disorder or something, you see? So I found that rather odd. But, well, it's not up to me to decide which reinsurance company our company enters into a contract with, is it. (C2, R, 2).

Yet, given the relevancy of these reinsurance manuals for an insurance company, it sometimes turns out that it is still the insurance company that has the final say in the deployment of risk categories. So insurance companies have some elbow room in their relative autonomy to diverge from the reinsurance company instructions. For instance, it may occur that insurance companies decide *not* to completely follow the reinsurance manual. Although the one used in case 2 lists smoking as a risk classification factor, the smoking rate, for example, was not applied in case 2. This was related in part to the particular company's history: their clientele largely consisted of public servants and "because these people all tended to smoke" (C2, J, 3), it would not have been a good business strategy to use this as a factor. A manager explained that because nearly every policyholder smoked, he therefore believed that

> they relaxed that guideline in the reinsurance handbook and only rate for smoking if there is also another disorder present. Because otherwise they have to rate everybody, isn't that right? ... And that's why, currently, we still don't use this smoking rate ... So now we often have potential customers who call us to tell us they are non-smokers. Well, then all we can say is: 'Congratulations, good for you! That's nice, but that is totally irrelevant here' (C2, V, 2).

In this regard, the reinsurance company also stresses the *advisory* role of the manual in its introduction:

> This manual is the first part of our work and also the most relevant aspect for everyday risk assessment. It is strictly meant as a guideline, designed both for the medical advisor and the non-medical trained underwriter. The individual guidelines are based on a new, flexible way of rating and on the most recent developments in medical knowledge (Re1, manual). [my translation]

Throughout the manual's introduction, reference is made to the room for manoeuvring individual insurance companies have:

> The excess mortality figures in this manual are a true reflection of current medical knowledge. They do not contain solvability or profit margins. Their aim is to enable the insurer to come to a risk assessment that is as accurate as possible. Whether or not the insurer decides afterwards to compensate for the increased risk is a purely commercial decision, which has nothing to do with the rating guidelines (Re1, manual). [my translation]

To some extent, it seems the reinsurance company wants to position itself as a "neutral" organisation, "only offering the scientific numbers" in its manual. It is then up to the insurance companies if, how and when to deploy these risk categories and ratings, and, above all, to strike a balance between the manual's data and their own underwriting policy. In practice, however, simply because most Belgian insurance companies lack the know-how found in the reinsurance manuals, they basically rely on these manuals in their risk assessment practices. But as the above example of smoking in case 2 has illustrated, some leeway may be available in deploying these devices.

However, apart from relying on reinsurance statistics, companies can build their risk rating on their *own* insurance population as well, based on their experience statistics. In case 1, the presence of such experience statistics derived from the company's previous activities. This company had a history of insurance, and it had always had a large stake in the Belgian life insurance market, with a clientele that is representative of the Belgian population as a whole. Data had been collected on policyholders since the company's establishment. By contrast, case 2 had always had a rather particular clientele, mainly consisting of civil servants. As a consequence, the management involved in case 2 did not feel much need to differentiate between risks and, therefore, to invest in experience statistics. As a manager explained:

> In our company we do not collect data on our own underwriting because, well, first of all, we do not have that many insurance policies here. We can't take that into account because we don't have large enough figures here to calculate it actuarially. And further, well, (case 2) is still a bit politically ... I mean, we are still bearing the consequences of the past. We used to be there primarily for civil servants, even though we are now privatised. But this his-

tory still haunts us, I mean, we used to be rather flexible in our underwriting. I mean, these civil servants, they were all the same and they didn't present large risks to us, you see; they just sit there at their desks all day, so they were not exposed to major risks (C2, V, 2).

What are the possible effects of collecting experience statistics? Let us explore this via case 1.

Observation case 1, underwriter D:
Underwriter opens a computer window, thereby coding the insurance result of the file in the computer.
D: "So, these are all codes [*shows code book*], ... and now [*looks at computer screen*], I'll code all the specific data of this file into the computer program. So the data of this file are stored in a statistical database and I code the type of product of this file, sex, date of birth, and here, that she [*the applicant*] was assigned a substandard rate, so that is code 1, and this here is for diabetes, code 34, and then the terms of the policy; I turn it all into statistical data."
IvH: "I see ... so actually you are now collecting data for future actuarial research?"
D: "Well, it is in fact for monitoring whether we are still doing our underwriting correctly. I mean, based on this database, by means of our coding, in the R&D department you have the 'actuarial research department', so there are people who regularly check these statistics, like: 'For these particular disorders, we have assigned a substandard rate of X%, does that in fact represent the same percentage in our actual mortality risks [*claims*]? And if not, they can react to this by changing the rating. Or they do particular selections in their studies, like: 'Give me all the males who have taken out a policy before the age of 45 and who have diabetes. How many have died in the meantime?' ... And if there is a clear significant difference between the underwritten percentages and the mortality risk over a longer period, then they take that into account in the future, which leads to changes in the substandard percentages" (C1, D, 3).

In other words, experience statistics allow the insurance company to change the risk categories and risk ratings. Consequently, the substandard norms in case 1, derived from their own experience statistics, could deviate from the norms inscribed in the reinsurance manual.

Apart from the reinsurer's manual and given that our experience studies have proven that our figures are more favourable in some cases and more adverse in other cases, new internal guidelines that differ from those of the reinsurer with different rating percentages were implemented. For example, the last study revealed that for some disorders, like epilepsy and diabetes with insulin treatments, we had far better figures than the reinsurance manual. Based on these experience studies, then, we now apply the lower rates for these disorders (C1, K, 2).

The opposite, however, is also possible. Based on the experience studies, some risks previously accepted at standard rates, may eventually end up being underwritten at substandard rates, resulting in an extra premium for the applicants. In addition, company experience studies could also help determine the type of risk decision. For example, whereas previously mortality risks above X per cent were underwritten as "excluded" from coverage, these risks might now be rated as a substandard risk. In other words, the cut-off point for "exclusion" has been readjusted. Consequently, applicants who were previously excluded from coverage might now be accepted at a substandard rate.

Again, we see that the risk categories can change. A company's experience statistics can turn normal risks into abnormal risks or vice versa, thus allowing some latitude in underwriting policy. This flexibility via experience statistics may be deployed to serve quite opposite commercial policy strategies, though. For example, by breaking down the unity of the product or the sub-population of policyholders, the company can tailor its prices to new market niches, thereby favouring certain applicants at the expense of others. Or it fine tunes its underwriting policy to fit its portfolio needs, thereby taking into account cost-efficiency concerns. Mast and Gaubast (2000) appropriately characterise experience statistics as the "strategic scalpel in dissecting the company's business." At the same time, these calculative tools may allow the company to produce better insurability results for substandard applicants. In this regard, we have already seen that applicants with diabetes were better off in case 1 (via the experience statistics) than in case 2 (via the reinsurance statistics).[43] Consequently, having detailed experience statistics can raise an insurance company's competitive edge over companies active in the same market. "The probability of gain," as Callon notes, "is on the side of the agency with the greatest powers of calculation, that is to say, whose tools enable it to perform, to make visible and to take into account the greatest numbers of relations and entities" (1998: 45). The availability of experience statistics may render an insurance company less dependent on the powerful reinsurance companies. The drawbacks of such dependency can be seen in terms of Callon's chess match between Kasparov and the IBM Deeper Blue (1998: 45-46). Callon refers to the "parasiting" of calculative agencies by another one, which by imposing its calculation tools and rules forces the host agencies to engage in its mode of calculation. "It is almost as if Kasparov... had to start calculating his moves not by playing like Kasparov but by imagining himself in the computer's position, that is to say, by borrowing from it its algorithms and calculation rules." Individual insurance companies are, like the Kasparovs, to a great extent dependent on the reinsurance companies for their statistical know-how. By establishing their own experience statistics, however, insurance companies can attempt to increase their independence, thus improving their competitive edge.

Regarding the Belgian insurance market, most insurance companies are dependent upon reinsurance companies for their statistics when underwriting insurance risks. After all, the availability of experience statistics is hardly a self-evident matter. As we have seen, the particular history of the company or its market niche might restrict its ability to invest in experience statistics. The choice of whether to capitalise on actuarial research also tends to be tied to a company's larger economic policy, including the relevance of medical underwriting as part of its general profit-making strategy.[44] Another potential restriction, insurance regulation, does not apply here because there is basically no specific regulation for Belgian insurance companies regarding this matter.[45] The Insurance Supervisory Authority (ISA) does not have any direct power to control or intervene in Belgian insurance companies in this matter. Yet, because of the strong dependence on the know-how of reinsurance companies, substandard underwriting is not a major competitive strategy among Belgian insurance companies. The specific routines of the general Belgian insurance market might be relevant in this regard. Belgian insurance companies, given their dependence on European reinsurance companies, usually embrace a mass underwriting approach, in which risk differentiation is merely done for some general risk factors. This differs significantly from another underwriting philosophy, that is, the preferred risks approach (cf. chapter II). Insurance markets in the US, New Zealand and (to some extent) the UK, for instance, are far more competitive in differentiating between applicants.

Finally, actuarial research at a national *inter-company* level (e.g., in national professional actuarial or insurance organisations) was considered impossible because of Belgian regulations on cartel information (cf. chapter III). Yet, again here, competitive concerns might also hinder this kind of inter-company research, given the importance of actuarial data as a competitive tool for an insurance company. As an informant explained:

> If we were to plan such an actuarial inter-company study, and we were to contact all of the individual companies, well, I wonder. What would be the response? Practically zero, I think. It would be very limited because each company – this is in fact still somewhat of a Belgian mentality, isn't it – would worry their competitor copying them. So here in Belgium it is nearly impossible to do actuarial research, given this kind of mentality. It is true, one should be more open, but ... (ARAB, B, 2).[46]

Currently, competitive considerations do very little to encourage self-regulative inter-company actuarial research on insurability issues, if it is not the market ideology itself that prevents this scientific-actuarial research from being conducted. It should be noted, however, that the Belgian Association of Insurers (BVVO) has organised working groups to discuss particular insurability problems. Recently, for example, a working group that included medical experts discussed the insurability of diabetes. The results were communicated as informal advice to Belgian insurance companies. As we have seen, at the beginning of the twentieth century, there was the same concern about the insurability of substandard risks. In order to rebuild public trust, insurers decided to establish inter-company actuarial research, thus reconciling their private and public roles (Horstman 2001; Porter 2000). Since public trust was perceived as too important an issue to be neglected, insurers have at least temporarily resisted individual profit-making and competitive concerns in order to solve the public trust problems of the industry as a whole.

Statistical risk categories have wheels

In this section I argued that the decisions on the use of risk classification factors were linked to several concerns, like accuracy, cost-efficiency, practicability, social acceptability and so on. Unlike the frequently used argument that insurers need medical information for adverse selection reasons (cf. chapter I), the above illustrates how other concerns are reflected as well. My argument highlights that risk categories are flexible and fluid rather than fixed. As we have seen, this flexibility can be at work at the level of reinsurance companies, insurance companies and inter-company organisations. Consequently, specific openings involving collective negotiations regarding the insurability of a particular risk group (e.g., patient groups) became apparent as well. Again, this "breaking of the laws" seems possible at various levels. Even though the Belgian market has specific limits regarding the malleability of these categories, the choice of whether to join collective negotiations on insurability problems seems to be rather a matter of political goodwill.

Measuring Risky Bodies

Whenever underwriters notice "abnormalities" in a questionnaire, they generally need extra medical information. To track such information, they deploy several measurement instruments, such as GP reports or lab tests. In this section, I focus on how applicants are linked to statistical risk categories and insurance ratings. How are applicants *measured* and what are they measured against?

The insurance industry, again, values the scientific character of its measurements greatly. Medical advisors, for example, emphasise that assigning a risk rating should involve an objective decision: "an applicant's cholesterol level is either less than 240 or it isn't. His weight is either is under 210 or it's not" (Biehl and Thieme 1998: 2). The cholesterol and weight figures are viewed here as *natural facts*. Typically, however, the data constructed by the insurance industry are the result of a whole range of concerns. I will support this point by discussing the various tools deployed in generating these facts, including (re-)insurance manuals, medical experts' protocols and lab tests.

Balancing acts in deploying medical tools

Over the years, the insurance industry has designed more test instruments to increase accuracy and efficiency, and in the past few decades, it seems, the relevance of these technologies for the insurance industry has only increased. For example, between 1970 and 1980, insurers introduced the use of biochemical testing in their business (Krinik in Society of Actuaries: 1999). Since the mid-1980s, urine and blood testing have been expanded and refined, in particular since the appearance of AIDS, while more advanced urine testing also resulted in the development of tests for tobacco (codeine testing). Since the 1990s, the insurance industry has been exploring the usefulness of "alternative fluids", such as simple urine samples used for testing for disorders that previously could only be diagnosed on the basis of blood tests (Hank 2000: 22).

In light of the above, it is not so difficult to understand the high level of interest in these technologies among insurers. New technologies can provide insurers with new numbers. Prognostic information previously unknown to the insurer can now be traced, which facilitates further differentiation between applicants, while information sources previously considered less reliable (such as the medical questionnaire) may be rendered more reliable. The development of codeine testing, for example, has provided insurers with an instrument to check individual tobacco use. As one insurer puts it, thanks to this testing device, insurers are no longer faced with "smokers' amnesia" (Hank 2000: 22). Innovations in testing technologies thus improve insurers' control on moral hazard and adverse selection.

As my fieldwork revealed, the underwriters requested test results as a way to improve the objectivity of their rating:

> Whenever somebody states on a questionnaire that he has an increased cholesterol rate and that, for example, he takes medication for it ... we ask for a cholesterol test ... Based on the information we already have, we may have a clear suspicion that something is wrong. And if that is the case, we request more evidence to verify our suspicion. In this case, for instance, we'll send a letter back asking: 'Is it possible to have a look ... ? If your GP has done cholesterol tests within the last 3 months could you please provide us with the test results?' Or: 'Here is the protocol of the medical examination, please could you go to our medical expert to have some blood tests?' (C1, B, 3).

However, the underwriters seemed to balance the advantages of these instruments against other considerations. For one thing, they did not always request extra lab tests but also resorted to other medical instruments, such as additional GP information. The instructions in the manual offer underwriters advice on *which* medical instruments to deploy and *when* to use them. Occasionally, however, these manuals merely provide recommendations on the company's policy regarding the use of specific tools. Consider the following fragments from the introduction of the reinsurance manual:

> A certain number of determining factors in a prognosis can be assessed based on the already available medical documents. For the rest, additional information is required. The decision whether or not to ask for this additional information is not just a medical issue (Re1, manual). [my translation]

Apparently, the reinsurance company allows the insurance companies some latitude as to the use of the prognosis-determining arrows. To determine the "global rate", that is, to put the individual into a statistical risk category (average percentage), the manual provides the insurance companies with some guidelines on the information that is required. In this case, as the manual indicates, only "summary information" is required. But the manual leaves it up to the insurance companies as to whether they want to customise the average rate dependent upon the applicant, as reflected in the guidelines regarding required *extra* information. In other words, the choice on how much and which medical information to require is left up to management's discretion. As already described in chapter III, such choices are tied to the relevance of medical underwriting as part of a company's overall profit activities as well as to the degree of accuracy a particular company wants to pursue. In this regard, the underwriters of case 1 received their guidelines from their own company's management, the "black cover", listing the details on the instruments to deploy regarding specific applicants.

My fieldwork revealed that the underwriters did not automatically apply all of the available types of medical instruments once they identified an abnormality on an applicant's questionnaire. The reinsurance manual and the "black cover" instructed them to be selective. The most accurate tools should only be deployed when the need for accurate data outweighed other considerations, such as the cost of using the tool. For example, requesting a GP's or specialist's report is initially preferred because it is less costly than an additional expert medical examination or lab test.

> So if a person declares a certain disorder on the medical questionnaire, we know that, most of the time, he'll be checked for this condition annually. This means we can simply ask the GP or specialist for the most recent report. This source provides us with a lot of information already (C1, K, 3).

> Why we prefer a GP's record over a medical examination? Because the latter is much more expensive... I mean, if we only ask for the GP record, it

> doesn't cost us a penny. While in the latter case, our expenses for each file are certainly to be higher ... (C1, E, 2).

Besides cost efficiency, marketing considerations were also a reason not to pursue more information on an applicant. As one corporate manager explained:

> When do we pursue more information and when do we stop? Well, it is... in part determined by the issue of how far can you go before you start to lose clients. I mean, if our client has already gone to a medical expert, we can't demand much more of him. So then we've incurred all these extra costs but the client is gone, you understand? (C2, V, 2).

In an attempt to reconcile marketing concerns with accuracy considerations, the guidelines instruct underwriters to gather as much necessary information needed immediately in order not to bother the applicant unnecessarily. Cost-efficiency considerations also played a role when additional lab tests were needed. The instructions basically distinguish between standard lab tests and more expensive comprehensive lab tests. Applicants who test positive on a standard lab test may have to go through a more expensive and elaborate test, as in the case of diabetes.

> It would be too expensive for the company to check the diabetes values for everybody. Therefore, we put the blood glucose concentration into the standard lab tests, and if that level is raised, you have already a serious presumption that something is going on, so then you can ask for further detailed tests and information around diabetes (C1, K, 3).

In line with chapter III, we see here that the norms for rating in insurance do not only depend on the norms from other practices (e.g., clinical medicine). The insurance business's own guidelines are motivated by several policy considerations that pre-format the use of particular tools or data for deciding on insurance ratings. These balancing acts also explain why standards and guidelines vary from one insurance company to the next.

Controlling acts in deploying medical tools

In addition to these devices on *when* to deploy particular medical tools, a whole range of considerations is involved in the particular *ways* insurance companies utilise this medical knowledge. Borrowing tools from peripheral actors (such as GPs, medical experts, laboratories) also entails their reconfiguration according to the needs and objectives of the insurance business. These are again tied to general insurance interests involving objectivity, efficiency and standardisation, but the company's underwriting policy also may "pre-scribe" them. These devices, which are specifically designed by the insurance company involved, *discipline* or *control* the actors from the other practices on which the insurance industry builds its business in several ways. Insurers "translate" tools from other practices so as to bring them in line with specific insurance objectives.

The information requested from the GP or medical specialist is a case in point. When the underwriters ask for this information, the cover letter already pre-structures that information.

> In the cover letter to the GP, we always ask him to produce a report with, for example, the following elements: the course of the disease, its evolution, the medication used and the patient's treatment compliance. So we're always asking for really specific aspects that he has to respond to (C1, K, 3).

This pre-formatted character of the service requested by the insurance company is even more apparent in the so-called "additional questionnaire". For several specific mortality risks, pre-printed additional questionnaires are sent to the GP. In case 1, for example, this instrument was used for a dozen types of disorders, such as asthma, arterial hypertension, and kidney stones – a selection based on the company's experience statistics. Because these statistics revealed excessive mortality for these particular risks, the company designed questionnaires for GPs, in order to gain more insight into these mortality risks. In other words, based on specific mortality statistics and choices in risk classification factors, the company has created a specific medical tool (the additional questionnaire), the format of which also carefully pre-structures – and restricts – the GP's reply by relying on yes/no categories and leaving little room for written comments. Moreover, the questionnaire is also accompanied by instructions on how to fill out the form. As to the content, questions tend to specifically concentrate on prognostic factors as listed in the reinsurance manual. For example, in the case of Karen, the determining factors related to hypertension as listed in the manual are: "recent ECG results, current treatment, urine analysis, and family history of cerebrovascular diseases". These address the questions in the additional questionnaire. It is obvious that the script limits and disciplines the GP's clinical framework. It pre-configures the clinical encounter Karen had with her GP in the context of her insurance application, while excluding other views and information on her health (which in turn contributes to more efficiency in the company's operations).

The appropriation of medical knowledge by the insurance company is also expressed in the reliance on medical experts and their written protocols. Their deployment seems subservient to the objectives of the insurance industry in particular. Medical experts, in fact, receive specific training from the company that hires their expertise in order to help them frame the applicant's body in a particular way. As a corporate manager explained:

> Before the experts start working for us, they are informed on the specific way an insurance company operates ... But, during their education they must have had some course in insurance medicine, don't you think? It is a specialty, after all. Because being a medical expert involves a radically different way of thinking than having a clinical practice, of course. But, on the other hand, we don't want to overdo it either. I mean, we don't want to have some kind of abnormal doctors here. We just need a doctor who represents the situation objectively (C2, V, 2).

The medical examination itself must obey a strict protocol, which functions as an extra control mechanism for the company to determine the medical expert's frame.

> IvH: "And the medical experts, do they 'think' like GPs or more like insurance doctors?"
> M: "Well, that's exactly why we designed a particular protocol for the medical examination, which has to be strictly followed by the medical experts ... All of our medical experts are given these forms. This means they just have to follow the directions and fill in questions like 'Have you ever treated this person before, yes or no?' This protocol automatically makes them insurance doctors of a sort, doesn't it?" (C2, M, 2).

In this regard, the protocol is based on yes/no responses and clear instructions, which includes boxes next to the questions with specific instructions. For example, at the top of the protocol, the following instruction is given: "The expert is kindly requested to answer all of the questions and offer comments on any pathological or abnormal situations" (C2, protocol). Moreover, these instructions function as an extra control on the reliability of the results. For example, the form combines blood pressure results with the question "Are there any signs of emotional distress?" (C2, protocol). Or the examiner is explicitly instructed to do a control test: "Whenever the values are above 15/9 or the pulse rate is above 90, please perform a control measurement after the examination" (C2, protocol). Clearly, these detailed instructions demonstrate the insurance company's great concern about the reliability of test results. As a way to avoid potential fraud, for instance, the applicant has to produce a urine sample in the expert's office. A last control mechanism on the medical expert's functioning is built in *a posteriori* and involves the insurance company keeping track of the performance of its medical experts. The company in case 1, for example, works with a record that lists its experts, each with their name and address plus a section for "remarks", which include performance evaluations.[47] Complaints from applicants or insurance company dissatisfaction, may lead to that the company no longer wanting to work with a particular expert.

As a final illustration of this process, it is instructive to have a closer look at the position of the medical advisor, who, as a company employee, is a central figure in insurance risk assessment. In general, whenever medical information from a clinical practice (e.g., GP reports) enters the underwriting process, the medical advisor is supposed to give advice on the insurability of the case involved. The medical advisor serves as the monitor of all of the clinical knowledge in the underwriting process. As an insurance company employee, he is also expected to keep up with progress in clinical expertise. In this regard, the medical advisor in case 1 argued that to do one's job as an advisor properly, "one still should have one foot in clinical medicine" (C1, V, 2). That he still worked part-time as a clinician helped him in assessing insurance applicants: "When I receive these GP records or protocols from medical experts, I always know what I'm reading and I can make my own interpretation" (C1, V, 2). However, his role is also geared towards insurance objectives in particular. First, the medical advisor also relies on the manual and the company guidelines when assessing files, and is as such disciplined by it in advance. Although the medical advisor in case 1 emphasises the autonomy of his role in the underwriting process, my observations established that he also mainly applied company guidelines.

> Indeed, I'm familiar with the general outline, I know the firm's statistics because they [the management] explained them to me when I started here. That's also the reason why I'm involved in discussions about portfolio management, you see, to keep up with things. When doing assessments I say something like: 'Okay, for this disorder, for this particular man, of that age, with that much insured capital, and this and that ... so much'. ... But decisions on the margins of that substandard rate, well, that is a matter that needs to be calculated; that's something I actually don't interfere with (C1, V, 2).

Although medical advisors have a medical background and a particular position in the underwriting process, they are ultimately tied to their company's underwriting policy. Significantly, in this regard, the medical advisors I encountered in my fieldwork all told me they thought it was pretty much impossible to get a job at another insurance company. Furthermore, in the end, it is up to the chief underwriter to take the medical advisor's advice into account in the final risk rating decision. As in the case of Karen, the medical advisor suggested a risk rating of 25 per cent, but the chief underwriter established the risk rate at 0 per cent. The medical advisor commented:

> I am only decisive in the sense that, well ... if I say 'it's this' and they [the underwriters] are not really sure, well, of course, it is clear that they won't follow my advice. I have seen several cases where they tended to give higher or lower ratings than I suggested ... because, well, they of course have to take the *market* into account ... [*sighs*], while I give *strictly* medical advice, don't I? So before the final risk decision goes to the client, there are these considera-

> tions like, 'is he or she a good client of the firm?' and ... well, these are things I don't bother with ... This means I can't have a take-it-all mentality; I merely propose how I would rate him, but in the end ... Will it be adjusted, or not? You'll have to ask them, it is not within my power ... I'm only doing my files here ... (C1, V, 2).

Apparently, concerns tied to marketing or customer relationships can be also taken into account in the final risk rating by the chief underwriter taking into consideration the medical advice.[48]

Measuring tools have wheels

The applicant's risk trajectory is contingent upon local considerations involving measuring tools and their deployment. Though these balancing acts are crystallised in the above described company devices, this framing is always provisional and subject to changes and alterations. Consequently, insurability is granted to an applicant in one situation while denied to the same person in another situation. Below, I briefly illustrate how the re-adjustment of a measuring tool can affect the applicant's insurance risk.

First, reinsurance companies periodically revise their manuals, including the instructions on which instruments to deploy and how to calculate the resulting numbers with the help of the manual's tables. One risk category in the manual, for instance, is "overweight". To define the percentages for rating, the manual includes a "height and weight" table for calculating the different degrees – "borderline", "slightly", "moderately", "seriously" overweight – on the basis of cut-off points for the different categories. For example, if you are between 169-172 centimetres tall and weigh between 84-91 kilograms, you are defined as "borderline overweight". These cut-off points or norms for the different categories are derived from clinical or epidemiological standards. They are based on changes in these norms in other medical practices or in the population's physical traits, and these norms may change along the way as well. As one underwriter explained:

> The body mass of a person ... is used as a cut-off point to calculate whether someone is overweight. But the average weight of the population has increased, hasn't it? People weigh far more than ten years ago, so the norm increases a bit, you see, it is not stable. This means that to calculate whether someone is overweight, you have to raise that norm, because otherwise you end up labeling far too many people as 'overweight'. You have to keep up with these developments, you see? This is why, for instance, the reinsurance company periodically reviews how risks evolve (C1, R, 3).

Secondly, the adoption of innovations in medical technology in underwriting (via instructions in the manual or guidelines) may have an effect on an applicant's final insurability. For example, the application of refined blood testing could reveal some extra mortality risks previously unknown to the insurance company, and turn the applicant from a standard risk into a substandard risk. In this respect, Brackenridge and Elder (1992: 97) note in their handbook that the advent of blood, urine and ECG testing "has progressively redefined and repartitioned the standard, substandard and declined proportion of new business at a time when the secular trend toward overall mortality improvement has generally continued." Innovations and refinements in testing technologies thus make it possible to detect more and more deviations from the normal values and, as such, these can also be taken into account in the norms for rating.[49] During my fieldwork, for instance, an underwriter mentioned the refinement of cholesterol testing with the introduction of the LDL level measurement. As he explained:

> K: "We always used to only look at the total cholesterol level: 'Is it too high or not?' But there are also the HDL- and the LDL levels within the cholesterol level, and we never used to pay attention to the LDL level. But recently, they discovered that it is precisely this LDL level that is so important. So if the LDL level is too high, there is a much larger chance that the veins become clogged ... "
> IvH: "This new fact was subsequently introduced into the underwriting process?"
> K: "Oh yes, we changed it right away. So what are we doing now? Well, we have two types of lab tests: the standard and the extended. In the past, the standard lab test for cholesterol did not require the LDL level. But we have done these cost-benefit studies, like 'How much does it cost to incorporate this LDL level test into the standard lab test?' It turned out it would only cost a euro extra for each test. So then we decided to add the LDL level test to the standard lab test, because we now know that this can be an important factor in mortality" (C1, K, 3).

As a consequence, the norms for being accepted at a standard rate based on cholesterol testing became more stringent. The acceptance norm considered standard now not only requires a standard normal value for the total cholesterol level, but also for the LDL level. Accordingly, the risk category for cholesterol has been adjusted. The company's cost-efficiency considerations were instrumental in determining for *whom* this innovation was meant. Because the LDL test was fairly inexpensive, corporate management decided to apply it in the standard lab test as well.

Thirdly, as we have seen, the company may also qualify the deployment of the various tools. This in part accounts for the fact that different insurance companies rely on different guidelines for deploying instruments. As one underwriter explained:

> But I don't think underwriters of other companies are using the same instructions. We hear about these people being rejected by our company but accepted by another. But who decides? ... Is it a correct decision? I don't know. The risk a company is willing to take varies from one company to the next. And I think that company X [case 1] takes fewer risks (C1, B, 3).

In this regard, insurance companies can favour a 'global rating' approach or a customised 'tailor-made' approach in underwriting, thereby balancing cost-efficiency concerns with accuracy concerns. This in turn might result in different insurability results for applicants across insurance companies. For example, in the case of Karen's hypertension, global rating actually meant that, based on the required information (questionnaire, medical expert), a substandard rate would be given (e.g. 50 per cent). But the insurance company followed a tailor made approach, requesting the additional questionnaire on hypertension from the GP, so that it was possible to apply the "prognosis-determining factors" from the reinsurance manual. The fact that Karen's recent ECG results were okay and that she was reacting well to the medication made the chief underwriter finally decide to reduce the substandard rate (50 per cent) to, in fact, 0 per cent (normal standard rate). Thanks to the extra information, the average substandard rate thus could be tailored to Karen's individual circumstances.

Conclusion

If anything, my argument in this chapter demonstrates that the *language of risk* in fact disguises a whole range of practices in the production of medico-actuarial numbers. Although the numerical rating system and the underwriting guidelines have all the trappings of *scientific objectivity* (medical terminology, elaborate matrices of diseases and point values), this empirical knowledge is only a final assemblage outcome – one that is based on a host of concerns and actively pursued efforts and constructions. As Stone convincingly put it: "Insurers use the term insurability as though it were a natural property of individuals, rather than a policy decision of a firm" (1993: 298).

It is exactly this preliminary work that is covered up afterwards (as in public policy debates) by calling on the "scientific character" or "givens" of these medico-actuarial numbers. Insurers invoke the language of risk to justify insurability results: one is not insurable because the laws and calculations of insurance say so. From this perspective, the decision to accept or deny applicants is nothing more than the result of the fit between the numerical rating system and the applicants, based on the information provided. This match between the applicant and the numerical rating system, then, looks like a simple input-output device: you insert an applicant into the medico-actuarial machinery and what it generates is an insurance risk. The various internal mechanisms of this machinery, however, remain invisible.

As a final remark, I want to draw attention to the specific way of calculating risks in insurance. Risk assessment in insurance has many elements of a mystery plot. If the applicant is the unknown victim whose identity has to be established, the risk assessor is the cool, hardboiled detective who has to solve the case in a logical, factual and unemotional way. A major distinction of course is that, typically, in risk assessment the victim is not dead yet: The case that the underwriter has to solve without becoming enmeshed in it centres precisely on how many more years the "victim" will live. In many ways, the applicant is absent from the risk assessment too, however. Who the applicant is and what kind of mortality risk he/she represents are features that are allocated *a priori* via the particular framing of how an insurance company pre-structures the risk assessment. In order to establish the true identity of the applicant as a mortality risk, so this chapter illustrated, various considerations and priorities are inserted *a priori* into tools and devices that constitute the core of underwriting as a practice. Underwriters need them as controlling mechanisms for filtering the information that, once the assessment process is underway, trickles in from (or onto) the applicant. These mechanisms all serve to push the applicant into the direction of a specific insurance profile based on a pre-formatted set of risk categories, cut-off points and classifications that contribute to the applicant's "objectification" (Callon et al. 2002). As a result, the applicants and their representations seem to overlap in insurance. Following an applicant's trajectory in the underwriting practice involves following the *representation* of the applicant as pre-shaped in writing devices and numbers.

What becomes clear is that the applicant is never physically present during the risk assessment but is only *made* visible via questionnaires, lab results, GP reports and reinsurance manuals. That is, the construction of insurance risk results depends on the way in which risk is rendered visible through a variety of distant representations. As we have seen, underwriters talk in terms of heights, measures, test values, deviations, borderline case and risk percentages; rather than dealing with "Karen" they refer to her as a risk, a case, a file, a life, and so on. Above all, Karen is (pre-formatted) "information" and as such she receives a number, is inserted into a computer program, and is combined with information from other sources, such as manuals and guidelines. As detectives, the underwriters gather data, find new bits of information, link data to other data, and try to piece everything together into a coherent story about Karen. As if she were a dead, absent victim, they finally arrive at a clear picture of who she is as a risk, without ever seeing her. Throughout the process, Karen continues to be a "file" to them: language and numbers, a fictional construct, a representation, an abstract informational artefact.

This disembodied approach constitutes the particular performativity of the insurance way of dealing with applicants. As we have seen, this particular approach has some clear functions for the insurance business. Standardisation via pre-shaped writing devices and distant numbers offers an efficient way of *fitting* the applicant into pre-shaped statistical risk categories, whereby guidelines and instructions help to streamline the overall process. This contributes to a well-run ordering or framing in the underwriting department. Thus the applicant is gradually transformed into a risk. As a file, Karen increasingly becomes an abstract object – one that is placeless, timeless and contextless. The standardised way of looking at Karen and the standardised way of *storing* her via coding in the computer system further enhances the actuarial nexus of the insurance company. "Stripped" from Karen, parts of the file's data can be assembled afterwards to make separate actuarial calculations for the deployment of future underwriting policies. This also explains why insurers are particularly interested in new medical technologies and ICT procedures in coming to closure. For the latter can provide images of the body-at-a-distance, thereby defining the body and its representation in specific ways (Brown and Webster 2004). But above all, that way, background "noise" or influences from applicants or from other practices (e.g., clinical medicine) can to some extent be prevented from disrupting underwriting's particular framing. The devices used *during* the underwriting process by the underwriters are scripted towards the objective of keeping the applicants at bay. In this phase of the risk trajectory, applicants are objectified, which leaves little room for external influences or negotiation. This can be attributed to the actual characteristics of underwriting, which, as we have seen, is deployed in order to select out moral hazard. In this context, "sincerity" or "truthfulness" is a mechanism that plays a central role in the underwriting process, notably in avoiding asymmetrical information between the two parties. It is precisely this element of trust which assures that insurers keep a distance from the applicants once they have entered the underwriting process.

However, despite this somewhat cool, hard-boiled attitude of insurers towards applicants *during* underwriting, I discussed some openings or room for negotiation in the *making* of the deployed statistics and measurement instruments. Although applicants are objectified during the risk assessment, they may function as subjects, co-constructors or co-writers in the *making* of the numerical rating system (beforehand). As suggested in chapter II, applicants are not necessarily powerless in the hands of underwriters. The example of the introduction of smoking as a risk classification factor shows how the insurance industry indirectly takes into account social imaginaries around disease or social acceptability considerations. Furthermore, the establishment of the statistics demonstrated how actuarial research might take into account current innovations in clinical medicine (e.g., better treatment) and, as such, contribute to improved insurability. I also discussed examples of collective negotiation between patient groups and (re-)insurance companies.

In the next chapter, the (in)direct influence of the *individual* applicant on risk assessment will be discussed further. Having illustrated the manoeuvring room available in the making of the medico-actuarial numbers, it will become clear that there is also room to manoeuvre in the underwriter's final decision making. By illustrating this presence of judgement in coming to final decision, the focus will shift from abstract numbers, guidelines and writing devices to the role of underwriters as pivotal actors in underwriting.

V Risky Bodies Stage 3: The Art of Underwriting

After years of trying to perfect the decision making process for myself and other underwriters, I can package everything I know into the commonplace image of an iceberg. The underwriting decision appears to me as the peak of vast, mysterious mental processes that are not seen and never quite fully understood by others than underwriters.
Balay 1994

Introduction

In the previous chapter, I addressed the various medical and statistical tools involved in risk assessment. Although this "numerical rating system" is considered an invaluable tool, the process of risk assessment is not finished here. Throughout its deployment there is room for the application of expert judgement in arriving at any decisions. This judgement dimension of the risk trajectory is the central focus of this chapter. As Balay notes above, it is specifically devoted to "the vast, mysterious mental processes" of underwriters.

Underwriters ground their decision making in the guidelines provided to them. How, then, do underwriters use these devices in arriving at risk appraisals? Consider the following remarks from underwriters on their manuals and data:

> Sometimes, when we are discussing a file with each other, we find it difficult to come to a final decision. Because one underwriter finds this aspect more important than another, while I think that... I mean, of course we have these statistics and the reinsurance manual, but, well, in the end it's not the Bible, you see (C1, K, 3).

> In theory it looks rather simple: you find a particular disorder based on the information you have and then you have your manual and your tables to tell you how to deal with it... But in reality, and even though you have to remain within certain boundaries and cut-off points from the manual, it is still a little up in the air; I mean, it is up to me to play around a little with these numbers, so to speak (C2, R, 3).

IvH: "But how do you know what is important information in the medical questionnaire?"

D: "Well, that's more of a matter of intuition; you develop a sense for it. I mean, as in this case: the person writes that he suffers from asthma, but I also find out that he is a smoker. These two details when combined are important. I mean, I'm now a little more cautious about him, which means that I won't rate him as a standard risk but, instead, ask for more information...." (C1, D, 3).

These comments demonstrate that the translation of an individual into an insurance risk is not a strict technical-arithmetical conversion of the individual's health characteristics into a statistical risk category. Despite the systematic and procedural nature of underwriting, there is *still* some room left for manoeuvring with data and their interpretation. In the final analysis, it seems, the carefully calculated data in the manuals and guidelines merely put underwriters on a particular track when it comes to articulating a specific insurance risk result.

It is important to ask, then, why the manuals and guidelines are not always sufficient as decision tools in underwriting. This concern will be explored in the first section of this chapter. Specifically, I will argue for the relevance of professional judgement in underwriting decision processes. Next, I take a closer look at the *subject* of these judgements and the effects of the underwriter's manoeuvring space on applicants' insurability. Subsequently, I focus on the end stage of the risk trajectory, that is, the communication of the insurability result to the applicant. It will become clear that the judgement dimension of underwriting is rendered invisible again by reverting to objective numbers, statistical risk categories and insurance ratings.

The Relevance of Judgement

Underwriters support their risk decisions by relying on a spectrum of data, such as lab tests, GP reports, expert opinions and statistics. It happens, of course, that different information sources are in conflict with each other, which produces contradictions or uncertainties in risk assessment. Such degrees of "interpretative flexibility" (Bijker et al. 1987) are not uncommon in settings where risks are routinely assessed (see also Prior et al. 2002). Vaughan (1996), for example, in her work on space engineering programs, argues that organisations can multiply uncertainties by constantly checking and rechecking engineering results using alternative methods and techniques, and that ultimately such differences have to be resolved not at the level of facts, but through organisational fiat. We see an echo of this in the manuals supplied to the underwriters. These manuals set limits on the amount of information needed, for example, because of cost-efficiency considerations, thus short-circuiting an infinite process of checking and rechecking procedures.

The manuals fix boundaries and set standards for underwriters, but they only do so to some extent. Although these tools are designed to solve problems related to indeterminacy, underwriters may sometimes encounter *more* uncertainty because of the limits set in guidelines. Moreover, the instructions in manuals are not always as straightforward as they seem. When numbers and guidelines fail to offer clear solutions, underwriters bring other strategies into play, such as past experience, practical knowledge, intuitions and deliberations or consultations. Below, I argue that such strategies are sometimes indispensable for underwriters in coming to closure on a particular risk.

Everyday experience and intuition

In the absence of clear guidelines, how do underwriters make decisions? An applicant's specific data from a lab test, for example, may situate him or her right on the edge of the established cut-off points. These borderline cases are considered difficult to assess because the instructions in the guidelines lose their (assumed) unequivocal meaning and no longer count as straightforward. In these cases, it appeared, the underwriters first of all tend to discuss the issue with each other. This strategy is well illustrated in the following words from an underwriter:

> Well, sometimes people's lab values are right in between two categories, and then the guidelines are not very helpful in classifying them. In these cases I'll deliberate with Jos and Tom. I first try to discuss the case with them, and ask them for their opinion about how I should interpret the applicant's information, if I should ask for more information, and so on. It often turns out that Jos knows a lot more than I do because of his years of experience, so I will follow his advice. And if it is still unclear, if I still don't know what to do, then I'll ask the chief underwriter (C1, B, 3).

This example shows how ambiguity and uncertainty are shared within the team. This strategy of peer-consultation is commonly used among underwriters. It enables them to cash in on the experience built up in the department over the years.

Occasionally, underwriters use their experience to bypass the restrictions in the guidelines on which information to ask. That is, they compensate for a deficiency in the required information based on the experience they acquired over the years. They calculate the most likely outcome in advance and *adjust* the required information accordingly. The following is an illustration of this practice from my fieldwork:

Observation of a chief underwriter – afternoon:

"Here we have a nurse, 40 years old, [*looks at questionnaire*], wow, she surely enjoys a drink or two! [*laughing*] Parents still alive, hmm.... so because of the size of the total capital, we have already requested a blood test. [*looks ups the results of the blood test*] Well, here we see that she suffers slightly from anaemia, [*reads from lab report*] 'too few red cells', 'the volume of the blood cells has increased', well, that's something I often see with people who drink... You know this after a while, that this can happen too... So that's why I also asked for an additional liver test, [*takes results of liver test*] and look: this value is three times higher than the average... So I would definitely give her a substandard rate" (C1, K, 3).

In this example, the chief underwriter establishes a hypothetical link between the available data from the outset. Based on his previous experience, he has a clear suspicion that something is going on and therefore he requests an additional liver test, the outcome of which in fact confirms his suspicions. This intuition potentially influenced the decisions on the information needed and the final risk appraisal.

Suspicions or hunches may even be experienced as more important than available risk assessment data. As one underwriter explains:

> Sometimes, on the basis of the information we already have, such as the questionnaire, we get a clear suspicion that something is going on. If that is the case, we need evidence to confirm our suspicion, so we'll ask for a standard lab test. But what if this test subsequently turns up negative? In that case, despite the negative results, we might still ask for more information, because of our suspicion that something is not quite right (C1, B, 3).

Remarkably, even if the hunches conflict with the immediate visual evidence, they may end up being more relevant to the underwriters for their risk appraisal. Despite the objectively established value, the underwriter here did not take the standard lab result for "true", but instead asked for more testing to confirm his intuition.

Finally, and above all, the judgement of the underwriters seems indispensable in the final stages of risk appraisal, that is, in the "adjustment" of the average substandard rate towards a "personalised" rate. Here it is left to the chief underwriter to assess the prognosis factors (cf. "+/- arrows"). This, of course, adds a judgement dimension to risk assessment. Moreover, it appeared there was in fact no other strategy for dealing with these determining factors. Consider for example this comment on the prognosis arrows in the reinsurance manual: "It is important to take into account that each arrow only has a purely qualitative value. There is no statistical evidence that allows one to quantify their prognostic value" (Re1, manual [my translation]). In other words, the insurance companies have to rely on judgement here because statistical evidence and numbers are unavailable. In such cases, underwriters resort to their individual experience and judgement:

> *Observation of the chief underwriter:*
> "Hypertension of 16/10 mm Hg, *and* she is being treated. And she is not overweight, does not smoke, short-term insurance, well, ... here it's clear I'll let her pay less than someone with 16/10, who is overweight, a smoker, and has all kinds of other problems. You see, so that's my interpretation" (C1, V, 2).

If an applicant suffers from two or more disorders, the underwriter's experience especially comes into play as a way to bypass the indeterminacy of numbers:

> The problem is: if one applicant has several disorders, or, moreover, if there is an interaction between these disorders, like with diabetes and high cholesterol level, well, there is no manual that can provide a solution. It doesn't exist. Only experience can tell you what to do in such a case (C1, J, 2).

The need to develop this hands-on judgement seems particularly important for new underwriters. One of my informants, called Arnold, is a young man with training in economics and two years of underwriting experience (case 1):

> Especially when I just started working here I would often experience that, well... that I had to ask a lot of the others because I felt that the information I had received from an applicant was not sufficient, as if I was missing some essential information. This was particularly true in the beginning, but, you know, meanwhile of course I have built up the necessary knowledge (C1, B, 3).

Underwriters become good at the art of underwriting especially by *doing* it. They learn the ropes by actually joining the underwriting department for a substantial period of time. Their on-the-job learning process is essential because the decision processes of underwriting in part rely on *tacit knowledge* – knowledge that can only be passed on to new underwriters by engaging in the practice of underwriting. For example, the chief underwriter of case 1, when addressing the recent new authority of the "junior coaches" to make final decisions, comments that

> they often come to my desk, as you might have seen already. They come to me with their files and then I assess their cases in terms of 'Well, for this, I think you might be too strict' or 'for this I would give a slight substandard rate'. In fact, it is only by constantly discussing things with me that they learn to do it on their own. Just as I learned how to do it from my predecessors (C1, K, 3).

This relevance of experience is also reflected in the way the training of underwriters is organised. In Belgium, there is no specific training program for medical underwriters. Newly recruited underwriters usually have different educational backgrounds. For example, the educational background of the underwriters in case 1 includes economics, nursing, accountancy and law. Of course the company does organise a training program for its new underwriters. But, apart from a basic introduction to the company's own insurance guidelines, this program largely consists of on-the-job training, a learning process in which the chief medical underwriter and senior underwriters play a central role. The new underwriters begin by assessing simple files, after which they are exposed to more complicated ones. Only by working with actual files do they learn to develop decision skills. Thus, this practical approach especially addresses the "common sense understandings", "tacit knowledge" (Polanyi 1958) or "thought habits" of underwriting. Only by dealing with files for some time on a daily basis do underwriters develop the proper intuition for risk appraisal and a feeling of certainty in risk assessment.

The role of mutual interaction

If interaction with experienced colleagues is crucial for new underwriters, mutual interaction more generally is a very important part of the routine in underwriting departments. This seems to be reflected in their spatial organisation. In case 1, for example, all of the underwriters are located in the same office space. Their desks are positioned such that everyone is able to see each other. Desks are grouped together. For example, the desks of the "junior coaches" are side by side, as well as those of the underwriters and those of the clerks who perform administrative tasks. Thus the similarity of the tasks of each group is reflected in the way the office space is organised. Furthermore, the chief medical underwriter's desk is located in the same space, which facilitates his accessibility in a structural way. Although the underwriters assess files on their own, in cases of doubt, they consult the chief underwriter. This has led in fact to a solid routine in the underwriting practice. In case 1, each and every day during the late afternoon (after 3 o'clock), the underwriters show up one after another at the chief underwriter's desk to discuss aspects of files they are working on. Consider the following extract from my observation notes:

> *Afternoon – I hear the chief underwriter calling the underwriters to his desk for 'consultation time', as he called it here.... Underwriter P begins to recapitulate how he came to the risk appraisal for a particular file. He starts with the questionnaire, shows what he found striking in it ...*
>
> P: "I thought she might be suffering from some kind of allergy. What do you think?"
>
> K: "Well, you may be right, it seems to be something like that indeed."

> P: "So that means requesting extra information?"
> K: "Yes, just go for it; you're right, this case does look a bit odd."

These interactions seem much like Socratic dialogues. In disclosing their basic views about a file, the underwriters recapitulate their argumentation, thereby showing the writing devices (e.g., lab test results, ECG, GP report). The chief underwriter then checks their reasoning in an attempt to discover potential logical mistakes, followed by his approval (in most cases) or his indicating what the underwriter had "missed". These interactions may also take the form of a quiz or have a more playful, game-like character. Consider this extract:

> R: "So I thought everything was fine, but then I realised, hey look here: the 'date of application'..."
> K: "Oops, indeed, yes, you're right: the contract was submitted too late!" (C1, K, 3)

This more informal, interactive process is crucial in risk appraisal. This kind of discussion helps underwriters to transform data into "evidence". Its dialogical nature – "Do you follow me?" "Yes, I see it now as well; you *are* right indeed." – contributes to building a kind of intersubjective agreement. By literally *arguing* the case (White 2002), both parties establish a shared sense of certainty about the risk decision.

In addition to this interaction with the chief underwriter, the underwriters are constantly interacting amongst themselves while each is working on his or her own files. This may take the form of small talk, of remarks or jokes on a file, or be merely a matter of handing over a manual, the guidelines, or a medical dictionary. But underwriters also discuss particular files with each other:

> If one of us has a particular medical, uh, or if there are specific new things or exceptional disorders or something like that, we'll discuss it and sometimes write a note about it, so that we are all informed about it. You learn a lot from your colleagues, of course (C1, R, 3).

> We discuss things we encounter in our work and that are not written down anywhere, exceptional things, the things you rarely come across. Well, I usually note these down here [*points to black cover*] and I try to figure out things like: 'What did the chief underwriter decide then?' [*shows notes: date, description case, decision*] and usually I adopt these decisions and sometimes I also discuss them with him again because, of course, in the meantime, things may already have changed as they say. But, when it comes to the exceptional cases, I always try to write myself a note (C1, B, 3).

As the fragments illustrate, underwriters learn from each other's experiences. They discuss and compare new data (from questionnaires and medical sources) with what is available in guidelines or manuals.[50] Thus, they not only use past experiences; as key players in the underwriting practice they in fact produce new experience-based knowledge. This they sometimes add in pencil to the guidelines they work with. This activity highlights the fact that experience in the underwriting department develops over a period of years.

> You learn a lot by doing it all the time. Thus you continue to build up experience. And, of course, it never ends, does it? When I started working here, I thought 'well, one year of training and I will pretty much know everything', but this turned out to be not the case at all because medical underwriting is always evolving (C1, E, 2).

The knowledge underwriters gain and develop is in large part collective knowledge, generated by the underwriting department as a whole on the basis of everyday practice. Over time, this gives rise to a collective mindset within the department that is used to increase the quality of risk decisions. As one underwriter explains:

> Normally I begin with the information we receive, such as that from a GP. Next I consider whether to send the applicant to a medical expert ... These things are often also a matter of intuition, aren't they? And hence a matter of interaction. For we tend to discuss these things, as you may have noticed. We go to the chief underwriter and we say: 'well, hmm, I don't know, I thought about this case like this and this, what do you think about it?' And we'll discuss it ... (C1, P, 3).

To some extent, then, the department operates on a collectively shared but unwritten knowledge base, consisting of insights from past experiences, anecdotal knowledge, intuitions, data from background cases, general information, and so on.

Mutual interaction, besides increasing a sense of certainty about risk decisions, also helps to standardise practical knowledge, thus raising inter-subjectivity. In this regard, it is striking to see the degree to which underwriters emphasise interaction, especially in the absence of guidelines:

> We always try to follow the guidelines as systematically as possible. For that is the only way to be fair to the clients. Because as underwriters, we can't differ too much from each other ... However, as in this case, concerning the duration of the contract there are in fact no guidelines because it is not mentioned in the reinsurance manual ... In these cases, we always try to talk to each other, because it is our intention ... to learn from each other, basically do things in the same way, so that there won't be too much difference between our individual risk appraisals (C1, K, 3).

Interaction is thus also perceived as quite useful for creating uniformity within the department, as a way to reduce, if not eliminate, subjective interpretation in risk assessment. The underwriters strive for a consensus and standardisation of their assessments. As the above quote illustrates, they believe that deploying the same standards means being fair to all of the applicants. In the absence of formal standards, underwriters try to compensate for them by establishing inter-personal standards of judgement through mutual negotiation. It is part of the effort to establish external legitimacy. Above all, however, their interaction serves the aim of realising internal legitimacy. After all, the underwriters have to account for their decisions among their colleagues in the claims department, as well as to the company's management. Their mutual interaction allows them to share the responsibility for their risk decisions. In this regard, underwriters may sign underwriting decisions jointly, as a way to back each other more formally:

> We tend to work carefully here. So, in cases of doubt, the other underwriters know I want them to first see me, to discuss it. It is not that I control them afterwards, by taking a sample or so, to check if the files are underwritten correctly. I also say to them: 'Well, if you have any doubt, come to me for consultation, or discuss it among yourselves, and you can also sign the decision jointly, because that too is a demonstration afterwards that, at least, you have reflected on the decision and consulted with the others (C1, K, 2).

The chief underwriter here indicates that mutual interaction and discussion among the underwriters contributes to spreading the responsibility and accountability within the *whole* department. Moreover, this quote demonstrates that *a priori* consultation is in fact an alternative to *a posteriori* control by superiors.

In sum, numbers are crucial to the legitimacy of underwriting, but where individual judgement cannot be avoided, mutual interaction is used to establish inter-subjectivity or objectivity so as to raise underwriting's legitimacy. The cases discussed above illustrate that numbers alone cannot enable underwriters. Numbers may be used to bring closure, but underwriters also bring practical knowledge, deliberation, background experience and intuition into play. They do not always "trust in numbers" (Porter 1995). In the underwriting practice, judgement may ultimately have a strong influence on the final risk appraisal.

The Manoeuvrability of the Final Risk Appraisal

Having demonstrated the relevance of judgement for underwriters in the assembling of insurance risks, in this section we will take a closer look at the *content* of these judgements. How do underwriters *fill in* the manoeuvring room they have? In conjunction with our observations in the previous chapters, I also illustrate how in this judgement phase applicants (in)directly seem to influence (or co-construct) their own insurability result or future underwriting policy.

Suspicious minds

> "Well, our job always comes down to perusing the files for something [suspicious]" (C1, K, 2).
> "You learn to have a good nose for it after a while ... " (C2, R, 3).

Risk assessment is grounded in the information that is at the insurance client's disposal, while incorrect or distorted information should be avoided as much as possible. In other words, underwriters are managers of "truthful" risk disclosure. They seek to control moral hazard and prevent fraud and insurance speculation. In the previous chapters, it was demonstrated how corporate management, in making and deploying questionnaires and other writing devices, uses control mechanisms as a way to manage the client's truthfulness. Below, I argue that these same efforts constitute an important aspect of the underwriters' judgement of the files.

In this regard, assumptions about the applicant's "truthfulness" may play a role in risk assessment, as a way to manage moral hazard. As such, several minor aspects may influence the way the underwriter perceives the applicant's reliability, sincerity, or openness. For example, if the GP co-signs an applicant's questionnaire, this increases their trust in the applicant. By contrast, whenever there is even the slightest suspicion that an applicant is withholding information, additional information is requested:

> If I find out an applicant has filled out his questionnaire incorrectly or if the answers to the questions seem ambiguous, I begin to get a sense of 'hmm, I think he is covering up something', then I'll ask for a medical examination by an expert or a GP (C1, B, 3).

This comment shows how the underwriter adjusts the measures, tools and guidelines towards assumptions about the applicant's character or sincerity.

Furthermore, when assessing the medical questionnaire, underwriters try to put together a coherent picture of the applicant in which subjective criteria like honesty or sincerity play a major role, especially if extra testing establishes the applicant's dishonesty:

> Currently this occurs a lot with regard to whether he or she is overweight or not. I get extremely annoyed by this. So when I find out that they have lied on this question, I may not rate them more stringently but I will surely not

> be inclined to rate them more favourably, you see? I mean, you don't reward them for that, do you? (C1, B, 3).

Moreover, suspicions of dishonesty may also influence risk categories on a more collective level. In the case of someone being overweight, my fieldwork has revealed that the guidelines and cut-off points in the manual are currently more strictly applied because of the underwriters' perceptions that today's applicants are more dishonest.

> Today we tend to interpret these cut-off points and related guidelines on when to ask for more information far stricter because we don't want to take the risk anymore, given all these concealed facts ... especially in cases involving a client being overweight, which are a disaster in our company nowadays ... What we used to do in the past, [*refers to height and weight table in manual*], here you have 'borderline underweight', 'normal weight', 'borderline overweight' and then 'slightly overweight' ... For 'slightly overweight', we used to request a medical examination, even if the rest of the questionnaire was okay and even if the amount of capital requested was rather low. This is what we used to do, but now I have become even more stringent. Today, even if they are 'borderline overweight', well ... I'm already inclined to request a medical examination, to check whether the results agree their responses. So this is something... you learn after a while here, after what you see every day... In the past we didn't encounter this problem as much. I think people were far more honest back then. Hmm, I think that's perhaps ... because many people disagree with the fact that they have to pay a substandard rate for being overweight (C2, R, 3).

Because the underwriters live with the perception that people tend to be less trustworthy, a more stringent underwriting regime is applied. That is, an increasing distrust of the applicants is translated here into a decreased reliability of the questionnaire as instrument. Consequently, those people who provide figures that put them in the category "borderline overweight" also have to undergo a medical examination, where previously the questionnaires' results were considered "reliable enough".

Evidently, the assumptions of underwriters about the applicants' trustworthiness regarding insurance policies influence insurability results and hence future underwriting policies as well. The previous quote suggests how the risk categories and numbers (involving being overweight) are changed or adjusted based on the assumptions of the applicants' conduct and their trustworthiness. To some extent, then, the applicants are co-producers of the underwriting policy. The way they inscribe themselves on the medical questionnaires and the judgement of their conduct by the underwriters affect the underwriting practice. In this regard, the underwriters function to some degree as trendspotters. Based on the written responses, they develop assumptions about their clients (their expectations regarding insurance, their perception of the product, their motivation, their honesty and so on) and may notice new patterns. This indirect feedback information, then, might be used in future underwriting policy.

Fair minds

If underwriters' suspicious minds can lead to stricter underwriting practices, the discretionary space they have in making judgements may also result in a more flexible rating system, especially with regard to the chief underwriter's final estimation of the risk involved. In allocating an insurance rating, the applicant's health characteristics, the statistics and measurement instruments all appear to be much less constant and none of them solely determine the final risk assessment.

First, in the process of assigning the applicant an insurance rating, the statistics and cut-off points are not always absolute. Diabetes is a case in point. As we have seen in chapter IV, recent treatments of diabetes have significantly improved mortality rates among diabetes patients. Yet these medical innovations were not yet reflected in the reinsurance mortality statistics (and the reinsurance manuals). Thereby, it was illustrated how in case 1 the company, by deploying experience statistics, could in fact offer a better substandard rate to diabetes patients than the reinsurance manuals. Although in case 2 no such experience statistics were available, it seemed that this treatment aspect of diabetes was taken into account as well. How was this possible in case 2? The chief underwriter told me he first heard about the innovations in the treatment of diabetes at a Belgian Association of Insurers' workshop he had recently attended.

> So, at the meetings I had with the other underwriters, we heard about the problem of insuring diabetes and so on ... And I think this is also a problem in our company. That's because the reinsurance manual we use still applies a heavy rating because the reinsurance company hasn't adjusted this yet. Well, we know they are busy changing these statistics, but apparently it takes them a long time before they get adjusted. So, in a sense, that's not fair to the applicants (C2, R, 2).

Based on this information, he assessed that the reinsurance manual the company worked with had not yet been updated and that this was unfair to diabetes patients. He solved this problem by taking this aspect into account in his risk appraisal decisions:

> So, what I do now with diabetes is ... I do have these cut-off points from which I can not deviate, you know, the percentage of substandard rate for diabetes in the reinsurance manual. Yet, I tend to, well ... if you see here for example [*refers to reinsurance manual*], here they state as a positive point [*shows "- arrows column"*]: 'that more than two values must be normal'. So they say that at least two measurements must have a normal testing value,

> for example, that there is no albumin in the blood and that the blood glucose concentration is under control. So this means that, lower than a certain percentage, the glycohemoglobin percentage falls in between two figures. That is a sign that everything is under control. Now imagine the case where there are two other diabetes facts lacking which could normally result in the lowest rate. Normally, this person would still get the average substandard rate and the '-arrow' would not count. But now, for diabetes, though this person does not fulfil all the conditions of the '-arrow', I would still give him the lowest rate. So, in the case of diabetes, I now tend to say rather easily: 'Well, if the glycohemoglobin percentage is fine, okay, then it is all right with me to give the lowest substandard rate. Because I realise that in fact this lowest rate is still rated too high in the reinsurance manual at the moment (C2, R, 3).

In other words, because he considers the average substandard rate for diabetes too stringent, he takes this into account by relaxing the conditions for the lowest rate for diabetes. Consequently, diabetes applicants in case 2 paid a lower insurance premium. This example illustrates that, besides the assemblage work in the establishment of the statistics and numbers (chapter IV), this room for manoeuvring is also available in the chief underwriter's final assessment. Thus, regarding diabetes, it is possible to improve the insurability by updating the insurance statistics on diabetes (case 1) or, as described here, by tailoring the old statistics to individual cases (case 2).

Secondly, it appears that within the available discretionary space the chief underwriter may deploy extra measuring results or instruments to come to a final decision. This happened for example when there was a disagreement between the medical advisor's and the chief underwriter's risk appraisal. Consider the following fragment:

> Most of the time, we follow up on the medical advisor's report. But, well, we are certainly not obliged to do so. For example, last week, the medical advisor recommended that we reject the risk. But the applicant then phoned our chief medical underwriter and the latter decided: 'Look, I am going to ask for additional advice from the reinsurance company.' And the reinsurance company then advised us to accept this client on a substandard premium (C1, D, 3).

By calling in the help of the reinsurance company, the chief underwriter tries to resolve the conflict, thus taking on the role of "intermediary" (Callon 1991). The reinsurance company's advice – despite that it contradicted the medical advisor's assessment – seems to have subsequently given him sufficient grounds for accepting the client. In other words, the applicant's interests were rendered justified here within the insurance framework by translating fairness or marketing considerations into scientific reinsurance advice. Thus the medical underwriter "presented a façade" to his superiors (Dodier 1994). He used the authority of reinsurance evidence as "objective evidence", thus legitimising insurance practice. Despite the conflicting underwriting considerations involved, in the end, the final risk decision is communicated as a neutral scientific result, and to the outside world it appears as if this risk assessment was never subject to any disagreement at all.

Calling on the reinsurance company for additional advice usually implies an increased workload on the part of the chief underwriter, which may disagree with efficiency and administrative considerations (in the guidelines). In addition, it may imply extra work for the reinsurance company as well. The chief underwriter explained his contacting the reinsurance company in the diabetes case by saying that

> of course they don't want me to send them these letters. This means I don't get an answer immediately and I really have to push them, write again, you know... So that's not easy for me. And you won't do that for everyone! But as in this diabetes case, lately we've been getting so many reactions from clients. And they're right, it's too restrictively rated (C2, R, 3).

In other words, although the reinsurance manual contains clear guidelines and norms as to the risk percentages, if the chief underwriter considers them as unfair in specific cases, he may go to some length in urging the reinsurance company to seek additional, more personalised advice. This suggests that reinsurance companies might also reconsider or adjust the substandard rates they themselves deploy in their manuals for particular applicants.

Together, these examples illustrate that the chief underwriter, given the discretionary space he has in the final rating, may take into account fairness or marketing considerations. As such, besides collective re-adjustments in the management's creation of the numbers (chapter IV), we see here another illustration of leeway, that is, of individual judgement. The chief underwriter has the authority to customise guidelines or standards. Whether he uses this authority depends on several factors: his own fairness considerations, the engagement level of the applicants, or other external influences. In the next section, I will once again explore these influences on risk assessment in detail.

Pliable minds

In his article *Mastering the underwriting decision*, the medical underwriter Balay (1994) refers to the underwriter's final decision moment as "a wizard at the moment of truth." At that point, he notes, external influences should be avoided as much as possible. My fieldwork reveals, however, that in that final stage underwriters may still have to deal with external influences and interests. Below I explore how applicants and bank agents specifically can influence the chief underwriter's final risk rating.

Angry phone calls

> Often we get angry phone calls, saying: 'I had better not mention it in the questionnaire, because then I wouldn't have received such a high premium' (C2, M, 3).

Calls from applicants who have questions or concerns are generally handled by one of the underwriters. The latter act as a buffer between the applicant and the chief underwriter. Only if applicants are particularly insistent are their concerns dealt with by the chief underwriter. Consequently, a (self-)selection process seems to occur: only a particular type of applicant (the "vociferous", assertive applicants) is ultimately able to come into contact with the chief underwriter. Evidently, the organisation of the underwriting department assumes a particular performativity. The departments I investigated tried to keep out external influences – including calls from applicants – as much as possible, thus seeking to preserve its particular arrangement. This organisational set-up seemed to function as a buffer to keep the staff from having to legitimate their decisions to outsiders. In case 1, moreover, answering calls was exclusively a responsibility of two underwriters, the "junior coaches". Given their specific instructions,[51] they acted as an even more effective barrier between the applicant and the chief underwriter. In comparison to case 2, this led to far fewer opportunities for direct contact with the chief underwriter.

But if indeed a client managed to get in touch with the chief underwriter, what would be discussed? During my observation it might happen, for instance, that the chief underwriter comes to his desk where he finds a message that a specific applicant would call him later in the afternoon. He seemed rather nervous about this message. He also told me that this was the most difficult part of his job. For during a phone call with an applicant, he was immediately confronted with the effects of his own risk decisions, while in normal circumstances, he said, he assessed risks "in a more detached way" (C2, R, 3). In this regard, he also mentioned that it was much easier to do risk appraisals for reinsurance companies, "because they deal with the files as 'cases', while I am afterwards confronted with the human individuals themselves" (C2, R, 3). In other words, phone contact with clients forced the the chief underwriter to confront the *human* side of underwriting much more intensely; it literally added a human voice to all the anonymous numbers and statistics. In some cases, he found it hard to maintain the insurance company's view, particularly when the reinsurance company's risk result produced a too-stringent considered rating:

> It's extremely difficult when I somewhat disagree with the reinsurance decision. Because telling people who call you 'well, it is not my decision but the reinsurance company's decision' doesn't help them much either, does it? So

what I try to do is ask the reinsurance company for very detailed arguments, because it can help me to deliver the message to the applicant in a better manner (C2, R, 3).

He suggests that experience is an important element in tackling this issue. In dealing with the applicants, underwriting requires specific skills and competence from the employees as well as a sense of identifying with the logic of insurance.[52] When later that same afternoon the applicant called back, the chief underwriter first resorted to a basic explanation of reinsurance principles, as reflected in phrases like "Well, I know, but we are obliged by our reinsurance company to take this factor into account... Well, I understand, but that is not our decision, but one by the reinsurance company, I'm sorry..." (C2, R, 3). Despite these responses, at the end of the phone call the applicant still managed the underwriter to promise to take another look at his file. As such, the call produced some effect. Applicants who manage to get in touch have a chance of influencing their insurability outcome.

Good customers

Furthermore, my fieldwork in case 1 revealed that external influences could also be wielded via the banks involved. Because bank employees are induced to sell their banking and insurance products, it was sometimes possible to discern tension between their relations with clients and the underwriters' concerns for accuracy.[53] The bank's network of offices was deployed in the risk assessment process for the communication between the applicant and the medical underwriting department. At the time of the application, for instance, applicants had already filled out the medical questionnaires in the bank; if more information was needed later on (e.g., a GP's report), this could also be communicated to the applicant via the same office. In order to eliminate possible sales input by the bank, the underwriting management built in specific control mechanisms. For example, the questionnaires always had to be signed by the applicants themselves. The underwriters paid particular attention to this aspect regarding questionnaires that were incomplete because they were aware that bank employees sometimes completed questionnaires for the applicants to speed up the procedure.

> "Oh, he hasn't filled out the question about his weight. I'll have to return the questionnaire because the questions about height and weight are very relevant to us. So I'll send it back to him now, and I'll mark the particular question and also ask him to sign the questionnaire again. Because otherwise a bank employee might quickly complete the questionnaire and..." (C1, E, 3).

Understandably, in its collaboration with the bank, the underwriting management attempts to maintain control over its business operations.

But the bank might continue to try to interfere in the underwriting process, for instance, by putting in a good word for one of its own good clients:

> Um, whether or not we take into account whether he or she is a good customer at this bank? We sometimes consider this aspect. Initially, we tend not to take it into account, but, well, it happens that a regional bank manager calls us afterwards, saying: 'Yes, I have seen my client has a premium for this, and ... could you please do something about it? (C1, D, 3).

In these cases, the chief underwriter discusses the matter with corporate management and makes decisions on a case-by-case basis. This same issue may come into play again when the applicant becomes a good customer of the insurance company itself. As a corporate manager explained:

> But then there is of course the commercial aspect: It may well be that we have a very good customer but we have rated him at a substandard rate of 50 per cent, so that means we would receive an annual premium of 125 euros extra from this client. But then we end up saying: 'Well, this is a guy who already pays us an annual premium of 5000 euros for fire insurance, car insurance, via his group insurance, which means he's a good customer. So to demand this extra 125 euro premium amounts to a very small portion of his total premium volume'. This is why from a commercial point of view, we tell him he won't have to pay the substandard rate because we don't want him to become annoyed. Especially over such a small amount. Of course it's important to first calculate the rate of that extra risk, but afterwards, we may decide to forget about it ... (C2, V, 2).

At the End of the Day

What happens at the end of the day, after the die is cast? In general, the final risk result is communicated to the applicant in a letter. But there may also be direct interaction, for instance, when an applicant calls the underwriting office. In this section I focus on how this interaction occurs. I also discuss what happens when a client decides to file a complaint against the insurance company. What power do applicants have to make their voices heard?

Numbers as token women

My discussion of the telephone conversations above showed that the chief underwriter tends to mobilise general insurance principles, objective numbers and statistics when explaining the final risk result to applicants. Another major strategy to defend a risk decision is to refer to the reinsurance company as the bad guy. This allows the chief underwriter to reach out to the applicant, the suggestion being that both are in fact the victim of some other organisation's rules and abstract numbers.

Statistics, numbers and insurance principles are thus discursively used as a legitimation of the underwriting decision. At the same time, these numbers also function as a way of disguising the expert's responsibility regarding the risk decision. At the end of the risk assessment process, numbers once again take centre stage because insurers need them in order to be able to leave the process, so to speak, as objective and credible professionals (which in turn facilitates their embarking on a new trajectory with a new applicant, new numbers, new calculations etc.). Yet, as we have seen in chapter III and IV, risk assessment, based as it is on *bricolage*, is a multifaceted process, one in which the numbers and facts have to be *established* or *built*. In addition, this chapter has illustrated the additional leeway and judgement available in assembling the final risk decisions. Again, these judgement elements are spread out toward the end, concealed behind numbers and (re) insurance principles.

> *Observation, chief underwriter in telephone conversation with a client:*
> "Yes, I know you take medication for your arterial hypertension, but there's still a risk for us. That's the reinsurer's principles for assessing the risks. It just means that you still have a higher mortality risk in the future than the average. No, not now, I know that, but we'll have to consider the future, we have to be able to assess your mortality risk in 20 years" (C2, R, 3).

In this regard, Glenn (2000: 802) labels this rhetoric of numbers in insurance as "the myth of the actuary":

> The myth of the actuary is a rhetorical process that conveys the impression that whether or not an individual is deemed insurable depends on basically nothing more than a fit between the objective characteristics of an applicant (such as age, weight, number of speeding tickets, or whether they smoke) and the rating classes of the insurance company.

Numbers as preventive pretext?

The letters sent to applicants informing them of the insurance risk decision also strongly rely on abstract numbers and figures. That these numbers are transparent, however, should not be taken for granted. Consider, for example, the following extract from an underwriter:

> *Observation, underwriter M – end of the risk assessment:*
> M: "So, now I'm going to compose the letter... so it doesn't say why this person is going to receive a substandard rate. It only mentions the figure of the rate, initial tax, annual rate ...
> IvH: But then ... he does realise that there is a substandard rate?

M: Yes, but he doesn't know why. Because, well, we are not allowed to put that in the letter because these letters, you know, where do they end up? You never know in whose hands they'll end up, you see?" (C2, M, 3).

In other words, applicants are intentionally left in the dark regarding the exact details of their risk calculation. This can be partly explained by the insurance company's concerns about technical information ending up in the hands of competitors. But, more importantly it seems, by leaving their decision process vague the company has much to win in its direct interaction with applicants as well. The lack of clear information may prevent applicants from articulating complaints about their risk result or from deciding *not* to purchase the insurance policy and trying another company. Moreover, in this regard, Glenn (2000) argues that by covering up numbers, insurance companies seek to prevent applicants from registering a legal complaint against the insurance company, for instance, on discriminatory practices. In other words, individuals must somehow first become aware that they are being discriminated against, and this can be difficult to do if they do not understand the underwriting process or if they are unaware that the insurance company categorises them in a certain manner (Simon 1988) – if, in short, they are kept uninformed. This effect is strongest in cases where the company leaves its risk-rating approach opaque.

The untouchables?

What happens if a client still wants to file a complaint about the medical underwriting procedure afterwards? How can clients make their voices heard *after* the actual risk assessment is finished and they have entered into a contract with the company? Apart from taking their case to court, complaints may be directed first of all to the Complaints Department of the Insurance Supervisory Authority (ISA). This department examines individual documents submitted by the insured, brokers, lawyers and others in all areas of insurance involving problems regarding the settlement of claims, the interpretation of contracts, etc. (Controledienst voor de Verzekeringen 2002). However, the ISA is an executive organisation and therefore its recommendations are not binding. Secondly, complaints may be registered with the ombudsman of the Belgian Association of Insurers (BVVO). The BVVO has established this complaints service in reaction to a public image study of the Belgian insurance industry (BVVO 2001: 2). This ombudsman publishes an annual report on the registered complaints and on the results of this mediation agency. The received complaints are statistically analysed as to origin, insurance branch, motivation, type of complaint, and type of outcome. A distinction is made between valid and invalid complaints. In this respect, the conclusion of the annual report of this ombudsman in 1999 states that for several years already

> We have found that complaints relating to communication, in other words, to the fact that the insurance company has not or has incompletely responded, has responded too late, or has not given any explanation ... are usually valid complaints. On the contrary, whenever the complaints relate to technical aspects of the management of the insurance company, they are mostly considered invalid (BVVO 2000). [my translation]

It is revealing that only communication aspects, such as the clarity of contract conditions and exclusionary clauses, are subject to valid complaints, whereas the medico-actuarial dimension (including the risk-rating categories used) seems to be entirely shielded from outside criticism. In other words, the technical side of underwriting is sacrosanct. Complaints are dismissed as "unfounded, from a technical angle" (BVVO 1999), and hence judged invalid. To complaints regarding, for instance, the insurability of bad risks in car insurance, the ombudsman responded:

> Unfortunately, the ombudsman only supports these persons in their *démarche* in part. After all, the insurance rates and underwriting terms regarding risks are part of the insurance companies' economic policy in which they can freely determine their own strategic choices (BVVO 2000). [my translation]

In this regard, a feedback mechanism like this has little to add: The numbers and risk decisions have already hardened into indisputable numbers. By the end of the underwriting process, they have been construed as watertight. How, in this logic, can a complaint about what is already established as objective – numbers, statistics, procedures – ever be a *valid* complaint?

The only option left in Belgium in such matters is to go to court. However, my respondents from both insurance companies and consumer groups expressed their dissatisfaction with this option, considering its many drawbacks. For individual clients, for example, lawsuits come with the risk of extremely high costs, which means that in practice only a group of applicants can register a legal complaint against an insurance company. Similarly, insurance companies consider a lawsuit a last resort because of the potential repercussions in the media on the image of the insurance industry as a whole.

Conclusion

This chapter addressed the relevance of judgement in the final translation of applicants into insurance risks. Numbers from guidelines are meant to bring closure to the risk result, but the underwriters also invoke their experience, intuition and background knowledge of past cases. So besides the assemblage work involved in the establishment of *objective* numbers, underwriters also have some manoeuvring room at the very end of the assessment process.

Given this discretionary space of underwriters, the applicant is not always just a passive actor. In more or less direct ways, applicants can influence their insurance results. Compared to the co-constructions of applicants as illustrated in the previous chapters, these co-constructions in the judgement phase are situated on an *individual* level. Underwriters, when assessing risks, may indirectly take into account clients' expectations involving insurance, its products and its medical selection via the writing devices received from the applicant. This kind of indirect feedback from applicants, however, reflects a meagre kind of clients' participation in the underwriting set-up. The applicant is mainly taken into account in insurance via *constructions* of applicants, based on the indirect tools (e.g., questionnaires) the underwriters receive from them. As an effect, the underwriters have to translate what is written into assumptions about the applicant's aspirations. This indirectness of course comes with the risk of "noise" between the two dimensions. Consequently, "truthfulness" in the disclosure of risk is rather difficult to attain because of the various translations and stagings of risks by the actors involved in the insurer-insured relationship.

Closing the black box

As argued in this and the previous chapters, a careful analysis of the entire risk trajectory hardly justifies the "givenness" of numbers. By opening up the black box of underwriting, it becomes apparent that risk assessment involves a process that has many openings. Even the applicants themselves can influence the company's efforts in this respect, albeit only slightly in most cases, and only as long as the risk is ultimately not yet established.

Despite this manoeuvring room, in the final communication, all of the options are again closed off by the reversion back to the language of risk. Although this language can also be productive in reconciling differing opinions within the department itself, its main purpose is to seal off the risk. It buries the assemblage work under the veil of objectivity and abstract numbers. In other words, underwriters once again close the curtain when resorting to the basic insurance principles at the very end of underwriting trajectory. What they cover up is that, in the name of risk, a new applicant's trajectory has meanwhile been paved, for which profit-making strategies are designed, bottom-line figures recalculated, communities divided, computer programs implemented, morals governed, numbers adjusted, cost-benefit studies applied, angry phone calls answered, internal disputes settled, medical advisors soothed, bank directors listened to, clients' preferences assumed, narratives told, statistics re-adjusted, figures moulded, experts controlled and so on.

In this manner, the recourse to the language of risk in the end communication serves the interests of the insurance industry. By hiding behind the language of numbers and principles of its own making, it silences the other parties involved or at least substantially narrows their opportunities to "voice" or criticise afterwards. Although the chapters have demonstrated that there are some openings or applicants' co-constructions available in the *making* of insurance risks, in the final stages these openings become unavailable. Thus the insurance language of risk renders underwriting as a social and commercial *practice* opaque – a mystery to outsiders.

VI Risky Bodies Future Stage? Risk Carriers and Risk Takers

The more there is about the individual that deviates in an undesirable direction from what might have been expected to be true of him, the more he is obliged to volunteer information about himself ... Here, the right to reticence seems earned only by having nothing to hide.
Goffman, 1964

Introduction

Having explored the general process of underwriting in the previous chapters, we now turn to the use of predictive medicine in life insurance. As already demonstrated in chapter I, the recent focus on genetics can be situated within a broader transformation in medicine, from a clinical, complaints-bound medicine to a predictive, risk-oriented medicine (de Vries and Horstman 2004). Since the 1970s, new disciplines have taken shape within modern epidemiology, public health and prenatal care that have contributed to a framework in which problems of health and disease have become problems of *health risks*, shifting the focus from symptoms and treatment to pre-symptomatic diagnosis and prevention. Where once health might have been defined quite simply as the "present absence of disease", it might now be better understood as the "absence of an increased statistical chance of future disease". New intermediate or in-between health categories have emerged where individuals are identified as "risk carriers", derived from risk probabilities and statistical correlations. People identified as being at high risk for, say, breast cancer, inhabit an intermediate disease state as neither necessarily healthy nor well, they are neither "already diseased" nor are they "disease free".

Given medicine's gatekeeper role in insurance, it is not so surprising that these issues are intriguing in the context of life insurance because assessing people's health forms the very criterion for access to life insurance. In this chapter, I will reflect on the introduction of this predictive medicine in insurance.[54] I will demonstrate how insurers highlight predictive lifestyle health information and how this articulates with a fault-based approach in underwriting. New predictive technologies allow insurers to evaluate our behaviour towards our self-capacity to control our health. Moreover, these developments create the possibility of tightening the norms for "suitable lives" in insurance, increasing the conditions that need to be fulfilled to become part of the insurance group. The chapter then moves on to a corresponding treatment of genetics and family history. Then I will reflect on the fault-based logic that is associated with this. Here it will be possible to see this as an effect of a "genetic essentialism" mobilised in social representations around genetics, which has been institutionalised in the Belgian legal prohibition on genetics in insurance (LVO 1992). I will then explore some of the side effects of this legislation before, in the conclusion, examining the implications for the insurability of people arising from predictive medicine. In other words, do we agree that our "fitness" for life insurance should be based on our moral qualities?

In doing so, I want to make connections with broader sociologies on risk society, neo-liberal governmentality and the individualisation of health (see e.g., Dean 1998; Rose 2000). For, as we will see, the framing of predictive medicine in insurance can be seen to articulate a wider individualisation of responsibility for health. In turn, we might consider in what ways and forms the private insurance industry represents the institutional expression of these neo-liberal discourses? By drawing on contributions from the sociology of insurance (see e.g., Ericson, Dean and Doyle 2000; Ericson and Doyle 2003; Baker 2000), we will see that insurance institutions do not simply or passively reflect wider societal visions. Rather, they actively produce a whole range of moral duties and cultural values, on, for example, what is meant by "suitable lives". In other words, we want to outline the role of insurance as a "normative technology" (Baker and Simon 2002) or an instrument in prescribing particular frames for responsibilities as an *effect* of the way it frames accountability around health.

Before we begin to explore this, however, it is useful to raise some issues on the meaning of predictive medicine and genetics in Belgium. Belgium was one of the first European countries to introduce a legal prohibition on the use of genetic data by insurance companies. The 1992 Law on Insurance Contracts (LVO) regulates this issue in its articles 5 and 95. Article 95 introduces a total prohibition on the use of genetic tests for predicting the future health status of policy applicants.[55] Article 5, section 1 of that same law requires insurance clients to knowingly supply accurate data that may be of interest to the insurer. It is not permitted, however, to pass on genetic information.[56] Legal commentary was however critical of this, and pointed to a lacuna for the law's interpretation. For one thing, Belgian legislators did not define "genetic data" (Freriks 1994: 28), or "genetic research techniques" (Nys 1992: 216). Consequently, it is not clear whether the legislator currently forbids the use of family histories or genetic information derived from routine medical examinations, like blood tests, for example. Given this lack of clarity, it has been a priority during my fieldwork to observe how predictive medicine is mobilised, defined and constructed by the involved actors.

How do insurers deal with risk factors that have to do with lifestyle and genetics?

Lifestyle as Predictive Health Information

In the course of my fieldwork it became clear that underwriters pay a lot of attention to applicants' lifestyle traits. In checking the information on policy applicants, for instance, they indicate that they mainly encounter "lifestyle risks" or "diseases of civilisation":

> Recently we have noticed a lot of depression. And also diseases of luxury such as increased liver values, high blood pressure, increased blood sugar and so on. All this has to do with ... stress and poor lifestyle habits. These are all things, it seems to me, that can be avoided, which is too bad in a way (C1, E, 3).

The instruments and forms used to request this information also mirror this attention to lifestyle. The medical questionnaire has a separate rubric devoted to questions on weight, blood pressure, alcohol use, smoking behaviour and drug use. Its heading, "major information", has a grey frame to emphasise the rubric's significance. During my observations it became clear that the underwriters attach a great deal of importance to the responses in this rubric:

> These questions [points to questionnaire and reads] 'weight, height, smoking behavior and alcohol use', we consider them carefully because to us these are major risk selection criteria. This is why we always return the questionnaire when an applicant has failed to respond to these questions (C1, P, 3).

The studies and statistics that underlie the premium calculation also reflect this attention to lifestyle. A recent actuarial study, for instance, listed the following "diseases" that are associated with excessive mortality: being under/overweight, alcoholism, hypertension, smoking, depression and heart conditions. Following this study, the department's management decided to institute a higher premium for these features, but at first it hesitated to do so exclusively on the basis of this kind of health behaviour. After all, if this lifestyle information is obtained via the questionnaire, it could easily lead to faulty data and fraud on the part of the applicant. To address this concern it was eventually decided to calculate higher premiums only if the same information was provided by more "objective" instruments, such as blood analyses, liver tests, lung X-rays or codeine tests. Thanks to these technologies, lifestyle features can be "measured" and thus serve as a legitimate basis for assigning higher premiums.

Similarly, the reinsurance guidelines on cholesterol, obesity and high blood pressure emphasise the relevance of predictive lifestyle information. Where these risk factors represent a statistically increased chance that someone will develop a particular disease, they are considered *primary* mortality risks in insurance, as independent bases for assigning a higher premium. Thus they are assessed in the same way as other "pre-existing conditions" like tuberculosis or asthma, as may be illustrated through the example of raised cholesterol levels. A high cholesterol level comes with an increased risk of clogged arteries or other cardiovascular diseases. In insurance practice, however, high cholesterol is synonymous with an increased mortality risk. This same logic can also be seen in how obesity and high blood pressure are considered. Apparently there is a tendency in the insurance industry to reify predictive lifestyle factors into autonomous mortality risks. These lifestyle risks are regarded as "prior-existing conditions", or as prior-existing "damage" or "deviation". In the case of high blood pressure, for instance, an underwriter explains:

> High blood pressure is not so bad as such. You do not die from it immediately. But the heart of someone who does not pay attention to it suffers a lot, becomes larger, the muscles weaken. This is how it is with many things. There is always a chance that problems will occur later on. So to us, this is already an increased mortality risk. We have to look at the long-term effects (C2, R, 3).

Insurers thus transform epidemiological risks (defined as probabilities for future disease) into diseases or deviations that already exist.[57] Probabilistic risk factors thus become physical abnormalities or deviations that require exclusion or a higher premium.

Aside from the use of lifestyle factors as primary mortality risks, these elements also play a role in the classification of those who are already suffering from an (other) disorder. For instance, lifestyle may play a role in *adjusting* the statistical average of higher premiums for a specific disease. By requesting additional information, via a report from the attending physician or an examination by a medical expert, elements come to light on the specific *circumstances* of the disease. These are taken into account as prognostic factors (+/-) in assessing individual rates. Thus it is possible to trace personalised, clinical information, including, for instance, the beginning of an illness, periods of relapse, the course of the illness and response to treatment. This is yet another way that lifestyle elements can be calculated by underwriters. Consider the following underwriter's comment regarding someone who on the questionnaire indicated that she was suffering from diabetes:

> So she fills in 'diabetes' on her questionnaire, but that is a little vague. I don't know how bad it is and such. So I send an extra questionnaire to her

> physician to find out her last blood readings and see if she has stabilised. We also want to know whether she controls her illness with insulin or just with pills and is it effective. All this, then, makes a difference. Thus we may potentially lower or raise the diabetes premium for this client (C2, K, 3).

In the case of high cholesterol, underwriters may request readings of tests performed at various intervals in order to assess whether the person involved has regularly used his or her medication for stabilising the cholesterol level:

> Here we have a letter from the GP with tests that cover the last two years, and as you can see [points to the rubric in the letter]: the blood values are fine throughout. So, I suspect this man takes his pills regularly, because I do not notice any extremes in the values. In other words, he is controlling his illness well. This is why I will accept him against a better premium (C1, B, 3).

In other words, we are dealing here with "compliant behaviour" on the part of the client. The applicants' premiums are fixed on the basis of their assumed sense of responsibility for their own health. If they are *good* patients, they are rewarded with a lower premium, but if they are *disobedient*, their premium will be higher.

The policy on smoking is particularly indicative of the prominent role of lifestyle. As illustrated in chapter V, smoking is used as a risk classification factor for charging smokers a substandard premium. In this regard, the reinsurers' statistical studies all point to smokers as a major category. A recent European study indicates that in the past smoking was undervalued in premium levels, both as a risk factor as such and in combination with other disorders. The study subsequently concludes: "Since smoking has a crucial impact on the mortality of both normal and medically substandard risks, all life insurance proposal forms should ask about smoking habits, and the resulting data should be recorded for statistical purposes and should be adequately taken into account in the rating guidelines" (Swiss Re 2002: 10).

Moreover, smoking has of late become a factor in the calculating of the standard premium as well. If the standard premium used to be put together on the basis of non-medical elements, such as age, insured capital and sex, smoking has been added as a factor:

> Before, there used to be a standard premium for smokers and non-smokers combined. And the smokers had to pay a higher premium. But in 1999, the managers said: 'Well, non-smokers clearly have a lower risk. We will reward them with a lower standard premium' (C1, K, 2).

In practice this means that at the start of the application process the standard premium is calculated on the basis of smoking. If it turns out that applicants are non-smokers, they will get a reduced standard premium. But if they smoke, the higher "standard" premium must be paid. And if they are "heavy smokers" (defined in the guidelines as: "more than two packages of cigarettes per day"), they have to pay an additional premium. By basing standard premiums in part on "smoking" behaviour rewards the non-smokers. When asked, the managers explained that this was a way of pointing out to clients that they are responsible for their own health. Aside from being a strategy for penalising unhealthy smokers, this has thus also become a strategy for attracting healthy clients:

> Instead of just having unhealthy people pay extra we chose the strategy of lowering the standard premium in the case of non-smoking. Thus we explicitly suggest to our clients that their lifestyles matters. If they do not smoke they are now rewarded via a reduced standard premium. It is, of course, a positive strategy to first assign a client the smokers' rate and so when it turns out he doesn't smoke you can tell him that he qualifies for a reduced premium. In cases of the reverse, when someone claims to be a non-smoker but the codeine test establishes that he is in fact a smoker, requiring us to inform him that he has to pay a higher premium. The first strategy is more customer-friendly (C1, K, 2).

Essentially, the new policy reinforces the difference between a healthy and an unhealthy lifestyle.

Making the normal deviant

The introduction of lifestyle predictive information in insurance practice raises questions about the significance of the standard premium in insurance. After all, the reliance on predictive risk factors (and innovative technologies) contributes to the idea of "the worried well", the idea that we are neither really ill nor entirely healthy (Harris 1994, quoted in: Davies 1998: 149). In insurance practice, however, we see that those who display risky behaviour are already seen as "ill". Ever more conditions are being tied to standard insurance rates. Predictive information thus causes more and more health characteristics to be applied during the underwriting process, which comes with the risk that the margins for being defined as "in normal health" are becoming increasingly smaller. What insurers defined "standard health" is ever more limited. Accordingly, the normality concept in insurance is shifting from a condition of *absence of illness* to a condition of *risk resistance*. In a way, predictive knowledge immunises the normal standard premium against disease by expanding the indicators for mortality. Ironically, although over the past decades our average life expectancy has steadily increased, the norm for being accepted as "standard" for an insurance policy has risen over that same period of time. Thus the *norm* in insurance increasingly deviates from the *average* health status. This raises the question of whether the introduction of predictive lifestyle factors has caused the standard premium in insurance to reflect rather a "more-than-standard-norm". Or does it imply that our social norm is shifting toward a stricter definition of health? On the one hand, these tendencies can be seen as a continuation of the common insurance logic. After all, insurers have always engaged in predicting people's health status. On the other hand, the increasing usage of predictive knowledge and techniques evidently creates new precedents for the insurance practice.

"Behave": Assessing the capacity to self-control

As has already become clear, potential clients are not only examined medically, but also increasingly on their moral conduct and their attitude toward their own health. The emphasis on lifestyle in insurance has caused insurers to begin stressing applicants' ability to control their own risk. Health is thus linked to the notion of "good citizenship" and meshes with sociological debates that arise concerning the discourse of the individualisation of health (e.g., Petersen and Bunton 1997; Baker and Simon 2002; Higgs 1998). Within these perspectives, it is argued that the concept of health is currently more and more embroiled in that of citizenship and neo-liberalism, where collective responsibilities give way to individual ones. Miller and Rose (1993) note:

> No longer is citizenship construed in terms of solidarity, contentment, welfare and a sense of security established through the bonds of organisational and social life. Citizenship is to be active and individualistic rather than passive and dependent. The political subject is henceforth to be an individual whose citizenship is manifested through the free enterprise of personal choice amongst a variety of options (1993: 98).

One's health choices constitute a crucial dimension here, no longer is health considered a consequence of fate, but increasingly of individual agency. Good health equals good citizenship whilst ill health excludes one from productivity and is seen as economically burdensome. "It is one's *duty* to achieve and preserve good health, so that one might fulfil the other obligations of citizenship" (Petersen and Lupton 1996: 65). Moreover, good health signifies good citizenship, by demonstrating one's self-control over the body and meshes with what some view as a discourse of "healthism," operating on the assumption that everyone should work and live to maximise their health (Metcalfe 1993: 35; Skrabanek, 1994). Those who are unable or unwilling to subscribe to the dominant health norms are likely to be labelled in a deregoratory way ("the fat, weak or lazy") and to be castigated for their lack of self-control. Consequently, the *healthy* body has become an increasingly important signifier of moral worth, a mark of distinction that serves to delineate those who deserve to succeed from those who will fail (Crawford 1994: 1354).

The pursuit of health through one's work on the body then has become a crucial means by which the individual can publicly express such virtues as self-control, self-denial and will power – in short, those qualifications considered important to be a *normal, healthy* human being. For Williams (1993), it is not so much health itself that is seen as virtuous, but the self-disciplined activity which produces it. Health thus becomes associated with "virtuousness" and managing one's own relationship to risk has become an important means by which individuals can express their ethical selves, fulfilling their obligations as good citizens (Scott and Williams 1991: 3).

Sociological work has illustrated that expertise plays an important role in this process of moral accountability, in, for example, the epidemiological and public health focus on lifestyle and individual responsibility rather than luck or misfortune (e.g., Petersen and Lupton 1996; Petersen 1998). Though expert risk assessment cannot be held exclusively accountable for individuals being held morally culpable for their own health, these perspectives all indicate its embeddedness within health promotion campaigns, governmental regimes and cultures of blame. Davies, for example, in her study on the discourse of weight control, writes of a "victim-blaming paradigm" (1998: 148). In current public health literature, excessive weight is understood to be self-inflicted and a result of failing to manage one's body appropriately. Being overweight becomes one's own fault where epidemiological "definitions of health are constructed around a concept of "optimal" well-being and are no longer simply understood as an absence of disease" (1998: 149).

My observations on the "normality" concept constructed in the insurance industry articulate the "victim-blaming paradigm" and the individualised self-control focus of health. By introducing more lifestyle risk factors into the underwriting process, the standard normal rate has been narrowed to converge on an optimal state of health as the health norm as prescribed by the insurance industry. Accordingly, insurance normality expresses a morally embedded civic notion of control over health. For, as the cases have illustrated, if you want to be accepted as a normal risk, you need to be in perfect health, and, what is more, you also need to be a good citizen. If you are responsible for your own health, you'll get your insurance at standard rates but if you display irresponsible behaviour you will pay the appropriate penalty.

The voluntary character of lifestyle risks

By "measuring" lifestyle variables one can trace to what degree individuals exercise control over their own health. If they cannot demonstrate this, they are financially "punished" with higher premiums. Individual control over one's health is thus translated into a selection criterion for insurance policy eligibility. Poor "body upkeepers" have to pay higher premiums. The moral claims that are thus linked to specific applicants allow insurers to contribute to the construction of the *voluntary* character of "lifestyle" risk liability. The identification of fault and guilt serves as the basis for penalisation. Where disease is, however, not a matter of fault but of fate, an ill person is seen as a *victim*. But insurers have increasingly begun to note the role of individual responsibility and they figure that those who do not take responsibility simply have to pay:

> We increasingly see people who are overweight, with high blood pressure, and diabetes. These are the main disorders today. And the heavy smokers of course ... This is counterbalanced by the cancer cases for instance. They in fact are the real victims (C1, K, 3).

The construction of the self-inflicted nature of lifestyle risks also returns in the way underwriters deal with remissions or modifications. It is permitted in specific cases to adapt a premium after a given timeframe. Insurers, however, only do this when it concerns "real diseases", rather than lifestyle diseases, such as obesity:

> In the case of poor lifestyle habits we will not issue an adjustment. If one used to have poor lifestyle habits this can no longer be entirely erased. There is always a specific lifestyle that automatically affects one's future. So this is not an issue. There are only a few serious diseases that return after a certain period. Of these you can say, okay, as in the case of breast cancer; when it appears the disease has been stable for ten years, we may issue a premium adjustment. So then we redetermine the premium because with breast cancer, it is not a consequence of lifestyle, it is beyond one's will. In these cases the disease is to blame. Meanwhile, lifestyle habits are dependent on people's decisions, and so in those cases we do not change our earlier decisions. Because if they used to have poor lifestyle habits, there is no guarantee that they have permanently changed their behaviour (C1, E, 2).

> Overweight people often say: 'Yes, I weigh too much, but from now on I'm going to do something about it.' So we get a lot of reactions like these, and questions like: 'How much am I allowed to weigh so I can get the standard premium?' This is not how it works of course. You can decide to lose weight but there is no guarantee that their weight will stabilize (C2, O, 3).

The same happens when underwriters are faced with the postponement of a decision. In the case of a pregnancy, for instance, the medical examination is postponed until after birth. For those with high cholesterol, however, postponement is impossible. These patients instantly receive an increase in their premiums:

> In the case of high cholesterol we will not postpone our assessment. We go right to a higher rate. With pregnancies we could do the same, but, well, I feel it involves an issue whereby those who are pregnant are being punished for something they have no control over (C1, R, 3).

As these examples illustrate, the introduction of predictive health information goes hand in hand with a distinction of the moral significance attributed to risks. According to Petersen and Lupton, this leads to a widening of the risk concept: a *moral* risk scale comes into being, "a continuum of moral judgement" (1996: 115) that extends from risks that arise beyond our control to risks that are purely indebted to negligence regarding our health. The insurance practice thus consolidates cultural judgements that are tied to specific risks. Such thinking reverses the cause of personal tragedy, which makes it seem that the risk has always been present as a risk, which may have been avoided if one had put in an effort to do so. As Lupton writes: "The experience of a heart attack, a positive HIV result... are evidence that the ill person has failed to comply with directives to reduce health risks and therefore is to blame for his or her predicament" (1993: 430). And: "Failing to protect oneself from this kind of 'internally imposed' risk is understood as an individual moral issue, highlighting personal failures or weaknesses" (1995: 89-90). The calculation of extra premiums for people with poor lifestyles, then, constitutes the basis for an *own-fault* approach.

Moreover, these observations on normativity in insurance also confirm and develop sociological work on decision making in clinical medicine. White (2002), for example, has shown that moral judgement is involved in the "story-telling" of paediatricians about their patients, based on a moral classification of cases. Pope (2002) similarly shows the presence of moral judgement in surgeons' decision making in treating women with urinary incontinence. When discussing whether surgery should be undertaken, some types of co-morbidity were characterised as the patient's fault (obesity, respiratory disorders caused by smoking) whilst others were non-attributable to patient behaviour or lifestyle: "a moral judgement was made about these co-existing conditions and the fault or blameworthiness of the individual" (2002: 382). Jeffrey's (1979) work on the classification of "good patients, bad patients and rubbish" in an A&E department is also noteworthy in this respect. Practical examples of *bad* lifestyles described above are similarly negatively sanctioned in the insurance industry, in the same way as Jeffery's (1979) "rubbish" cases.

Two more remarks can be made here. First, these studies illustrate that moral judgement in health operates beyond the specific confines of insurance. As such, the insurance approach to predictive medicine should not be analysed as an isolated practice. Underwriting is shaped by, and shapes, broader societal images and epistemologies, articulating parallel expert practices like epidemiology and clinical medicine. Secondly, whereas the above studies mainly deal with the moral work involved in the judgement phase of clinical decision making, my analysis demonstrates that these moral judgements are present throughout *all* phases of the risk trajectory. That is, beyond the final decision making of underwriters, my data illustrates that moral distinctions about culpability are also inscribed in numerous materials, technologies and writing devices. This is evident in the choice of risk factors used, in the selection of insurance statistics, in inscription devices (e.g., questionnaire) and in marketing towards some customers rather than others.

The measurement of trustworthiness

The deployment of insurance statistics, underwriting guidelines and other devices on predictive lifestyle factors not only emphasises responsible health behaviour but also fabricates the trustworthiness of applicants. Insurance institutions distribute responsibility by marking people along the continuum of trustworthy or not.

This positioning of people in a trustworthiness continuum is not new, quite the reverse. Insurance institutions have always been primarily concerned with the management of moral hazard and adverse selection (Heimer 1985). The underwriting process is then precisely the *raison d'être* of insurance for predicting and controlling moral hazard. Rating and underwriting techniques predict where dishonesty and non-performance are likely to occur, refusing insurance in some instances and adjusting premiums in others. Whenever moral hazard is identified, individual financial responsibility is claimed by refusing cover or having to pay a substandard rate. In other words, making the "morally hazardous" share *a priori* (via higher premiums) the cost burden of risk encourages people to act in a responsible manner. To be "beyond insurance" is therefore often seen as a moral assessment that a person is imprudent or even irresponsible. Rather than simply bearing more risk than others, those who are unable to get insurance find that technical and normative assessments are conflated and they are also unable to get loans, drive a car, or operate a business (Heimer 2002: 119). Insurance is a form of "discipline" or social control, of inculcating norms, supervising behaviour and enforcing compliance (Foucault 1995; Simon 1988). In managing moral hazard, insurance regulates behaviour rather than simply spreading risk. In other words, attempts to manage moral hazard reflect and reinforce moral attitudes and cultural values on trustworthiness. To keep adverse selection or the "immorals" at bay, insurers have always had to carefully select the so-called "quality lives." In the nineteenth and early twentieth centuries, these "quality of life" assessments mostly meant that the company had to be satisfied that the applicant was honourable and trustworthy. It was very difficult for any medical expert to know as much about an applicant's health as the applicants knew themselves. In this regard, Porter (2000: 229) writes that medical knowledge was subordinate to a general assessment of dignity and morality. Moral character meant worthiness to associate with a select society, but it was also taken as a good predictor of longevity. In time, this moral judgement found *objective* expression in medical diagnostic and actuarial knowledge. In other words, the control of moral hazard is now medically and technically mediated.

The argument here is that the emergence of predictive lifestyle risk assessments has taken shape within these historical continuities. Increasing the scope of lifestyle predictive risk factors in epidemiology and actuarial techniques, insurers are increasingly able to take into account these characteristics in the underwriting process. Nineteenth-century assessments of moral judgement (e.g., "the total abstainers") have however undergone important shifts, notably a "metrication" through predictive knowledge and technologies (Mol 2002: 222). Objective predictive measures are therefore increasingly the basis upon which the citizenship and moral duty of applicants is shaped. More importantly, normative moral judgements have been scripted and translated into diagnostic devices considered morally *neutral*. This builds upon and extends the classic tension between framing people as citizens who behave rationally or irrationally, properly or improperly, responsibly or irresponsibly and framing people as fragile bio-psycho-social systems who happen to be normal or disturbed, capable or incapable, together or broken apart.[58] Consequently, framing lifestyle characteristics and health behaviour within a medicalised discourse (as part of a bio-psycho-social system) results in a greater scope for policing the individual responsibilities of applicants and the requirement for them to pay substandard rates.

And yet there are also some inconsistencies here. The increasing availability of predictive lifestyle technology further enhances, or takes beyond its limits, the idea of the controlability of death in life insurance.[59] By metricating health behaviour, predictive medicine suggests that we are ourselves responsible for our own morbidity or mortality. Consequently, it suggests not only that death is manageable, but that there is a lot we *ourselves* can do about it. From the fatalism of an inevitable death, we are now enmeshed in a view of mortality that is *individually* controllable. As Heimer (1985) notes, losses over which the insured has no control do not raise major problems of moral hazard. However, where the insured has substantial control, the price for buying insurance often includes giving up a measure of that control.[60] Where managing moral hazard may once have been the main concern of insurers (via risk selection), it has increasingly become that of individuals, embedded inter-subjectively and mediated medically. The shift has been from a collective risk management (via risk selection) position, towards an *a priori* individualised risk management position. Moreover, by stressing the moral healthy behaviour, insurers are, to some extent, requesting that applicants institute "safety measures" as preconditions for insurance coverage – as would be the case, for example, with building insurance where a policy would only be offered to those who have installed fire and theft prevention devices. Predictive lifestyle technologies increasingly play a similar role, especially as financial inducements for people to alter their levels of risk. A good lifestyle (and a good citizenry) has become decisive in offering coverage and at what cost. And of course, this is likely to play an important role in reshaping the wider public and cultural dynamics of accountability for health. Offering substandard premiums to people who exhibit substandard lifestyles forms the basis of a *fault-based* insurance logic. Below I build on this discussion about predictive medicine by examining the way underwriters deal with genetically related predictive information, specifically the family history.

The Involuntary Character of Genetic Risks

How do insurers deal with predictive *genetic* information? As indicated above, this is very much determined by Belgian legislation that prohibits the usage of genetic information. As a consequence, underwriters only rarely encountered genetic test results or genetic information (on, for example, Down syndrome, cystic fibrosis, Huntington's disease). Underwriters in these cases solicit the advice to the reinsurance company. Since Belgian law does *not explicitly* prohibit the use of a family history, the two insurance companies where I did my fieldwork asked for family history data in their medical questionnaire, while the underwriters could further deduce information on serious genetic and familial disorders from reports presented by the attending physician or specialist.

However, my respondents proved to be reticent in taking this information into account in risk assessment. For one thing, they did not consider it necessary to send back medical questionnaires where the responses about family history had not or had been incompletely filled in. Moreover, this family information was only meant to confirm or negate data on diseases from which the applicant himself was already suffering. As in the case of a person with cardiovascular complaints:

> If we establish symptoms for him that have to do with heart problems, we also consider the family history. It is possible, then, [grabs guidelines] where heart infarcts have at least occurred in the family, that we have to charge a higher rate. But if a person indicates that his father suffered from a heart affliction, while this person has no such problems at this point, we do not charge a higher premium (C1, E, 3).

The applicant's current pathology determined whether or not family history should play a role. A *tainted* family history might raise the average premium for a specific disorder (60 per cent instead of 50 per cent). For instance, as one underwriter explained with respect to familial hypercholesterolemia (FH):

> When the applicant indicates a family history of FH but he himself has no raised LDL cholesterol levels at this point, he will be accepted against a normal premium. But if he proves to have high cholesterol levels and if we also can prove that there are specific relevant conditions in the family, these things are added up and he will end up paying a premium that is slightly higher than the average raised premium for FH. And if he discloses no family history and there are also high cholesterol levels, he will end up with the average higher premium for cholesterol (C1, P, 3).

Although family history is taken into account, then, this element plays less of a role than lifestyle. In general, the insurers make no distinction between applicants with a good or bad family history *per se*; these applicants are not penalised just because of their family histories.[61] Thus, in contrast to lifestyle, predictive familial risks are not reified to autonomous, primary mortality risks. A family history of disease does not automatically make a person a high risk.

These examples demonstrate that insurers attach less significance to family history than to lifestyle factors. Underwriters also articulated normative objections against the use of family history as a decisive risk factor:

> We cannot afford to give a higher premium merely on the basis of family history. We cannot tell our clients that they'll have to pay more because of their father's heart problems. This is not client-friendly. If someone honestly declares that he is not suffering from anything and our tests confirm that there is nothing wrong with his heart, charging him a higher premium is hard to defend (C1, E, 3).

Again we see that moral connotations are embedded in the underwriting process. Charging somebody because of his genes or his family's medical history alone is considered un-delicate or unjustifiable, because having "bad genes" is something this person cannot help. The same objection is advanced more fiercely when it involves behavioural diseases among family members. As an underwriter noted in the case of alcoholism:

> If we consider whether the mother and father have an alcohol problem? This is even a more delicate matter. You have to realise that when we charge someone a higher rate because his mother was an alcoholic, that leaves a bad impression commercially. After all, can this person be blamed for his mother's alcoholism? So why penalise him for his mother? (C1, P, 3).

Family history or "bad genes" are not considered to be a matter of choice or self-control. In other words, this is how the *involuntary* character of genetics is constructed.

Risk Carriers vs. Risk Takers

If we compare the underwriters' approaches to predictive risk factors, lifestyle risks are far more pressing with regard to risk assessment than genetic risks. In the first case, the risk pool will not subsidise the applicant; he must bear his own risk. In the latter case, insurance companies are often willing to take the risk. Consequently, insurers construct the voluntary or involuntary character of, respectively, lifestyle and family history risk factors.

According to Petersen and Lupton (1996), the moral judgements involved in predictive medicine create on the one hand "at-risk people", that is, people with risks which are perceived as completely out of individual control and, on the other hand, "risky selves", or people whose risk derives from their ignorance or lack of self-control. The same tendency seems to occur in the Belgian insurance industry: lifestyle *risk takers* are treated differently than genetic risk *carriers*. This results in a fault-based approach to underwriting: Risks are assessed differently according to whether they are a result of the applicant's own fault or not. In the first case, you are made a culprit, in the latter, you are considered a victim. Implicitly then, insurers disseminate moral judgements on the responsibility for one's own health. Although both lifestyle and family history are predictors of an individual's future health status, lifestyle has gained ascendancy in the risk calculation process.

This prompts questions not so much about the emergence of these judgements but what they *imply*. That is, by stressing the difference between lifestyle and genetic risks, we see how distinct moralities are attributed to applicants, and, consequently, different (financial) responsibilities are assessed. Other sociological studies have argued that genetic knowledge production is associated with new forms of determinism, a "geneticisation" or "genetic essentialism" in which genes are attributed an overly deterministic role (see e.g., Lippman 1993; Kitcher 1996). This means there is a tendency to distinguish people along genetic characteristic lines and to categorise diseases into genetic and non-genetic ones, resulting in different levels of responsibility attributed to genetic and non-genetic diseases. So where genes are linked to fatalism or lack of control, lifestyle is associated with individual control or responsibility.[62] The same approach is found in Belgian insurance companies. The Belgian legal prohibition on using genetic information in insurance policies can be considered the institutionalisation of "genetic essentialism". Where genetic risks are seen as "fate", as "involuntary" or "uncontrollable", lifestyle risks are considered as self-induced, voluntary and one's "own responsibility". The outcome is a financial solidarity or collective responsibility for the genetic *risk carriers* – the collective risk pool is prepared to pay for them – and individual financial responsibility for lifestyle *risk takers* – they have to pay for their risk taking themselves via higher premiums.

This further clarifies how insurance is a normative technology and practice. Risk selection is neither a purely technical procedure nor simply the application of insurance principles – but much more of a social and normative undertaking (Stone 1993). On the one hand, we see that insurance institutions are dovetailing with social judgements originating in epidemiology, regulation or, more generally, public opinions about health and disease. On the other hand, when insurance institutions become relevant expert risk assessors in society they can also innovate, thus propagating or enhancing particular morals (or not). The business of insurance is thus not simply confined to the distribution of risk (Abraham 1986) but also of duties and responsibilities. Normative judgements are disseminated in insurance on who "deserves" solidarity and which criteria citizens have to fulfil to be included as members of the insurance pool. The introduction of predictive medicine in underwriting contributes in this regard to new standards for the distribution of responsibilities between the applicant, the insured and the insurer. On a wider front, such practices reflect how we, as a society, consider the criteria for solidarity with the sick.

The question arises, however, to what extent such normative distinctions in assigning responsibility for disease are desirable or tenable and how these criteria can be determined. Which characteristics can we identify as controllable or uncontrollable? (Shklar 1990) What does it mean to have control over your health? In other words, the geneticisation of disease and the associated fault-based approach present us with major challenges. In the next section, I address this in more detail by discussing the effects of the Belgian ban on genetic information in the insurance industry.

Side Effects of a Genetic Essentialism

As we have seen, articles 5 and 95 of the Belgian Insurance Law (LVO) are formulated to prevent genetic discrimination in insurance. In this respect, the Belgian law can be viewed as the crystallisation of the above-described "genetic essentialism". By thus treating genetics separately, it is emphasised that genetic information should be characterised as fundamentally *different* from non-genetic information. This particular distinction, however, creates some major side effects. The legal imposition of a "wall" between genetic and non-genetic information prompts new questions, notably about the workings of general insurance policy.

One of these side effects has to do with the emergence of new forms of discrimination. For instance, Rouvroy (2000) notes:

> a discrimination between, on the one hand, people who are carriers of specific 'predispositions' or 'genetic susceptibilities' and, on the other hand, those who are carriers of mere pre-symptomatic signs of specific disorders,

> which are not identified via genetic analysis but via routine clinical tests (2000: 601). [my translation]

This can be elucidated by numerous examples I encountered during my fieldwork. Take, for instance, George, who while filling in his insurance application is in perfect health but is also carrier of a genetic mutation for colon cancer, which, according to Belgian law, he was not allowed to mention. Next, there was Peter, whose health was as good as that of George's but who via routine tests was diagnosed for specific pre-symptomatic symptoms of colon cancer. In Belgium, George is accepted based on a standard premium while Peter has to pay a higher premium. Still, both basically represent the same mortality risk because they have a similar chance of contracting colon cancer in the future. When I confronted the underwriters with these cases, they responded: 'I know, it is hard to defend. That boundary is hard to define, isn't it?'" (C1, K, 3).

Along the same line, one may ask what this ban implies for the equality principle in insurance. It seems that, paradoxically, the law itself, by thwarting genetic discrimination, undermines this principle. As Lemmens notes:

> Statutes singling out genetic susceptibility as a category, and offering it much wider protection than other similar health conditions, although intended to promote equity in access to social goals, may themselves be ineffective and to some extent even inequitable (2000: 349).

The "right to conceal information" thus benefits those who are carriers of a genetic risk. This can result in the undermining of the equality principle.[63]

Furthermore, one should question the tenability of such legal boundaries between genetic and non-genetic information. Through its juridical embargo, the law affords disputable, undeserved *certainty* to the predictive character of genetics. In medicine, it is however increasingly acknowledged that the distinction between genetic and non-genetic information is quite artefactual. Alper and Beckwith (1998), for example, indicate how difficult it is to maintain a distinction between genetic and non-genetic factors. According to them, many clinical tests may also provide information on the genetic code. In addition, while genetic tests are commonly defined as information derived from a DNA-analysis, there also exist more indirect forms of genetic testing, like genetic information derived from chromosomes, proteins or via routine urine or blood tests.[64] As this indirect genetic testing becomes more commonplace, genetic and traditional medicine will probably be administered alongside it. Thus it might become difficult for physicians or underwriters to differentiate genetic from non-genetic information. Consequently, it is important to ask whether an exclusive legal ban on genetic information will be tenable in the future.

Finally, the fault-based approach of the Belgian law embodies major implications for insurance industry. This approach may indeed provide a new meaning for justice in insurance: Insurers have to calculate higher premiums when it is the applicant's own fault, otherwise insurers are acting unfairly. Differentiation according to a fault-based approach, after all, denounces the actual meaning of "actuarial fairness" in insurance. In this regard, insurers have always applied involuntary features in their risk differentiation. For example, various premiums are calculated for men and women, but for the time being individuals do not yet have control over their gender distribution (Brockett et al. 1999: 12). The fault-based approach – as institutionalised in Belgian genetics legislation – may affect the concept of a "pre-existing condition", which is used as the basis for risk classification. This may cause the mere presence of disease to lose its primary legitimisation as the basis for risk selection. In other words, the moral judgements that involve the controllability of diseases as introduced by the Belgian law on genetics appear to have a cascade effect on the general "disease" concept in insurance. Insurers tend to fix a premium level that is based on whether the disease is controllable or not for those who are already ill and who want to take out insurance. Accordingly, individual responsibility in the form of higher premiums should only be applied in cases of "self-inflicted" diseases or risk factors. This trend can potentially have major effects on general insurance principles. Thus, genetics serves as a *catalyst* for a debate on the general workings of insurance policy.

In summation, and to resume Callon's (1998) argument, the establishment of the Belgian law on genetic information can be considered a way to internalising the externalities of genetics in insurance. But the above illustrates that *new* externalities seem to appear, externalities which in fact have significant implications for the *general* insurance process. These side effects include new forms of discrimination, the destabilisation of the equity principle in insurance and the creation of new meanings of actuarial fairness.

Conclusion

In this chapter, I have shown how the introduction of predictive medicine in the Belgian underwriting practice has resulted in a fault-based approach. This in turn has generated a new attribution of responsibilities: while genetic "risk carriers" are attributed responsibility collectively, lifestyle "risk takers" are expected to take their responsibility individually. As noted, this approach is the result of a "genetic essentialism" in Belgian legislation on genetics in the insurance industry. As such, I explained how regulatory initiatives in the context of genetics can determine a certain practice. In this sense, this legislation is accompanied by major, unanticipated side effects. The legal imposition of a "wall" between genetic and non-genetic information raises new questions for the general insurance branch in particular. One of the side effects discussed here is that moral judgements on the controllability of disease, which are institutionalised through law, can have ramifications for the general disease concept in insurance.

My argument shows that it is questionable whether legislative initiatives can provide adequate solutions to the issue of genetics. It even appears that such initiatives, instead of solving particular problems, may actually cause new ones. This becomes visible when we consider the feasibility of the transformation of socio-normative judgements into legal distinctions or definitions. What does it mean to have control over one's own health? And how do we define the dividing lines between risks that must be carried and risks that are actively sought out? In this respect, the further development of genetics may confront us with new surprises. It may put additional emphasis on lifestyle and individual responsibility. Current developments in behavioural genetics, for example, suggest that genetic factors are partially the cause of many behavioural traits and psychiatric diseases (cf. Moore 2002). If one assumes that genetic factors contribute to disorders such as alcoholism (see e.g., Carmelli, Heath and Robinette 1993) or nicotine addiction (e.g., Straub et al. 1999), the question arises whether people who smoke or have alcohol problems are in fact responsible for the health effects of their behaviour. Ironically, today smoking and alcoholism are presented as the primary examples of bad lifestyles. But this view can also be reversed: The discovery and "spread" of genetic disease could actually strengthen the notions of lifestyle and individual responsibility. Consider, for instance, a genetic mutation for smoking. Recent studies have aimed at establishing genetic factors for smoking, nicotine-dependency and the inability to quit smoking. This implies not only that the *involuntary* smoker – the gene carrier – is seen as a victim, but also that in the case of those who smoke and who are not gene carriers the issue of responsibility for their behaviour is likely to be highlighted. Detection of genetic components of lifestyle diseases, then, causes the voluntary aspect of non-genetic lifestyle diseases to be emphasised even more.

Surprisingly, the main effect of developments in the field of genetics may well be that individual lifestyle will continue to grow more important regarding issues of health and disease. This becomes even more plausible when we take into account the notion that most diseases are *multifactorial*, meaning that they originate in a complex interplay of lifestyle factors, genetic factors and environmental factors. For example, one may contract specific diseases that have a genetic component largely on the basis of certain types of behaviour, meaning that these individual types of behaviour can be a major factor in the actual occurrence of a genetic disease (McGleenan 2001: 41). Instead of assuming a "genetic determinism" for carriers with a predisposition to some diseases, it seems more plausible, therefore, that we are (all) subjected to various susceptibility levels in relation to disease. In this context, Rose (2002) speaks of "the susceptible self". It implies that if a genetic mutation in individual cases is discovered for some disease, individual lifestyle habits and preventive measures regarding this predisposition may be pursued in a more sustained manner. Predictive medicine with its early detection of risk factors, then, might help encourage people to deal with their predicted risks properly. In this sense, predictive medicine differs from our traditional way of looking at disease by shifting the focus to the fact that we are the main source of our own health – that even if we do not all draw the same health card there is plenty we can do about it. According to Ewald and Moreau:

> With the arrival of predictive medicine, disease can no longer happen to us blindly. It uncovers a predisposition, a domain that we used to consider as more or less predestined. It affords all of us the possibility – at least in theory – to know our own predispositions. Where disease used to be considered fatal, it now becomes an issue of individual destination. Undoubtedly, this will significantly change our political anthropology regarding health and disease ... Being ill is no longer something one goes through; it becomes instead a moral risk, which depends on our own conduct (1994: 115-116). [my translation]

The risk factors we are aware of make us more responsible for controlling the state of our own health. Thus we are to some degree urged to join "the worried well" (Harris 1994) or "patients *en vie*" (Rouvroy 2000: 595). According to Petersen and Lupton (1996: 56), it is possible that those who are seen as "at risk" and who take no preventive action in this respect are also automatically perceived as failing in their duties as citizens. This same approach is currently being developed in Belgium's insurance practice. Individual responsibility for managing one's risk factors becomes the golden standard for assessing one's *fitness* for membership in the insurance pool. In this way, insurers increasingly assess insurance applicants with respect to their *decent citizenship* as the basis for their ultimate insurability.

These developments present society with some important challenges. Do we agree that risk assessment should be based on our health behaviour or our capacity toward self-control? In addition, by applying predictive technologies, a form of economically imposed solidarity between those included in large risk groups may disappear. This is how insurance policy continues to contribute to the increases in differentiation – and the emphasis on difference – between people, which enacts further appeals to individualisation in society. Moreover, these developments create the possibility of tightening up the norms of "suitable lives" regarding insurance. This might further contribute to the classification of increasing numbers of individuals as uninsurable or insurable only at much higher premiums. Apart from this, it is also doubtful whether it will be ever possible to determine one's level of control or individual responsibility over one's own health. Where do fate, blame and bad luck stand in this regard? For example, the US debate about the risk classification of women who have suffered repeated domestic violence might highlight this issue. The victims of domestic violence were evidently substandard risks from the perspective of the life insurer. Though it was also argued that charging them increased premiums was unfair because the increased risk was beyond their control. One suggestion then was that victims of domestic violence should be insured at ordinary rates but that the difference between the ordinary rate and the substandard premium should be passed along to the abuser (Dicke 1999a). In other words, financial accountability was redistributed here to the "cause" of the "uncontrollable" risk. It is of little surprise, then, that penetrating socio-political issues arise in these highly plastic risk debates about who should and who should not carry the burden of blame.

Just as the innovative capabilities of predictive medicine expand our knowledge of the future of health and mortality, so too do the many uncertainties and ambivalences about the actual utility of that information in the real time present. However, for Ewald (1986), such ambivalences are far from insurmountable for insurance institutions and adjusting to such novelties is far from uncommon: "*La science actuarielle n'a pas précédé la pratique de l'assurance, elle l'a bien plutôt suivie. L'histoire de l'assurance est aussi politique que technique et scientifique*". In the same way, Callon (1998) describes how insurance principles are first assembled and constructed throughout the located practices of underwriting and, once stabilised, can pre-format the insurance market. The making of these insurance principles presents difficult socio-political choices, reflecting larger socio-cultural representations on disease and the accountability for disease. Moreover, implicit within such choices are quite formidable re-workings of collective and individual responsibility. Predictive medical innovation constitutes new ground in the old debates about individual control, responsibility and blame for health. This goes to the heart of the basis for *citizenship* and how this articulates membership – and indeed non-membership – in the insurance pool.

VII Towards Experimental Learning

Learning by Travelling

A research trip is not complete without reflection on the sites visited and the distance covered. The main objective of my retrospective effort in this chapter is to analyse what my own journey, such as it is, contributes to my object – to the world of underwriting in the context of the life insurance business, with special attention for one of its major challenges in recent years, the genetic turn. What, in other words, have we *learned* along the way?[65]

By opening the black box of medical underwriting, this book demonstrates the *making* of insurance risks and traces openings, co-constructions or mutual learning in the making of insurance products. In so doing, I want to contribute to the qualification of insurance products as a way of cooperating with the actors involved in a process of *experimental learning* towards the "hot" issues involved in medical underwriting.

To this end, I will now recall some insights from Callon and introduce the work of economist Hirschman on concepts – in this case "exit", "voice" and "loyalty" – as different approaches to accountability in institutions. Hirschman has formulated a theory of social learning in private and public organisations. I use this framework to discuss its potential in life insurance with regard to medical underwriting. In the wake of Hirschman, I focus on the the concept of "voice" and elaborate his views on voice as a mechanism for social learning. In illustrating the effects of insurance on social order, I argue that this does not require that much attention to individual voices, but reflection geared towards *public* concerns, what I call "normative voice". This is how I set the terms for new institutional arrangements as occasions for actors to engage in reflection on forms of markets or the definition of insurance products to converge. Such occasions of course may bring out what these accounts imply and what we can learn from each other.

The Organisation of Voice to Stimulate Learning Processes

As we have seen in chapter II, Callon (2001; 2002) argues that within the "economy of qualities" the *joint* involvement of actors becomes more and more crucial in realising profits as a firm within a technico-economic network (TEN).[66] Companies increasingly need to link up with consumers while consumers, on their part, need to be involved or active in collaborating in the qualification of goods. According to Callon (2001), the economy of qualities favours talkative, or "voicy" consumers.

> In order to function, the economy of qualities needs consumers who involve and express themselves, who talk, argue, suggest, criticise and share their feelings and emotions. "What do you want?" says the producer. "Just wait a moment!" replies the consumer. "Start by involving me in your TEN and let me participate actively in the process of qualification of products intended for me. Let my spokespersons talk to your marketing people and engineers. But, above all, let me interact, talk with other consumers, with my friends and family, my elected representatives or those who more generally share my tastes and expectations (Callon 2001).

Moreover, because the economy of qualities creates more and more externalities, it increasingly affects identities and consumer groups that can be a source of "overflowing" as well. These groups collectively formulate and express demands, calling for certain actions to be undertaken so that their interests and projects can be taken into account. As Callon (2001) puts it: "In the economy of qualities consumers are thus a constant source of overflowing. And it would be counter-productive to simply suppress those overflowings, because, in order to function, markets of the economy of qualities need them." In this regard, he suggests two particular kinds of voices, "orphan groups" and "hurt groups", that suffer from overflowings caused by TENs and that progressively realise that their identities and interests are not (yet) included in economic calculations (Callon 2001; Barry and Slater 2002b). For Callon, a market can be effective only if it is framed, that is, if, at least for a while, overflowings are not taken into account. But it is necessary to ensure that this exclusion is not permanent. The groups involved must, in some way or another, be taken into account in the qualification of the product. Consequently, he argues, new institutional arrangements like "hybrid forums" are needed, in which the organisation of markets becomes a subject of (political) debate that takes into account points of view developed by these groups. Such processes are needed in order for all actors to *learn* about the qualification of the product.

This focus on "voicy" consumers and firms as *learning institutions* suggests a direct link with the work of economist Hirschman (1970). Although published more than thirty years ago, Hirschman's theory is inspiring because it focuses in particular on how private or public institutions and users relate to each other and which mechanisms are available to customers in co-participating in these institutions. Hirschman was intrigued by the fact that while most economic models basically assume a perfect economic equilibrium, in practice, the dysfunctional aspects of companies, industries and other economic institutions are the rule. Accepting that the ideal of "perfect functioning institutions" cannot be reached goes hand in hand with the idea that institutions and people are capable of improving by *learning*. The untenable aim of perfection is thus replaced by that of learning, a process that never stops. Consequently, Hirschman asks what mechanisms may stimulate learning processes in institutions and thus stimulate the improvement of the quality of products and services.

For his answers he relies on the usefulness of concepts of exit, voice and loyalty. Hirschman considers both "voice" and "exit" as relevant mechanisms for consumers to respond to the dysfunctional aspects of economic institutions, and, as such to stimulate learning processes about the organisation and the qualification of products. People can leave the firm and turn elsewhere for better products or services ("exit"). As a result, revenues drop and the customer base declines, which forces management to search for ways and means to correct whatever faults have contributed to their customers' dissatisfaction. But customers may also raise their "voices" to articulate their dissatisfaction in order to stimulate the improvement of the quality of the products. This once again is supposed to challenge management to search for causes and possible improvements. The voice of the customers can be raised in various ways. They may complain, file grievances, appeal to a higher authority, leak information, participate in governance, bargain collectively or participate in the making of the organisation. They may express their concerns to the management, potential customers, or influential outsiders such as policymakers, the press or consumer groups, each of whom may be willing to take up their cause. Voice can be exercised episodically, as special circumstances arise, or continuously, through established consultative mechanisms.

But under what circumstances do customers choose voice or exit? Hirschman's theory advocates the empirical exploration of the exit and voice options in specific institutional practices as well as their interplay. His pragmatic socio-philosophical approach holds that the meaning of the concepts cannot be defined *a priori* and apart from the particular practice in which they function, but will develop while in use. Sometimes exit and voice reinforce each other, while at other times they may be at cross-purposes. Each has its strengths and limitations. In this regard, he argues that voice is most typically employed where exit is difficult or limited, where alternative firms are limited, or where unusual features of the market exist. Exit may be an efficient means of signalling consumer demands, but with monopoly supply or if the quality of a product deteriorates across firms in a market simultaneously, consumers have no place to go or they may end up constantly exiting one firm's product for another without ever attaining satisfaction while none of these firms will ever receive a signal. In this regard, Hirschman calls attention to what he calls lazy monopoly or collusive behaviour (1970: 57-60). In a restrictive market, a firm may choose to get rid of its difficult customers rather than change its behaviour to please them. If a problem is endemic among all rival firms, dissatisfied customers will only be able to switch to an equally unresponsive competitor. Here the only means of signalling discontent is to express concerns verbally. These kinds of markets may thus increase voice because customers are held captive while exiting to another supplier is not an option. Voice is the only chance for improvement, but its efficacy obviously increases if exit is an available option and both voice and exit are more or less equally powerful as weapons.

A more solid understanding of the conditions favouring co-existence of exit and voice is gained by introducing Hirschman's concept of "loyalty". This concept is the key to forestalling premature exits, for it gives voice a chance to remedy organisational failure or group disadvantage. It is loyalty that buys time for voice to remedy inadequacies in the firm before exit drains away its customers. The particular importance of loyalty is that it can serve, within certain limits, as a brake on the tendency to exit. As a result of loyalty, customers will stay on longer than they would ordinarily, hoping or reasonably expecting that improvement or reform can be achieved *from within*. Loyalty, far from being irrational (it is not blind faith), can serve the socially useful purpose of preventing exit. Thereby, loyalty often tends to activate voice.

Although Hirschman introduces the exit and voice option symmetrically, his book can be read as a powerful argument for the establishment of voice options in economic institutions. Hirschman argues that private firms can benefit more from voice than from exit for several reasons. First, markets may often involve "ignorance and uncertainty, shared by consumers and producers, about the manner of producing a desired good or service, and, in fact, about their precise nature... In such situations, then, the use of voice rather than exit is to be expected and recommended" (Hirschman 1981: 221). The reason is that voice, in contrast to exit, is informative. The "contribution of voice can clearly be of the greatest importance, simply because the information it supplies is rich and detailed as compared to the bareness and blankness of silent exit" (220). While exit may only inform a firm of the fact of customer dissatisfaction, voice also explains *what* is wrong as a way of improving the product's qualification. In consumers' exit options (simply by no longer buying a company's product) the *reasons* for action do not necessarily reach the company, although the result certainly does. Consumers simply "vote" with their wallet, and hopefully some astute manager (or available calculative device) will draw the right conclusions based on *indirect* information. Voice options, on the other hand, provide potentially relevant qualitative information to the firm. This is all the more the case, Hirschman argues, with complex goods, like insurance products, where no standards are readily available for determining their quality. The quality norms that are at stake in an insurance product are far from straightforward because of the "inversion" involved in the purchase of insurance and the time-interval between the purchase of the product and the actual delivery of the product. So the complex character of the insurance product makes quality control in this market pre-eminently suitable to voice. Interaction between clients and firms in the qualification of the product and the definition of the value of the good are of crucial relevance. Moreover, as Hulbert et al. (2000) argue, it might be more efficient for a firm to invest time and resources towards engaging customers in discourse instead of managing (afterwards) defections (exit). While most economic research exhorts firms to strive for zero defections, and suggest exit interviews as a means of achieving this, they perhaps overlook the importance of giving customers more voice, which may reduce defections in the first place. So firms can use voice as a pro-active means of reducing exit, rather than as a reactive means of understanding it.

Another argument Hirschman advances in support of voice as an appropriate feedback mechanism for complex goods is that the availability of dialogue and opportunities for expressing experiences and being heard is itself often part of the quality of a service. We might call this participation or user involvement. Voice, then, is not only a mechanism towards quality improvement, but often an intrinsic element of quality (Horstman et al. 2004). For users, being considered and heard by an institution or service is sometimes more important than just being a satisfied customer. They want to experience that their expectations and definitions of the value of the product *matter*, not merely in response to a particular complaint but as a matter of self-evident involvement in institutions. This user involvement or voice as intrinsic element of quality also matters to loyalty to a firm. According to Feurst (1999) and other marketing researchers, encouraging and responding to customer voice is an essential condition for building customer loyalty. Often loyalty is *bought off* through cheap prices, extras and discounts by marketing strategies of a firm. But loyalty that is built on money, she argues, can be bought again. It is a loyalty to the treat or to the money itself, not to the supplier. If the objective is to *earn* loyalty in a more lasting and sustainable way, there is something missing in these programs: customer involvement and trust. A company can keep its customers (satisfied) in the long run only by caring about, taking into account and considering their best interests.

Because of its pragmatic tone, Hirschman's analytic frame is useful for the analysis of ways in which institutions function. Along with Hirschman and Callon, below I will give a retrospective of my travels through the insurance world while tracing the possibilities of exit and voice in regard to access to life insurance (medical underwriting). I will now concentrate in particular on *attempts to speak* by individual and collective applicants by tracing back the moments during my trip when such attempts became evident or the locations where these attempts were particularly encouraged, or rather nipped in the bud, by the insurance companies.

A story on complexification – voice – noise?

With Callon, this study has considered insurance markets or underwriting practices not as abstract givens but as embedded and collectively organised devices that make it possible to reach compromises, not only on the nature of goods to produce, but also on the value attributed to them. This process of qualification is a controversial process through which qualities are attributed, objectified and arranged. So, a firm has to regularly allow *complexity* to proliferate, by taking into account a growing number of aspects or to facilitate negotiations that lead to compromises. As such, I have illustrated the balancing acts, compromises and building efforts in the underwriting practice aimed at framing the underwriting process or designing a particular underwriting policy. These balancing acts involved a wide array of actors, objectives and considerations, such as accuracy, preventing moral hazard, solvability, cost efficiency, marketability, social acceptability of using risk classification factors or technologies, the relevance of underwriting for the firm's general profit-making strategy, underwriting strategies, clients' expectations, underwriting's public image, innovations in technology, changes in the definition of mortality risks, practicality of certain medical tools, available statistics and so on. These balancing acts were often confined or determined in part through broader aspects, such as the particular history of the company, the type of insurance company, regulation and located regularities in the insurance market. So the assemblage of means, strategies, interests and objectives constitutes the heart of underwriting as a practice, as the joint work of a host of actors. Above all, this qualification of the life insurance product involves a *learning process*, a process of trial and error aimed at organising the encounter between supply and demand most effectively. Based on this learning process, then, an insurance company is able to frame the specific outcome of these balancing acts in a particular underwriting policy. This script is afterwards *in-scribed* into the writing devices of underwriting – including the table, the medical questionnaire, the reinsurance manual or guidelines, and the medical expert protocol – that are all deployed in order to "meet" the applicants. The outcome of these balancing acts affects the final insurability result of applicants. The insurability of an applicant is not an inherent, universal quality of the applicant but the result of historically and locally *specific* circumstances, compromises and balancing acts.

By tracing an applicant's entire risk trajectory, I demonstrated the diversity of possible forms of organisation of insurance markets, underwriting practices and underwriting strategies, all having their particular effects on the insurability result. For this reason, a life insurance good can be made calculable, or objectified, in numerous different ways. Or an underwriting practice can be organised in various ways, whereby the question is how to strike a balance or find compromises between different conceptions (of the value) of goods (Callon 2001). From there, I argued that insurance principles like actuarial fairness are not givens but produced along the particular, variable localised underwriting practices and regularities of the insurance market. In other words, insurance principles, the laws of the market, underwriting technologies or statistics and insurance risk results are a consequence of a continuous balancing of temporary agreements, suspended beliefs, or mini-social contracts (in Rousseau's sense of that term).

Callon et al. (2002) argue that within this process of qualification supply and demand are not discerned but that there is constant interaction and, indeed, co-construction of clients. As to our life insurance case, we have seen how clients' expectations and reflections on the life insurance product and the process of medical selection were taken into account by insurers when framing the underwriting policy. For example, in reflecting on reforms regarding the medical questionnaire, clients' expectations were taken into account via the data of previous applicants, which after being processed in statistics offered the management insights for their future underwriting policy. Or management took into account perceptions they had on clients' incentives to buy insurance while sorting out various considerations in positioning the life insurance product. In the same way, the underwriters themselves could inform management about clients' expectations and incentives based on their daily experience in underwriting. Furthermore, occasionally there was direct negotiation between the insurers and insureds, as in the case of the collective patient groups' talks with insurance companies on the deployed statistics, medical knowledge and related insurability rates.

However, this co-construction of clients in life insurance qualification mainly occurred *indirectly*. No direct surveys or other feedback mechanisms were available in the insurance companies (in contrast to the customer satisfaction surveys or exit polls one finds in other service economies like, e.g., telecommunications). This kind of indirect feedback or voice reflects a minimal kind of voice in the set-up of medical underwriting. The public is mainly taken into account in insurance via *constructions* of applicants, based on indirect, disembodying tools by which the underwriters receive information from applicants during the underwriting process. As an effect, the underwriters had to translate what is written into assumptions about what the public aspires to. This indirectness comes with the risk of "noise" between the two dimensions.

Because of this indirectness insurers internally discuss and reflect on what *the client* or *the public* actually wants. What is the value of the life insurance good to clients? What does it *mean* to potential buyers? How do applicants act when buying life insurance: as individual profit seekers or as solidary individuals?

A story on simplification – Voice-barring

At the same time, as I illustrated throughout this book, the above-described process of qualification, or "complexification", results in a (temporary) framing of the insurer-insured transaction. In other words, a process of *simplification* is necessary to be able to perform the insurance market transaction. Thus a particular outcome of balancing acts is always reflected in a specific underwriting policy and inscribed in the various writing devices designed and deployed to "meet" the applicant in the underwriting process. The focus on these devices is theoretically relevant for several reasons. First, it makes clear how these devices frame the action of the underwriting process and, as such, perform a particular normativity. As a script, these writing devices supervise and control the other actors in a particular way, including the applicants themselves. As I illustrated with our fictitious applicant Karen, these mechanisms all serve to push Karen into the direction of a specific insurance profile based on a pre-formatted set of risk categories, cut-off points and classifications that contribute to her objectification. *During* the process of underwriting, Karen is thus literally "objectified". That is, little space is available for her to speak up or represent herself to the insurance company. On the contrary, the writing devices all *enact* Karen in a particular way. Who she is or which mortality risk she carries are features that are allocated *a priori* via the particular framing that is prestructured in the writing devices. In other words, *during* the underwriting process, Karen is basically represented by the various writing devices. If her voice is a factor at all, it is pre-structured in prepared response categories or via *distant* technological devices. As an embodied person she is essentially non-existent. During the underwriting process she is only performed as printed "information".

At this point, then, the asymmetry of these writing devices becomes important. Throughout this book, I have chosen to show how these devices were put in place by the management of the insurance companies. This makes it easier to show the asymmetries that they produce and the effects of domination. In line with Callon (2002), we see how the final author of the writing devices, that is, management, prevails over those who are excluded from writing. In fact, it is management that finally objectifies the applicant by pre-structuring the specific enactment of the applicant's risk result. In a similar way, Law (1991b) has clarified the way material devices support strategies and make possible the "storage" of power. Following Foucault, Law (2001) notes that power is not only a matter of domination or of asymmetry, but also a matter of enabling, constructing, and making possible. In other words, the writing devices used by insurance companies have power in the sense that they can and do *produce* certain forms of realities, along with the subjectivities that these entail. The associated devices enact the insurance risk result of applicants in particular ways.

As we have seen, this distancing approach of insurers *during* the underwriting process is performed precisely in order to block applicants' influences or interactions related to the inherent nature of underwriting. Underwriting finds its *raison d'être* in deploying bona fide answers, to select out fraud, moral hazard or adverse selection. At the moment of the market transaction, the object of transaction has to be as "disentangled" as possible in order to make the transaction possible (Callon 1998). What insurers thus try to avoid most of all is applicants attempting to *recruit* their risk on their own. At this "moment of truth", all of the other entanglements that the applicants have with their body or health should be prevented. Consequently, no opening or space for the voice of applicants is available. What this asymmetry highlights is that insurers have more power than other actors to define this moment of disentanglement – insurers, after all, ultimately control the underwriting process. Consequently, *uberimmae fides* or "truthful answers" here means "truthful *according to* the insurance logic". Other perceptions of risk and health (e.g., lay experiences, clinical risk perceptions) are muted at this stage of underwriting. Thus insurers *enact* applicants without the latter being capable of having a say about this enactment *during* the underwriting process. Moreover, applicants are enacted by insurers precisely to disable their *voice-in* during the underwriting process.

A similar case can be made for the very *end* of the risk trajectory. As we have seen, once the insurance company has established a risk result basically no openings are left: a risk is a risk is a risk. Here, then, the voices of applicants are silenced by the language of numbers, technical facts and the insurance logic. Thus, to outsiders, the insurance language of risk (in the end communication or in public policy debates) renders underwriting as an assemblage *practice* opaque – a black box. As we have seen, the only way applicants can voice their concerns at this stage is through complaint or grievance mechanisms. For instance, applicants may try to call the underwriting department before the final contracting of the policy. However, as I have shown, the companies I studied installed several buffers to keep applicants from reaching the person they wanted to talk to. Consequently, only the most assertive voices manage to get through. What is more, the complaint mechanisms in place are usually designed to resolve individual concerns, not the underlying institutional problems or contradictions. The underwriting management may sometimes accede to some individual concern or demand by making an exception or working out some special modification – rather than deal with the source of a specific problem that affects those who complain but also those who remain silent. In this regard, companies may settle disputes with clients on an individual basis to prevent them from complaining to public authorities or other consumers. But the ombudsman of the Belgian Professional Association of Insurers, as I discussed above, also viewed technical insurance data as sacrosanct and only considered complaints about communication issues as potentially valid. A feedback mechanism like this has little to add in this regard: the numbers and risk decisions have already hardened into indisputable numbers. Moreover, organising the possibility for individuals to express their voice via the ombudsman does not automatically result in the insurance market *hearing* these voices. The ombudsman's annual recommendations to the insurance industry cannot be enforced; whether they are taken seriously depends on the *goodwill* of the insurance industry. A final option for clients is to go to court, but, as we have seen, this has many drawbacks for all of the actors involved. For individuals, lawsuits come with the risk of incurring extremely high costs via the legal counsel. Moreover, those with complaints are usually already in a vulnerable position, an account of their being sick or disabled, which suggests that the emotional costs associated with raising their voice are likely to be even harder to bear (Hirschman 1970). Typically, in fact, those who are silent or most powerless are often those who are also the most ill. For insurance companies a lawsuit or litigation is only a last resort because of the potential repercussions in the media on the image of the insurance industry as a whole and the threat to public trust.

A final note should be made on the exit options in the life insurance market. The economic models of private markets give much credence to consumer exit, or switching insurers and policies. If the performance of an insurance firm declines, its customers will become dissatisfied, and their defections will signal to the firm to clean up its act (Hirschman 1970). Market models favouring exit is one thing, but the market reality is another. Those who are most in need of insurance, the ill and disabled, tend to have few exit options. Shopping for private insurance can be physically and emotionally exasperating (Horstman et al. 2004) and, moreover, is there a genuine alternative for these customers? As we have seen, given the entanglements and shared understandings of insurance companies in the insurance market, the argument that one can always choose freely to go to another insurer (including its associated free market ideology) is often invalid. Insurance companies tend to take the other market players' strategies into account in their own, which results in a rather uniform underwriting strategy within a particular insurance market. Furthermore, some insurers ask applicants directly whether they have been rejected elsewhere. The range of options for customers is often quite small because of these features of the insurance market. They may go to another company but that does not automatically or necessarily increase their satisfaction. Meanwhile a company may receive no clear information on why clients go elsewhere, or it may choose to be rid of its more difficult applicants rather than change its behaviour to please them (Hirschman 1970: 57-60). Evidently, in this case a company will hardly mind losing its high-risk applicants because their exit is to the company's gain. Under these circumstances the threat of exit will not encourage improved performance. If a problem is endemic among all of the insurers in one market, dissatisfied customers will only be able to switch to an equally unresponsive competitor.

These exit qualifications in life insurance markets increase the relevance of voice. But as I argued above, *during* the underwriting process and *at the end* of it only minimal openings are left to applicants to let their voice be heard. In underwriting the sequence of actions is precisely directed at silencing applicants, while only minimal space for voicing concerns is available at the very end of this process. The only genuine openings are in the process of the insurance product's qualification, that is, *in the making* of the underwriting strategies, policies, devices, statistics, medical tools, tables and so on. However, in this context the consumer's voice is *indirect* at best, which increases the risk of potential "noise" between insurers and insureds. Especially in the case of complex goods, such as insurance products, the effort of introducing more direct voices in the qualification of products might be considered an advantage, rather than a cost, because it allows the company to receive feedback and, when it is seen as constructive, change track accordingly. However, once the insurer-insured relationship has been framed, this feedback mechanism has to some extent little to offer; in fact, it might come too late, as a voice *after the facts*. Therefore, the issue is not so much how consumers can represent themselves or participate during the underwriting process, but rather how they *are* represented in underwriting practices. In other words, the crucial moments are not those were applicants (can or are allowed to) act as an agent, but rather those where they are defined, measured, observed, listened to, or otherwise *enacted* (Mol 1999: 86). Given that the qualifying of the insurance product basically entails a weighing of different considerations and underwriting strategies, the voice of consumers is most directly effective in that very process. The crux of the qualification of the insurance product is indeed the actor(s) who decide between the different options. Participation or consumer involvement is a fiction when consumers only have a say after the rules of the game have been written down. By contrast, there is real involvement if the voice of the consumers is heard and listened to in the *making* of insurance risks.

A story on performativity – normative voice

Of course, this argument for a "voice incorporated" in the process of qualification begs the question: *which* voices? In this regard, insurance companies may decide to hold, for example, a *selective* hearing of particular voices. As we have seen, one underwriting strategy focuses on the average population, while another tries to attract healthy applicants in particular and ignore those who are not empowered to offer a loud voice to insurance organisations. Hulbert et al. (2000), for example, refer to the many managers who mistakenly used small, non-representative samples of customer opinion to generalise. A manager will indicate that "our customers are saying..." whereas in reality only one of their most vociferous customers says so. Thus a manager's decision, while benefiting one or two customers, can potentially be to the detriment of the majority that remains silent. As Hirschman (1981: 244) explains: "Suppose that different consumers have different ideas about what sort of improvements are needed and further that the ideas and tastes of the activists differ systematically from those of the non-activists. To the extent that it is successful, the voice of the activists will then cause the quality of the product or policy to vary in such a fashion that benefits are bestowed primarily or exclusively on them. The reason is simple: voice is information rich and is able to give precise instructions to management." In this situation, the company reacts exclusively to the loud voices, at the possible expense of customers who do not engage in discourse.

To avoid ending up with a hearing that is too selective, if not exclusive attention for those who raise their voice, I argue that attention be paid to the role of "normative voice". This concept expresses a critique of the linking of voice to an individual reservoir of knowledge. In everyday language, the voice is considered an instrument of the individual. Only individuals are able to speak, to formulate opinions, to give voice. This common-sense conflation of voice and the individual seems also to characterise Hirschman's use of voice. Focusing on voice *per se* comes with the risk of its being conflated with individualism (Benschop et al. 2003). As we have seen, some underwriting strategies enact better insurability for some, while disadvantaging others. Or they enact better insurability for only a particular group of individuals. On a wider front, however, these underwriting strategies have an effect on who we define as different, on the formation of citizenship, on social equality, in short, on our social order. Such issues then do not so much require concern for individual interests, but reflection directed at *public* concerns (see also de Vries and Horstman 2004). So with the concept of "normative voice", I want to stress the *public* character of insurability issues and the need for collective deliberation on the effects of insurance on the social.

I will now briefly recapitulate these effects of insurance to show how Hirschman's ideas might be sharpened and amended. First, I will illustrate the constructive role for voice as the inclusion of *different* voices in the formation of social values and in the understanding of needs, rights and duties. In line with Sen (1999), voice – or the freedom to express opinions, the interplay of voices – is pivotal to the formation of values or priorities and understandings of economic feasibility, as well as to the conceptualisation (or comprehension) of "economic needs".[67] I will also introduce a more pragmatic concept of voice, "hesitant voice" (Benschop et al. 2003), which implies that opinions are not given (regardless of their being voiced or not), but constructed in the *process* of giving voice. My points are both motivated by the effort of trying to move away from a too-narrow conception of the individual right to voice on the one hand,

and the institutional obligation to heed individual voice on the other. To deal with the public issue of genetics and insurance, I argue, we need new institutional arrangements that enable public normative deliberation and voicing on these issues.

First of all, what can be said about the effects of insurance on our social order? Insurance is a normative technology, or "norm-giver" (Baker and Simon 2002), promoting particular images of responsibility (of insurers, individuals, state and so on). Private insurers do not just manage risks; they *produce* risks, risk categories and individuals at risk. They *regulate* by excluding some and mandating the conditions of inclusion for others. In short, they define who is part of the group and who is not. In other words, private insurance contributes to the shaping of community. Choices regarding insurance impact on the way a community defines itself. It thus contributes to the development of the ideals and competencies linked up with citizenship. It creates a situation in which control of social interdependency is largely fought out on the body (Horstman 2001) by co-producing norms on health and disease. The body, or rather, the maintenance of the body, becomes a sign of "decent citizenship". As we have seen in chapter VI, the use of predictive technologies in particular enacts individual responsibility for health. Those who are categorised as "at risk" in insurance, or who have not taken preventive action, are seen as failing in their citizenship duties. So people who do not act sensibly when it comes to their own health risks and who fail to adequately care for their own bodies not only display little concern for themselves, but they also neglect their duties as citizens. In addition, by applying these predictive technologies, a form of economically imposed solidarity between those included in large risks may disappear. That way insurance contributes to an increasing differentiation – and emphasis on difference – between people, which enacts further appeals to individualisation in society. Finally, these developments in predictive medical technologies might contribute to the classification of increasing numbers of individuals as uninsurable or sub-standard. They imply a changed concept of health, in which a normal standard in insurance increasingly means to be in perfect health. While the standards of citizenship in a regime of predictive medicine thus become more strict, the possibility exists that fewer people will receive access to the infrastructure they need for acquiring the norms of this mode of citizenship.

In this respect, there is ample reason to ask ourselves whether insurers should be the ones making these decisions on insurability. If insurance access is based on "decent citizenship", should we not want some more direct form of citizen participation to co-reflect on what this citizenship is comprised of? That insurers' decisions are constitutive factors in the genesis of risk and its related risk subjectivities, or that, in other words, they do not so much assess risks but *produce* them, is rendered largely invisible through medico-actuarial science's image of objectivity and the language of risk. As Heimer (2002) notes, as a regulator, private insurance operates by stealth. Rather than being publicly debated as are regulations that originate with the state, insurance regulations or the way we are *enacted* by insurance are largely imposed: "The public may debate whether or not to require insurance as a precondition for participation in some activity, but it does not participate in decision making about the conditions under which insurance is granted" (Heimer 2002: 119).

Given the effects insurance has on citizenship or how it enacts the social, I argue for a process of "normative voice" in order to discuss the value of insurance goods. Via a collective, deliberate approach, we might reflect on the way people are enacted in the insurance industry, on the way we are cast, invented or imagined as citizens. Moreover, this normative voicing does not so much imply formulating strong opinions, but rather expressing uncertainty and reflections on these normative-political dilemmas. With Benschop et al. (2003), we might call this a "hesitating voice". It is acknowledging, listening and engaging in uncertainties, doubts, discomforts and differences the actors involved might experience. Such arrangements can be seen as occasions on which different ways of qualifying the life insurance product and the way insurance enacts individuals converge, as well as what this implies and what we might *learn* from one another. The latter, amongst other things, suggests the relevance of having a say when it comes to the criteria for insurability, while also underscoring the significance of reflection on what "decent citizenship" and its conditions signify.

Risk Taking as Experimental Learning with Genetics

I designed this study of underwriting-in-action in part to establish the terms for new institutional arrangements in which the actors involved can *learn* from each other in the qualification of the insurance product. My journey capitalised on the experimental character of insurance markets, the assemblage work involved in medical underwriting and the effects these practices generate on the social. In so doing, I provided insight into the openings and the locations for reflection and negotiation where these learning processes can take place. As such, I do not envision my role as that of a "voice-over"; instead, my function is that of an actor who cooperates in the process of experimentation, innovation and learning about dealing with the overflows of medical underwriting in life insurance (Callon et al. 2002).[68] Consequently, I am interested in learning how life insurance might be made more accountable by being more "socially robust" in the qualification of life insurance products. This involves a broadening of the terms on which the medical underwriting process is built, a moving towards a "socially distributed expertise" (Nowotny et al. 2001; 2003; Nowotny 2003) that is both more accountable and inclusive of a wider range of understandings of the world.

This shift towards accountability is receiving increased attention from the life insurance industry itself. If insurance asks policyholders to behave like *good* policyholders, it is equally important of course for insurers to act like *good* insurers. As we have seen, there may be several good reasons why insurance companies should worry about their reputations. One simply involves the concern that behaviour considered to be *bad* may provoke costly litigation or legislation with sometimes unintended consequences for the business as a whole.[69] The other, more crucial, is damaged trust. A company that lacks the confidence of its stakeholders (policyholders, shareholders and employees) is likely to suffer. This is all the more the case in an industry in which consumer trust is paramount. As the CEO of Fortis, an insurance company, recently suggested: "We sometimes say we are in the 'risk management' business, but I submit that we are as much in the 'trust management' business" (Van Rossum 2004: 55). In various ways, the industry has been working to raise its social and ethical accountability. For example, in the US, life insurance industry leaders responded to the crisis of damaged consumers' trust by creating the Insurance Marketplace Standards Association (IMSA), "to strengthen trust and confidence in the life insurance industry by requiring member companies to demonstrate commitment to high, ethical marketplace standards" (Atchinson 2004: 41).

This implies, amongst other things, an even larger relevancy of voice. After all, accountability, or the obligation of companies to justify their decisions and actions, depends in part on public questioning and examination. Moreover, in the face of accountability, voice almost automatically becomes an active voice. Simply listening and doing nothing in response to insistent demands evidently discredits the idea that promoting voice is central to improving human well-being (Goetz et al. 2001). The obligation that firms or markets explicitly justify their actions drives passive voice into active voice. As illustrated in this chapter, such processes of "giving voice" or accountability might be institutionalised in two ways, after the facts or – far more preferable – before the facts as "voice incorporated."

Similarly, reflexivity can be routinised in two ways. In a first version it involves the move towards what Lynch (2000: 31) has called "systemic reflexivity", whereby in late-modern society reflexive monitoring takes the predominant form of cost-benefit, risk-benefit, measurable indicators or performance benchmarks. In insurance, we see this expressed through the above-described corporate social responsibility initiatives, with increasing weight given to evidence-based underwriting practice, actuarial tables, the rise of management consultancy or auditing and an upcoming "ethics industry."[70] Power (1997) speaks in this regard of the "Audit Society." Exploring why society invests so heavily in an industry of checking when more and more individuals find themselves the subjects of formal scrutiny, the author critically examines the reasons, means and consequences of this audit explosion. The audit is in fact all about being able to verify *ex post*. So we see here the rise of experts convincing the public of their authority to having made *accessible* risk decisions as a way to increase public trust. One of these mechanisms is the current manifestos for transparency. Professional experts have to account for the decisions they make, give clear fact sheets of their programs and managers are required to deliver yearbooks, annual reports and other accounts. In insurance, we see this for instance in the shift towards insurers having to demonstrate accountability for their risk assessment decisions.[71] Transparency is most of all performed in communication to the public of the "accountable" numbers and figures. This in fact applies to the *effectiveness* of insurance markets' performances and involves accountability *after the facts*, or *ex post*.

The second version considers a reflexivity based on pluralism and uncertainty – a reflexivity that welcomes a much wider range of interpretations, including from non-experts, in order to arrive at "inclusive accountability" or what I refer to as "normative voice". According to Callon, this experimental learning approach requires the search for institutional innovations aimed at the organisation of "hybrid forums" (cf. chapter II). Instead of delegation, this focuses on the politics *of* economic markets, that is, *within* the process of knowledge production, or "the market as a public space" (Latour and Weibel 2005). Such arrangements might entail inclusive debates with all stakeholders involved on the organisation of the insurance market, the underwriting criteria to be used and the value of insurance. This kind of reflexivity deals with the *effects* of insurance markets' performances. We might call this an accountability *ex ante*.

Genetics and insurance

Finally, I return to the issue of genetics and insurance. The same strategies of a technocratic, procedural and a learning, experimental approach are also present in today's insurance industry in dealing with the genetics issue. As we have seen in chapter II, the insurance industry originally grasped the genetics issue as an external or public relations problem, while proclaiming a defensive approach by resorting to its insurance logic. Genetics was *not an issue* because genetic information was merely seen as medical information and therefore it should not be handled differently. Yet, in several countries this framing of genetics prompted regulative initiatives that intervened in the insurance market. This has gradually evolved into a substantial problem for the life insurance industry. Again here, genetics is *not an issue*, because insurers realise that its underwriting practices and principles *in general* might be at stake.

My examination in chapter VI of Belgian underwriting practices in the context of a prohibition on genetic information (Law on Insurance Contracts 1992) provided empirical insight into the practical operation of such a statute-based system of regulation on genetics. I demonstrated how such legislation (and its embedded genetic essentialism) might have side effects for the insurance business as well as society at large. These side effects were introduced as new forms of discrimination and the creation of new meanings of actuarial fairness in insurance. I argued that statutes that single out genetic susceptibility as a category and offer it much wider protection than other similar health conditions, even though intended to promote access to insurance goods, may themselves be ineffective and to some extent inequitable. This once more illustrates that we cannot expect too much from legislation in dealing with these issues.

At an international level, the insurance industry, confronted with these legislative cross-fires, felt provoked to embrace a proactive and self-regulating approach. As we have seen, this is institutionalised in a technical, procedural approach of actuarial devices aimed at calculating the effects of genetics, whereby insurers have to demonstrate accountability for their risk assessment decisions. The UK Genetics and Insurance Committee (GAIC) is a case in point in this regard. However, as illustrated in chapter II, this approach has many shortcomings. Apart from "internal" problems associated with the uncertainties surrounding genetics and a shortage of proof for actuarial evidence in regard to research of genetics and insurance, this approach can also be considered as a typical example of accountability *after the facts*.[72] This is why some actuaries and economic agents in the industry have considered this actuarial approach useful but incomplete. In line with our opening of the black box of underwriting, they called attention to the diversity of underwriting practices, the normativity involved in actuarial science-making, and the forms of insurance markets. Moreover, as we have seen, such reflections have a wider scope and apply to medical underwriting in general, rather than to the issue of genetics alone. Although it is not unreasonable to pay particular attention to the social effects of genetic testing, the issue highlights already existing problems regarding, for example, access to financial security or the effects on the social that private insurance generates.

To some extent, then, insurers rightly suggest that "genetics is not the issue." The issue of genetics in insurance and the dilemmas it raises are indicative of a larger debate on the status quo of the basic tenets of insurance. Genetics might be seen as the force that is gradually exerting more pressure on the medico-actuarial principles and the rules of the insurance game. Perhaps a greater challenge overall for the life insurance industry is the focus of public policy entities in relation to the use of genetic information which could lead to a general questioning of medical underwriting with respect to all medical concerns. Thus genetics serves as a *catalyst* for a debate on the general insurance workings. As the actuaries Daykin et al. (2003: 38) recently argued: "Gone are the days when applicants had a deferential attitude towards highly respected financial institutions." While in the early twentieth century medico-actuarial science was used precisely as a vehicle for building public trust in insurance, today there is more and more pressure on insurers to demonstrate the scientific basis for all of their underwriting decisions and, moreover, to broaden the terms of this scientific basis, as a way of integrating the "can do" orientation of science with the "should do" questions of ethical and political analysis.

Risky business: Insurers take a risk

For the insurance industry, the question remains how to respond to increasing distrust in the industry and the associated uncertainties. Holding on to their "mystique card" (Goford 2002) and their basic operational principles as "givens" has indeed become a risky strategy in its own right at a time when transparency, public participation and public access to assessment procedures are the order of the day. The insurance industry feels the heat regarding genetics as well as the urgency to respond to it, but neither sufficient information nor the predictive knowledge needed is available. Jasanoff (2003), in her recent call for "technologies of humility", pleads for a turning away from the technologies of predictive policy analysis (e.g., insurance modelling) by replacing them with methods that try to come to grips with the fringes of human understanding – the unknown, the uncertain, the ambiguous and the uncontrollable. Under such a regime of humility, the existing predictive approaches would be complemented or replaced by an approach that makes apparent the possibility of unforeseen consequences, to render explicit the normative within the technical and to acknowledge from the start the need for plural viewpoints and collective learning (2003: 240). Thus, the concept of "expertise" would be opened up by changing the experts' epistemological approach and their basic political attitude. An example of such change of tacks can be found in a recent paper by the Institute of Actuaries (UK). Instead of demonstrating the statistical significance of genetic testing (in the GAIC) (for which they currently do not have proof) they proposed that the insurance industry demonstrates "vulnerability" as a "demonstration that insurers are financially exposed to the aggregate risk that single applicants, or groups of applicants, will take advantage of an insurer's vulnerability resulting from an asymmetry of information about the applicant's medical condition" (Daykin et al. 2003: 31).

This focus on vulnerability and uncertainty does not mean that risks are not calculable or manageable. Therefore, this is not a denial of the need to assess, manage and contain risks, but a recognition of the fact that in modern societies there can be no safe way of making decisions (Luhmann 1996). For the world of insurance this is hardly news: Since its beginnings it has been involved in taking on risks for the long-term future, thereby accepting uncertainty. In 1921, the economist Knight celebrated radical uncertainty in effect as a position that inspires and motivates the entrepreneurial behaviour that is required for profit-making – capitalist innovation, in other words, is essentially governed by a lack of a certain knowledge. In everyday language, we would call this "risk-taking" behaviour. In political science, Wildavsky (1987, in: Raman 2003) similarly used uncertainty to argue against "excessive" caution, his point being that "searching for safety" precludes the possibility of *learning* about risk – knowledge that can only be obtained from practical *experience*. Risk-taking, then, for the insurance industry, implies that it must experiment with the social overflows of medical underwriting, as a process of trial and error. Paraphrasing Haraway (1997: 190-191, cf. chapter I), just like the social sciences, or the science of ethnography, insurance can be said to be "a method of risks.... It is about risks, purposes and hopes – one's own and others – embedded in knowledge projects." This risk-taking might take the form of investing and experimenting in "socially robust knowledge," in looking for creative solutions to reconcile economic realities of the insurance industry with social needs and in trying out new institutional arrangements. Together, they may contribute to bridging the apparent gap between corporate social responsibility and profitability in a seemingly autonomous insurance logic, founded on the "givens" of statistics, insurance rates and principles. Between unconditional acceptance and hostile rejection, there is always space for negotiation.

Glossary

This glossary is intended to be a short guide to the relevant subset of the terminology used in association with human genetics and insurance. It also includes the abbreviations, names and translations of relevant organisations.

ABI	Association of British Insurers (UK)
ACLI	American Council of Life Insurance (US)
Adverse selection	When an individual with more knowledge of his or her own level of risk than they need to disclose to the insurer, still chooses to apply for insurance when they would not otherwise have done so, or to apply for a larger amount of coverage than they would have applied for in the absence of such information about their own risk
Autosomal dominant disorders	Disorders where the inheritance of a genetic mutation from one parent is sufficient for the disease to manifest itself. Examples include Huntington's disease, adult polycystic kidney disease and neurofibromatosis
Autosomal recessive disorders	Disorders where the inheritance of a mutation from both parents is required for the disease to manifest itself. The parents are usually unaffected carriers as they carry only one copy of the affected gene. Examples include cystic fibrosis, sickle cell anemia and thalassaemia
BVVO	Beroepsvereniging voor Verzekeringsondernemingen (Belgium) (Belgian Professional Association of Insurance Companies)
CEA	Comité Européen des Assurances (The European Federation of National Insurance Associations)
CDV-OCA	Controledienst voor de Verzekeringen (Belgium) (Office de contrôle des Assurances / Insurance Supervisory Authority (ISA))
DNA	Deoxyribonucleic acid; the chemical substance in chromosomes and genes in which genetic information is coded
Family medical history	Information about the illnesses suffered by parents or other close relatives, and, in particular,

	where applicable, the cause of their deaths, usually in the context of disclosures required by an insurer of a prospective insurance client, in order to inform the underwriting process
Gene	The biological unit of heredity; a sequence of DNA which codes for one protein or other molecule
Genetic code	A mapping of the genes of a particular organism
GAIC	Genetics and Insurance Committee (UK)
HGAC	Human Genetics Advisory Committee (UK)
HGC	Human Genetics Commission (UK)
Information asymmetry	The situation which arises when one party to an insurance contract has more information relative to the risk propensity than does the other party; this typically arises when the client does not fully disclose all information to the insurer
KVBA – ARAB	Koninklijke Vereniging van Belgische Actuarissen (Belgium) (Association Royale des Actuaires Belges / Royal Association of Belgian Actuaries)
LVO (1992)	Wet op de Landverzekeringsovereenkomst (1992) (Belgium) (Law on Insurance Contracts)
Life insurance	Insurance payable on the survival of people for particular periods or upon death within certain periods, including full-term life insurance, endowment insurance and temporary life insurance (also know as term insurance or term life insurance, see Term life policy)
Monogenetic condition	A hereditary disorder caused by a mutation of a single gene
Moral hazard	Occurs when individuals behave differently in insurance situations. *Ex ante* moral hazard can occur when a client does not fully reveal all relevant information prior to the conclusion of an insurance contract. *Ex post* moral hazard can occur, for example, when an insured person manipulates the level of loss after the occurrence of an insured event
Multifactorial genetic disease	A genetic disorder resulting from the combined action of more than one gene, or from the combination of genetic and environmental factors
Mutation	The change in a gene or chromosome that causes a disorder or the inherited susceptibility to a disorder or the ability to pass on such susceptibility to one's heirs
Mutuality	Principle according to which private commercial insurance operates. Each person should pay an

	insurance premium which is commensurate with his or her actual or perceived level of risk. The higher the risk of the client the higher the premium, and there is no assessment of either ability to pay or of the adequacy of benefit entitlement in relation to need
Penetrance	The penetrance of a genetic mutation refers to the proportion of people with that genetic mutation who develop the disorder. This is usually expressed as penetrance by a particular age
Premium	Sum received by the insurer or reinsurer as a consideration for covering risk
Proposer/applicant	Person who applies for an insurance policy
Reinsurance company	Procedure whereby an insurer insures himself with an outside company (the reinsurer) for part or all of the risks covered by him, in return for payment of a premium
SOA	Society of Actuaries (VS)
Standard rate	Premium for people who, according to an insurer's medical underwriting standards, are entitled to purchase insurance without extra premiums or special restrictions
Sum insured	The sum payable under the insurance policy
Term life policy	Life coverage provided for a specified number of years. The insurer only pays out if the policyholder dies within this time
Whole life policy	A policy where premiums are paid for the rest of an individual's life, or up to a specified advanced age, and benefit is paid upon the death of the insured, whenever that occurs

Notes

Chapter I

1. Individuals in the first group have few problems getting insurance. Because they present a 'normal' risk, they just pay the standard premium. Individuals in the second group must pay higher than average premiums (= substandard premiums) because of the higher mortality risk they represent. Individuals in the third group are excluded because the cost of their coverage is considered "unquantifiable" or would exceed any reasonable premium.
2. The tools used to develop regulatory frameworks vary from one country to the next. Besides genetics-specific legislation in insurance (e.g., Belgium, Norway, France, Austria), other (self-)regulatory initiatives include moratoria to provide time for policy formulation, discussion and decisions or codes of conduct (e.g., UK, the Netherlands). For an overview of these regulatory initiatives in Europe and the US, see, e.g., McGleenan (1999); Nys, Dreezen et al. (2002).
3. The rational calculation model of risk has its roots in the nineteenth century. One of the most important changes in the development of risk was the emergence at that time of a whole new practice consisting of specific measures and statistical techniques that was aimed at gauging and thus controlling the processes of social change associated with industrialisation and urbanisation. Risks became actuarially conceptualised and notions of standardised risk and compensation became part of the regulatory regimes of nineteenth-century society in Europe and the US (Ewald 1986, 1991; Hacking 1990). This notion of risk and the related expansion of the insurance industry represented a modernist way of viewing the world, its contingencies and uncertainties. It assumed that unanticipated outcomes were an effect of human action, and as such it largely replaced earlier concepts of fate or *fortuna* (Giddens, 1990: 30). This idea of controlling what is unpredictable – such as death – via statistical calculations became exactly the philosophical foundation of the development of life insurance. By calculating risks and framing death as a risk, death turned into something to be managed. In the twentieth century, this process continued, aided by increasingly sophisticated information sources based on computing technologies and the new science of risk assessment.
4. According to Callon, framing is "an operation used to define individual agents... who are clearly distinct and dissociated from one another. It also allows for the definition of objects, goods and merchandise which are perfectly identifiable and can be separated not only from other goods, but also from the actors involved, for example in their conception, production, circulation or use. It is this framing that allows the market to exist and distinct agents and distinct goods can be brought into play" (1998: 17).
5. Paraphrasing Chamberlin, Callon et al. note that consumers are just as active as the other parties involved: "The qualities of a product depend on the joint work of a host of actors and there is no reason to believe that consu-

mers do not participate, like the other actors concerned, in the objectification of those qualities" (2002: 202-203).

6. According to Ewald (1986, 1991), four characteristics can be attributed to insurance: institutions, forms, technologies and imaginaries. The latter emphasises the normative act of insurance arrangements, meaning that the particular form insurance technology takes in a given institution at a given moment depends on an insurantial *imaginary*, "on the ways in which, in a given social context, profitable, useful and necessary uses can be found for insurance technology" (1991). Insurance "imaginaries" or "visions" (Baker 2002: 9) are ideas about insurance that animate the development of insurance technologies, institutions and forms. Again this work thus stresses the variability of the forms of insurance.
7. My choice for an international perspective was prompted by the fact that the insurance discussion on genetics is largely an international affair. Genetics is a topic discussed in many national countries, but the relevant expertise is based internationally, which is mainly due to the innovative and cutting-edge nature of genetics. The period of research was basically suggested by the Human Genome Project (HGP), which formally began in 1988. Prior to this date, genetic technology was hardly on the insurance agenda.
8. The first site was the underwriting department of an international bank insurance company, one of the market leaders in the Belgian life insurance industry. Since this case belonged to the market leaders, I opted for a second case with a more average market player. I thought it fruitful in this second case to choose a company with a different profile in terms of its economic policy and market position.
9. For an argument in favour of shifting the attention from thinking to practice, see, for example, Latour (1988). Originally, this perspective on "do-ing" was elaborated in sociology by Garfinkel (1967). It refers to "the ways in which ordinary people ("ethno") methodologically construct their social world".
10. My use of 'trajectory' follows Strauss's definition of the term (1993), highlighting the on-going, practice-based and thereby processual nature of ordering.
11. Whenever I use materials from my fieldwork, these fragments are coded to safeguard the anonymity of the respondents. These codes (e.g., C1, B, 3) are designed along three categories. The first one deals with the cases or main organisations. Reference to the cases is made via the codes C1 or C2. Codes for other organisations are e.g.: for reinsurance companies: Re1, Re2, ...; for consumer organisations: Consum1, Consum2, ...; for experts: Exp1, Exp2; for the Belgian Professional Association of Insurance Companies: BVVO and for the Royal Association of Belgian Actuaries: ARAB. For the second category, letters are used to refer to respondents (e.g. A, B, C,...). Finally, figures are used to refer to the type of material (talk = 1; interview = 2; observation = 3). References to figures, percentages, numbers, names or locations from the fieldwork are made fictitious in the text.

Chapter II

12. An earlier version of this chapter was published in *New Genetics & Society* (Van Hoyweghen et al. 2005).
13. Illustrative in this regard are the arguments put forward by Dr. Cignoli, a member of the Life Insurance Association, when legislation for a ban on genetic information was introduced in 1996 in Massachusetts (US):
"We feel that the insurance industry has always dealt responsibly with medical information such as family history, height, weight, cholesterol, blood pressure ... and all these have a genetic basis, and we've always used them in our underwriting. Just because the tests become more sophisticated in the future.. we would still want to be able to use the information" (cited in: Hartnett-Barry 1996).
14. A test will be deemed suitable for insurance purposes if it meets three conditions:
    (i) technical relevance – Is the test technically reliable? Does it accurately detect the specific changes sought for the named condition?
    (ii) clinical relevance – Does a positive test have any implications for the health of the individual?
    (iii) actuarial relevance – Do the health implications make any difference to the likelihood of a claim under the proposed insurance product?
15. Note thereby that the interim recommendations of the Human Genetics Commission (2001) in fact included an exception to the genetic information for policies in excess of £ 500,000. Furthermore, the HGC also recommended a method of independent enforcement of the moratorium. Persuaded by the findings of a previous report of the House of Commons Select Committee on Science and Technology (House of Commons, 2001) that not all insurers were equally observing the ABI Code of Practice, the HGC believed that back up legislation would be necessary. It is instructive that the ABI, on the same day of the recommendations of the HGC (1 May 2001), had already published a set of proposals for genetics and insurance (ABI, 2001), thereby recommending a financial limit of £ 300,000 (backed up by statistical figures). It might have been that the ABI felt the HGC breathing down (with its heightened ceiling limits and regulative recommendations) and that they therefore have set these proposals as a way to be proactive.
16. This was, for example, observed in a Report of the Public and Professional Policy Committee of the European Society of Human Genetics. This document is an evaluation of the EuroGapp project 1999-2000 *Genetic information and testing in insurance and employment: technical, social and ethical issues.* After intense consultation and debate with insurance experts, the results of the report seem to have a way towards an actuarial, scientific solution to the issue of genetics for insurance. The conclusions of the report were phrased along these lines: "The validity and consistency in use of genetic information in insurance should be researched... The question of how to meet the (insurance) needs of those at genetic disadvantage should be solved" (European Society of Human Genetics 2001).
17. In casu: the Genetics Group of the Social Policy Board of the institute and the Faculty of Actuaries.

18. To illustrate this claim, the author of the editorial related the following anecdote:
"The 4 April 2001 issue of *The Times* reported that the Alzheimer's Society was looking for clarification as to what the rather woolly term 'actuarially significant' meant. They phoned the Institute of Actuaries, which reportedly clarified the situation by saying that a result was actuarially significant if an actuary said so. You can see how this reply would have opened up a world of insight" (Dolan 2001).
19. More specifically, the British Genetics Group of the Social Policy Board of the Institute and the Faculty of Actuaries.
20. In this regard, some actuaries argue that, from a purely academic point of view, it could be possible to make every kind of "distinction between people" actuarially relevant. Consequently, the actuarial relevancy criterion is considered not a sufficient condition for resolving the dilemmas of genetics and insurance. Therefore, it is suggested that the GAIC approval criteria – besides/instead of the actuarial relevancy criterion – should include the (more strict) criterion of "adverse selection". Whereas the latter one might indeed constitute a real danger to the insurance industry, the choice to implement an "actuarial relevant" risk factor is merely related to economic policy and profit-making strategies. "Where certain aspects of social policy might be held back by lack of access to insurance, we should note a difference between freedom to underwrite in order to protect the insurance pool from adverse selection, and freedom to underwrite simply to allow insurers to compete in a free market, and therefore to fragment existing and working risk pools at will. For example, there was no suggestion that life insurers' risk pools 20 years ago were threatened by an influx of smokers that had to be controlled by charging them higher premiums; the latter course of action was taken purely for commercial advantage." (Daykin et al. 2003: 36)
21. For example. in the US, some insurance companies have some 12 subcategories of people, ranging from the "super healthy" down towards the other end of the spectrum.
22. Currently, it seems that the European insurance market, unlike the American market, has not been involved much yet with these preferred underwriting strategies. Most European market players hold a more "conservative" underwriting strategy, characterised by mass underwriting (few risk classification categories).
23. In other words, these agents realise that keeping the public trust in insurance is one of the most important variables for profit-making strategies. For if public trust fades, the entire life insurance industry could be harmed. Therefore, the insurance industry should take into account public concerns regarding genetics. In this regard, Chuffart (1996b) also argued for a "give-and-take" approach relative to the issue of genetics to keep the flourishing European life insurance business established.
"In many European countries, the most commonly sold individual insurance contracts have very limited, or even no death benefits. It is therefore understandable that maintaining the right to underwrite risk products does not appear to be the priority no. 1 of many European insurers: fiscal advantages attached to life insurance are far more important to preserve, and in order to keep these advantages, a lot of European carriers are prepared to

forego even the basic principles of the risk classification process" (1996b: 23).

24. This is the Chair of the Genetics Issue Committee of the ACLI.
25. Illustrative in this regard is a recent internal note the Comité Européen des Assurances (CEA) sent to the national trade organisations. In this document, the national associations of countries where there has yet been no legislation enacted are encouraged "to be proactive and take action" by introducing self-regulating moratoria and codes of practices, appointing a genetics advisor and having the support of the other parties involved (CEA 2000).
26. The first results of the actuarial research projects on genetics suggest that when a ban is introduced on genetic information, adverse selection is currently not particularly dangerous to the industry because so few people who apply for insurance have been genetically tested. The existing tests only apply to rare, monogenetic conditions, whereby a defect in a gene causes a specific disease. Though such tests have a high predictive value, these diseases are relatively rare, and there is usually a family history that already enables insurers to identify those at risk (Berberich 1999; Regenauer 1998b; Lowden 1998b; MacDonald 2003a). Slesenger (1997) goes so far as to state that in some areas family history may be even more accurate than genetic tests. Examples are tests for the Huntington's disease gene and breast cancer genes (BRCA1 and BRCA2). Tests for multifactorial genetic defects, indicating a prediction of a disease when combined with certain environmental and lifestyle factors or triggers, are currently not very useful to insurers because their predictive value for life insurance purposes is not very high while the tests are not reliable enough (e.g., Lowden 1998a; Lockyer et al. 1997). However, as to the future, if multifactorial genetic testing will be introduced on a large scale, insurers still fear adverse selection as these tests will apply to far more people.
27. This "economy of qualities" is characterised by an increasing reflexivity of markets and mobilisation of socio-technical capacities or firms operating in a Technico-Economic Network (TEN) (Callon 2001). Science and technology are so present here that they are difficult to control. In this regard, he refers to controversies on GMOs, BSE, mobile phones, nuclear waste and therapeutic cloning. We might add the issue of genetics in insurance markets.

Chapter III

28. The "PV" or "procès-verbal" is the report of a medical examination performed by a medical expert. These experts are appointed and employed by insurance companies. They may be clinicians who do examinations as an extra source of income.
29. It is relevant here that management may include a mixed group of actors. In case 1, corporate management was the main underwriting policy actor, operating in close contact with the CEO of the company's insurance section, the General Board and the financial corporate management. At an intermediate level, echelon managers were involved, such as the heads of actuarial research, the claims and medical underwriting departments. In addition, chief underwriters may also be involved in underwriting policy matters.

30. This distinction between overall economic and underwriting policy is not always straightforward. In a firm's underwriting policy, broader economic strategies are also taken into account (e.g., particular profit-making strategies like targeting on a particular product (e.g., investment funds), relevance of medical underwriting for overall profit making). In other words, these economic strategies may affect or confine the particular underwriting policy.
31. As a common interest body, the Insurance Supervisory Authority (ISA) was introduced by law on 9 July 1975. The ISA is authorised to do the "prudential, financial inspection" of Belgian insurance companies (Controledienst voor de Verzekeringen (CDV) 2002).
32. Note that case 2 is not a bank-insurance company.
33. Callon's notion of "intermediaries" highlights the way in which relationships can be characterised in terms of the entities that pass between them (1991: 134-135). Besides things like literary inscriptions, computer software, technical artefacts and instruments, persons can be characterised as intermediaries. One might parallel this notion of "intermediary" with the concept of "compromise" or "compromised device" (Boltanski and Thévenot, 1991). The term "compromise" is used as an attempt to make compatible two (or more) orders of worth within the process of justification (Thévenot 2002: 64).
34. This double role of actuaries is also a factor *within* the Belgian Association of Actuaries (KVBA-ARAB). This professional organisation aims to be "neutral" by relying on a purely scientific-actuarial point of view (ARAB, A, 2). As also can be read in their magazine *Actuanews*: 'We limit ourselves... to focusing on the actuarial side of the moon' (KVBA-ARAB 2001:7). However, the organisation represents some 700 actuaries who work in *various* contexts, such as consultancy, private insurance, social insurance and government. This shows that actuaries may have to wear different hats from time to time. As a consequence, it can be difficult to find a consensus on 'neutral actuarial principles' within the organisation. For example, at the time of my fieldwork, the KVBA-ARAB was developing a "code of good practice" for the adjudicated actuaries of the Belgian insurance companies. This proved quite a challenge, mainly because of the fact that actuaries tend to adopt the economic policy of their particular employer. An informant commented on the establishment of these guidelines as follows:

    "Well, yes, it turned out to be rather difficult in the end to reduce these five different points of view into a single perspective and into a guideline; after all, if one is active in a particular company for a while, one starts to identify with that company's views ... So that meant making compromises and probably not everyone was too happy with these guidelines ... But yes, in the end, it is a matter of finding a compromise, isn't it? But the problem is that one is really dependent on the company itself and its management" (ARAB, A, 2).

    In other words, the actuarial professional organisation is confronted with a variety of economic policies. Although they all represent the same profession, different views and perspectives are combined in the development of the guidelines. As such, economic accounts also enter the meeting rooms of the actuarial professional organisation, rather than stopping at its doorway. Actuaries cannot simply *brush off* their affiliations.

Chapter IV

35. Large-scale research, such as the Framingham studies about risk factors related to cardiovascular diseases, are illustrative of this multi-factorial epidemiology.
36. Note that these risk categories and statistical categories in insurance are often closely associated with epidemiological categories. The same mechanism of statistical correlations between research variables that are wrongly seen as causative factors has been demonstrated in epidemiology (e.g., Petersen and Lupton 1996: 43; Davies 1998: 144). Again here, it is argued that many of the epidemiological 'facts' presented as 'truths' to the lay public are the product of a whole range of concerns. For example, Kriegler (1994) argues that some risk factors are privileged as explanations over others because they are relatively contained and closest to the outcome under investigation. More attention is paid to a risk factor like smoking than to a *fuzzy* factor like socio-economic status. Other concerns my be related to vested commercial and professional interests pertaining to certain risk factors.
37. Swiss Re, (n.d.), accessed in September 2003 at http://www.swissre.com.
38. Swiss Re for example has over 70 offices in more than thirty countries with over 8,100 employees, providing risk transfer, risk financing and asset management to its global client base. In the financial year 2002, gross premiums written amounted to CHF 32.7 billion (Swiss Re, accessed in September 2003 at http://www.swissre.com).
39. For example, a recent study of a European reinsurance company comprised of some 200,000 policies analysed with around 1,400,000 observation years (Swiss Re, 2002: 3).
40. Today the same seems to occur as well in the development of genetic knowledge (cf. chapter II). The actuarial research on genetics must be secondary to any advances in genetic research. This factor may lead to significant time lags in the generation of crucial actuarial information.
41. For example, the Belgian Haemophilia Patient Association recently had a meeting with the reinsurance company Gerling Global Ruckversichering-AG. The association's major complaint was that today these patients have a standard mortality risk but that reinsurance statistics are not updated and still rate them at substandard rates. This negotiation resulted in better insurability rating for *some* patients: haemophilia patients without HIV or HCV contamination and in good health condition can now be accepted at standard rates in the company. Another condition was that patients are under treatment in a haemophilia centre and can present a medical file to the reinsurer.
42. This will be explored further in chapter VI.
43. This might be realised because experience statistics generate an expected mortality rate (statistics), which can in fact be very close to the actual mortality rate because experience statistics are based on a similar kind of population. Relying on experience statistics could turn out to be a major advantage over reinsurance companies, which rely on mortality data from different countries or other populations.
44. As was illustrated in the previous chapter, companies could follow different profit-making strategies. Investing and innovating in the medical statistical

risk categories is thus (just) one of many profit-making strategies for an insurance company.

45. For the exception on the prohibition of genetic data in Belgian insurance as inscribed in the Law of Insurance Contract, see chapters I and VI.
46. Along those same lines, most respondents noted that the yearly collected statistics on Belgian insurance companies by the Belgian Association of Insurers (BVVO) were not "sufficiently reliable" to be used for actuarial research. Again, concerns related to competition were mentioned as the main cause. When conveying their information to the BVVO, individual companies might disguise competitive information ("Everyone here is afraid of disclosing data to competitors". (C1, M, 2)).
47. The cover of claims experts employed in case 1 listed remarks like: "very good expert"; "to avoid"; "moderate report"; "expensive!"; "very good report, but expensive!", "client of the bank", "needs incentives to send his report". The record on medical experts also includes remarks on complaints the insurance company has received from applicants.
48. This will be elaborated upon in chapter V.
49. Moreover, the increasing ability of insurance companies to determine signs of some sort of extra mortality risk through refined medical technologies sometimes results in diagnoses for disorders the applicant was not yet aware of.

Chapter V

50. For example, if the information reveals some new risks, the underwriters compare these to similar cases or risks. An approximation of a numerical evaluation of the unknown risk can be inferred from knowledge about known risks that resemble the one's to be assessed (Mol 2002). Earlier cases or "model narratives" are used as a standard to help the underwriters in assessing new files.
51. This telephone training of the junior coaches has obvious advantages for the underwriting department. If underwriters would be in direct contact with applicants, there is the danger that they will be taken aback by callers or overwhelmed by their concerns. The coaches seemed especially trained in avoiding this and they were also very knowledgeable about the general insurance frame and principles.
52. This aspect is also reflected in the distribution of tasks and the hierarchy in the underwriting department. For example, in case 1, only the more experienced junior coaches were applied to do "public relations".
53. Cf. chapter III.

Chapter VI

54. Earlier versions and parts of this chapter were published elsewhere (Van Hoyweghen 2004; Van Hoyweghen et al. 2006).
55. Law of 25 June 1992 concerning the agreement on land insurance, articles 5 and 95 (Wet op de landverzekeringsovereenkomst, 1992). Article 95 states that "the physicians nominated by the insured shall submit to the insured,

at his or her request, the medical certificates necessary for the completion and execution of the private insurance contract. The medical examinations necessary for the completion and execution of the contract may only depend on the anamnesis of the present health condition by the candidate and not on genetic research techniques which are capable of determining the future state of health" (translation from Nys, Dreezen et al. 2002: 24 and McGleenan 2001: 61). It should be noted that article 95 of the LVO was replaced in 2002 by art. 19 of the Act on Patients' Rights (WPR) (Wet op de patiëntenrechten 2002). Furthermore, Belgium has neither signed nor ratified the European Convention on Human Rights and Biomedicine.

56. Article 5 states: "The policyholder is obliged to declare, at the time of completing the contract, any particulars known to him or her which he or she could reasonably be expected to consider as constituting risk assessment elements for the insurer. However, s/he does not have to disclose details which are already known to the insurer or which the insurer should be reasonably expected to know. Genetic data cannot be transmitted" (translation from Nys, Dreezen et al. 2002: 24 and McGleenan 2001: 61).
57. Note that the reification of risk factors for disease is a tendency also apparent in epidemiology (see chapter IV). Atrens (1994) for example points to the vested commercial and professional interests that surround and are reliant upon the belief that high blood cholesterol levels cause heart disease, not only for medical research, but also for coronary health foundations, the health food industries and drug companies who market drugs to lower cholesterol. In the face of these powerful interests, studies challenging this hypothesis have often been ignored or down played.
58. For the classic analysis, pointing to the tensions as well as the analogies between irresponsibility and insanity, see Foucault (1995).
59. Note that this idea of "managing death" was exactly the philosophical foundation in the development of insurance (Ewald 1986). By calculating risks and framing *death* into *risk*, the governmentality of death became visible.
60. An example is the sprinkler requirements in commercial fire insurance contracts.
61. Persons with a family history of Huntington's disease, however, were an exception.
62. This is illustrated by a recent comment in the *British Medical Journal* on the fault-based approach that such geneticisation of disease entails. The author asked whether the discovery of genetic defects in particular individuals does not automatically make those people *powerless*. He argues that a geneticised approach brings these people "to a learned and licensed helplessness" (Smith 2002). The new biomedical distinctions implied by the "discovery" of genetics thus result in normative effects in the distribution of responsibilities.
63. Genetic risks, in other words, receive preferential treatment in comparison to other probabilistic information. In this respect, it is interesting to compare a positive HIV test with a genetic test (cf. Sandberg 1995): until recently the positive result of an HIV test was seen as a diagnosis of imminent and inevitable serious disease. Over the last decade, these people's survival rates have increased dramatically, however, in part as a result of new experimental drugs. Studies also show that some HIV "patients" do not even develop the

disease. An HIV test, then, might well be less predictive than, for instance, a test for Huntington's disease.

64. Examples are the detection of phenylketonuria via blood tests or Tay-Sachs via measurement of mutated proteins.

Chapter VII

65. My argument in this chapter is reflective of the recent "shift towards performance" in STS. Earlier research efforts in STS basically proceeded from the assumption that it is possible to offer pragmatic descriptions of technological and scientific practices. In recent years, some authors have exposed this "normative inconvenience" in STS studies. It is increasingly argued that researchers, while delineating the different workings of a particular practice, should also be able to say something about the *effects* of these workings. But the researcher also produces a particular performance with regard to the study's object (Law 2000; Law and Urry 2002; Law 2003). Our research methods and accounts may have effects or make a difference precisely because they enact realities or "give voice".
66. As such, in recent years, there has been in private business increased attention paid to managing better relationships with customers, for example, by encouraging and responding to customer complaints. Industries ranging from banking to fast food, and from airlines to industrial solvents, try to gain a competitive edge in the marketplace by focusing on customer relationships via retention analysis, listening and managing customer complaints or customer defection analyses.
67. In this regard, Sen (1999: 12) argues that the practice of giving voice "gives citizens an opportunity to learn from one another, and helps society to form its values and priorities. Even the idea of 'needs,' including the understanding of 'economic needs,' requires public discussion and exchange of information, views, and analyses."
68. As Callon et al. (2002) argue: "In the economy of qualities... cooperation between scholars and economic agents and the constitution of hybrid forums are inevitable, for the questions they raise are to a large degree identical." In this view, the role of the sociologist is neither legislative nor interpretative, but *experimental* (cf. Bauman, cited in: Barry and Slater 2002a).
69. For unintended consequences of genetic legislation, see chapter II and chapter VI.
70. For example, accountancy firms offer to audit the ethical performance of insurance companies or financial services. See for example a recent research paper by PricewaterhouseCoopers, "The trust challenge: How the management of financial institutions can lead the rebuilding of public confidence" (2002).
71. The recent tendency in legislation to shift accountability from insureds to insurers is illustrative. In the UK, for example, this *reverse approach* is taking shape in the development of the GAIC. Whereas in the past, based on discrimination law, it was up to the insured to submit a complaint by going to court to prove insurers were wrong, the development of the GAIC means that it is now up to the insurance industry to prove that they have a right to

underwrite (in the case of genetics) via the criteria of "technical, clinical and actuarial relevance" (cf. chapter II).

72. For example, the GAIC terms of reference continue to be based on the insurance standards or rules of the game of insurance, which require insurers to meet the "technical" criteria of actuarial significance. Thereby, they are provided with actuarial research based on abstract modelling, founded on assumptions about the insured, such as individual purchasing behaviour, where the approach is broadly to assume that individuals may withhold information from insurers and that some adverse selection occurs, and then investigate whether a market under those assumptions is stable. Moreover, this research is frequently not peer-reviewed by academics but performed by actuaries who work in the private insurance business.

Bibliography

Abraham, K.A. (1986). *Distributing Risk: Insurance, Legal Theory and Public Policy.* New Haven: Yale University Press.

Akerman, S. (1999). "Introduction to the Sessions: At the Geneva Association", *Selected Papers from the Seminar on Genetics and Life/Health Insurance held in Paris, February 11-12, 1999.* (pp. 5-8). Paris: Geneva Association.

Akrich, M., and Latour, B. (1992). A Summary of a Convenient Vocabulary for the Semiotics of Human and Nonhuman Assemblies. In W.E. Bijker, and J. Law (eds.), *Shaping Technology/Building Society* (pp. 259-264). Cambridge: MIT Press.

Alonso, W., and Starr, P. (eds.) (1987). *The Politics of Numbers.* New York: Russell Sage Foundation.

Alper, J.S., and Beckwith, J. (1998). "Distinguishing Genetic from Non-genetic Medical Tests: Some Implications for Anti-discrimination Legislation". *Science & Engineering Ethics,* 4, 141-150.

American Academy of Actuaries. (1998). "Genetic information and voluntary life insurance. Issue Brief" [Web Page]. URL http://www.actuary.org/pdf/life/genet.pdf [07/04/2003].

American Academy of Actuaries. (2001). "Genetic testing: what you need to know. Capital Hill Briefing" [Web Page]. URL http://www.actuary.org/briefings/genetic_082901.htm [07/04/2003].

American Council of Life Insurance (ACLI) & Health Insurance Association of America (HIAA). (1991). *Report of the ACLI-HIAA Task Force on Genetic Testing.* Washington, D.C.

Association of British Insurers (ABI). (1997). "Genetic Testing: A Code of Practice" [Web Page]. URL http://www.abi.org.uk [2001, January].

Association of British Insurers (ABI). (1999). *Genetic Testing: ABI Code of Practice.* London: Association of British Insurers.

Association of British Insurers (ABI). (2000). "Raising Standards Quality Mark Scheme" [Web Page]. URL http://www.raisingstandards.net/news/bulletin/september_2000.pdf [2004, February].

Association of British Insurers (ABI). (2001). "Insurers confirm decision to extend moratorium on use of genetic test results". Press release 32/10 [Web Page]. URL www.abi.org.uk [2002, March].

Atchinson, B.K. (2004). "Walking the Talk: Ethics as Corporate Culture". *The Geneva Papers on Risk and Insurance,* 29 (1), 40-44.

Atrens, D. (1994). "The Questionable Wisdom of a Low-fat Diet and Cholesterol Reduction". *Social Science & Medicine,* 39 (3), 433-447.

Baker, T. (2000). "Insuring Morality". *Economy and Society,* 29 (4), 559-578.

Baker, T. (2002). "Risk, Insurance and the Social Construction of Responsibility". In T. Baker and J. Simon. (eds.), *Embracing Risk: The Changing Culture of Insurance and Responsibility* (pp. 33-51). Chicago and London: University of Chicago Press.

Baker, T., and Simon, J. (2002). Embracing Risk. In T. Baker and J. Simon (eds.), *Embracing Risk: The Changing Culture of Insurance and Responsibility* (pp. 1-25). Chicago and London: University of Chicago Press.

Balay, K.A. (1994). "Mastering the Underwriting Decision". *Reinsurance Reporter,* 1994, 141, 3 [Web Page]. URL http://www.lincolnre.com/eprise/main/lre/Publications/Reporter/Issues/141/141_06.htm [23/03/2001].

Barry, A., and Slater, D. (2002a). "Introduction: the technological economy". *Economy and Society,* 31 (2, May), 175-193.

Barry, A., and Slater, D. (2002b). "Technology, Politics and the Market: An Interview with Michel Callon". *Economy & Society,* 31 (2), 285-306.

BBC News. (2001). "Moratorium on genetic data use", Tuesday, 23 October 2001 [Web Page]. URL http://news.bbc.co.uk/1/hi/business/1615397.stm [07/04/2003].

Beck, U. (1992). *Risk Society: Towards a New Modernity.* London: Sage.

Beck, U. (1999). "Risk Society Revisited: Theory, Politics and Research Programmes". In U. Beck, J. van Loon, and B. Adam, *The Risk Society and Beyond: Critical Issues for Social Theory* (pp. 211-229). London: Sage Publications.

Benschop, R., Horstman, K., and Vos, R. (2003). "Voice Beyond Choice: Hesitant Voice in Public Debates about Genetics in Health Care". *Health Care Analysis,* 11 (2), 141-150.

Berberich, K. (1999). "L'importance des Tests Génétiques pour l'Activité de la Kölnische Rück". *Köln, General & Cologne Re, Thèmes N° 7,* 7 (4), 38-41.

Bernstein, P.L. (1998). *Against the Gods: The Remarkable Story of Risk.* New York: Wiley.

Best, J. (ed.). (1995). *Images of Issues: Typifying Contemporary Social Problems.* New York: Aldine de Gruyter.

Biehl, J., and Thieme, K. (1998). "What do you mean my client isn't preferred?" *Reinsurance Reporter,* 1, 53 [Web Page]. URL http://www.lnrc.com/eprise/main/lre/Publications/Reporter/Issues/153/153_05.htm [2001, March].

Bijker, W.E. (1995). *Of Bicycles, Bakelites and Bulbs: Toward a Theory of Sociotechnical Change.* Cambridge: MIT Press.

Bijker, W.E., Hughes, T.P., and Pinch, T. (eds.) (1987). *The Social Construction of Technological Systems.* Cambridge: MIT Press.

Bloor, M., Goldberg, D., and Emslie, J. (1991). "Ethnostatistics and the AIDS Epidemic". *British Journal of Sociology,* 42 (1), 131-139.

Boltanski, L., and Thévenot, L. (1991). *De la Justification: les Economies de la grandeur.* Paris: Gallimard.

Brackenridge, R.D.C., and Elder, W.J. (1992). *Medical Selection of Life Risks.* New York: Stockton Press.

Braun, R. (1999). "Keeping Life Insurance Affordable in the Era of Genetic Medicine". *Journal of Financial Service Professionals,* LIII (5), 46-53.

Braun, R. (2000). "Insurance, Genetic Testing and Regulation around the World". *Medical Resource,* 12 (3), 6-7.

British House of Commons Science & Technology Committee. (2001). "Genetics and Insurance: Fifth Report Commons Science and Technology Committee" (HC174) [Web Page]. URL http://www.publications.parliament.uk/pa/cm200001/cmselect/cmsctech/174/17402.htm [01/2004]

Brockett, P.L., and Tankersley, E.S. (1997). "The Genetics Revolution, Economics, Ethics and Insurance". *Journal of Business Ethics,* 16 (15), 1661-1676.

Brockett, P.L., MacMinn, R., and Carter, M. (1999). "Genetic Testing, Insurance Economics and Societal Responsibility". *North American Actuarial Journal*, 3 (1), 1-20.
Brown, N., and Webster, A. (2004). *New Medical Technologies and Society: Reordering Life*. Cambridge: Polity Press.
Bury, M.R. (1986). "Social Construction and the Development of Medical Sociology". *Sociology of Health and Illness*, 8 (2), 137-169.
BVVO. (1999). "Termijnen inkorten en communicatie verbeteren. De ombudsman vraagt dat er maatregelen worden genomen". *Assurinfo*, 28 October 1999.
BVVO. (2000). *De Ombudsman. Jaarverslag 1999*. Brussel: BVVO.
BVVO. (2001). "Imago". *Assurinfo. To the Point*, February 2001, 1-12.

Callon, M. (1986a). "The Sociology of an Actor Network: The Case of the Electric Vehicle". In M. Callon, J. Law, and A. Rip (eds.), *Mapping the Dynamics of Science and Technology: Sociology of Science in the Real World* (pp. 19-34). London: Macmillan.
Callon, M. (1986b). "Some elements of a sociology of translation: Domestication of the scallops and the fisherman of St Brieuc Bay". In J. Law (ed.), *Power, Action and Belief: A New Sociology of Knowledge?* (pp. 196-233). London: Routledge and Kegan Paul.
Callon, M. (1991). "Techno-economic Networks and Irreversibility". In J. Law (ed.), *Sociology of Monsters. Essays on Power, Technology and Domination* (pp. 132-161). London: Routledge.
Callon, M. (ed.). (1998). *The Laws of the Markets*. Oxford: Blackwell Publishers.
Callon, M. (1999). "Actor-network theory – The Market Test". In J. Law, and J. Hassard (eds.), *Actor Network Theory and After* (pp. 181-196). Oxford: Blackwell Publishers.
Callon, M. (2001). "Economy of Qualities, Researchers in the Wild and the Rise of Technical Democracy" [Web Page]. http://www.cts.cuni.cz/seminar/callon.htm [2004, January].
Callon, M. (2002). "Writing and (Re) Writing Devices". In J. Law, and A. Mol (eds.), *Complexities. Social studies of knowledge practices* (pp. 191-217). Durham and London: Duke University Press.
Callon, M., Lascoumes, P., and Barthe, Y. (2001). *Agir dans un Monde Incertain: Essai sur la Démocratie Technique*. Paris: Le Seuil.
Callon, M., Méadel C., and Rabeharisoa, R. (2002). "The Economy of Qualities". *Economy & Society*, 31 (2), 194-217.
Callon, M., and Muniesa F. (2002). "Economic markets as calculative and calculated collective devices" Paper presented at the New York Conference on Social Studies of Finance, Columbia University and the Social Science Research Council [Web Page]. http://www.coi.columbia.edu/ssf/papers/callon-muniesa.doc [2004, January].
Campbell, C.A. (1998). "Lecture presented to the Society of Actuaries, Session 1GS. Overview of Insurance Industry Issues and the Role of the Actuary". Maui I Spring Meeting, June 15-17 1998. *Record*, 24, 1. [Web Page]. URL http://www.soa.org/library/record/1990-99/rsa98v24n11gs.pdf [07/04/2003].

Carmelli, D., Heath, A.C., and Robinette, D. (1993). "Genetic Analysis of Drinking Behavior in World War II Veteran Twins". *Genetic Epidemiology*, 10, 201-213.

Castel, R. (1991). "From Dangerousness to Risk". In G. Burchell, C. Gordon, and P. Miller (eds.), *The Foucault Effect: Studies in Governmentality* (pp. 281-298). London: Harvester Wheatsheaf.

Chambers, D.C. (1993) "Insurers Unite! Genetic Testing is Coming of Age". *Reinsurance Reporter*, 135, 1, 14p.

Chambers, D.C. (1999). "The Future of Risk Classification in the Age of Predictive DNA-based Testing". *North American Actuarial Journal*, 3 (1), 21-33.

Chiche, Y. (1995). "Genetics and Life and Health Insurance International Aspects". *Geneva Papers on Risk and Insurance*, 76, 274-278.

Chuffart, A. (1996a). "Genetic Testing in Europe". *Journal of Insurance Medicine*, 28 (2), 125-135.

Chuffart, A. (1996b). *Genetics and Life Insurance in Europe*. Presented at the Swiss RE UK's conference "Ringing the Chances", May 1996. Zurich: Swiss Re.

Chuffart, A. (1997). *Genetics and Life Insurance: A Few Thoughts*. Zurich: Swiss Re.

Chuffart, A. (1999). "Public Perception of, and Concern about, Underwriting - related activities in the Life Insurance Industry". In Geneva Association, *Selected papers from the Seminar of Genetics and Life/Health Insurance* (pp. 87-98). Paris: Geneva Association.

Comité Européen des Assurances (CEA). (2000). *Some Helpful Guidelines for National Associations confronted with Restrictive Legislation Regarding Insurance and Genetics*. Brussel: CEA.

Commission of the European Communities. (2001). *Towards a Strategic Vision of Life Sciences and Biotechnology: Consultation Document. COM (2001) 454 final.* Brussels: European Commission.

Controledienst voor de Verzekeringen (CDV). (2002) *Presentation – Role* [Web Page]. URL http://www.cdv-oca.be/en/index.htm [2003, August].

Crawford, R. (1994). "The Boundaries of the Self and the Unhealthy Other: Reflections on Health, Culture and AIDS". *Social Science & Medicine*, 38 (10), 1347-65.

Davies, D. (1998). "Health and the Discourse of Weight Control". In A. Petersen, and C. Waddell (eds.), *Health Matters: A Sociology of Illness, Prevention and Care* (pp. 141-155). Buckingham: Open University Press.

Daykin, C. (2001). "Genetics and Insurance: Lecture to the Royal Institution, 23 march 2001 UK Forum of Genetics and Insurance (UKFGI) " [Web Page]. URL http://www.ukfgi.org.uk/text%20-%20%20daykin%20RI [2003, July 4].

Daykin, C.D., Akers, D.A., MacDonald, A.S., McGleenan, T., Paul, D., and Turvey, P.J. (2003). "Genetics and Insurance – Some Social Policy Issues". Presented to the Institute of Actuaries, London, 24 February 2003, and to the Faculty of Actuaries, Edinburgh, 17 March 2003.

Dean, M. (1998). "Risk, Calculable and Incalculable". *Soziale Welt*, 49, 25-42.

Dean, M. (1999). *Governmentality: Power and Rule in Modern Society*. London: Sage.

Department of Trade & Industry, Office of Science & Technology (DTI). (1998). *Government Response to the Human Genetics Advisory Commission's Report on the Implications of Genetic Testing for Insurance.*
De Vries, G. and K. Horstman (eds.) (2004). *Genetica van Laboratorium naar Samenleving. De Ongekende Praktijk van Voorspellende Genetische testen* Amsterdam: Aksant (*Genetics from Laboratory to Society.* (2006). London: Palgrave Macmillan, forthcoming).
Dicke, A.A. (1999a). "Discussion after Chambers 1999". *North American Actuarial Journal,* 3, 31-33.
Dicke, A.A. (1999b). "Discussion after Jones 1999". *North American Actuarial Journal,* 3, 65-66.
Dodier, N. (1994). "Expert Medical Decisions in Occupational Medicine: a Sociological Analysis of Medical Judgement". *Sociology of Health and Illness,* 16 (4), 489-514.
Dolan, C. (2001). "You wouldn't understand: Editorial". *The Actuary,* Jan./Feb. 2001 [Web Page]. URL http://www.the-actuary.org.uk/backissues/index.asp?Section=3 [03/2002].
Dupree, M.W. (1997). "Other Than Healing: Medical Practitioners and the Business of Life Assurance during the Nineteenth and Early Twentieth Centuries". *The Society for the Social History of Medicine,* 10/01, 79-103.

Engman, M.L. (1998). "Risky business: The collision of genetics and the life insurance industry. Product development". Lecture presented to the Society of Actuaries. Palm Desert Spring Meeting, 21-23 May 1997. Session 111SM Risky Business. *Record,* 23, 1. [Web Page]. URL http://www.soa.org/library/record/1990-99/rsa97v23n1111sm.pdf [2003, July 4].
Ericson, R., Dean, B., and Doyle, A. (2000). "The Moral Hazards of Neo-liberalism: Lessons from the Private Insurance Industry". *Economy & Society,* 29 (4), 532-558.
Ericson, R., Doyle, A. and Dean, B. (2003). *Insurance as Governance.* Toronto: University of Toronto Press.
Ericson, R., and Doyle, A. (2004). *Uncertain Business: Risk, Insurance and the Limits of Knowledge.* Toronto: University of Toronto Press.
Ericson, R., and A. Doyle (2003). *Risk and Morality.* Toronto: University of Toronto Press.
European Society of Human Genetics. Public & Professional Policy Committee. (2001). *EuroGapp project 1999-2000. Genetic information and testing in insurance and employment: technical, social and ethical issues. Background document.*
Ewald, F. (1986). *L'Etat-Providence.* Paris: Bernard Grasset.
Ewald, F. (1991). "Insurance and Risk". In G. Burchell, C. Gordon and P. Miller (eds.), *The Foucault Effect: Studies in Governmentality.* (pp. 197-210). London: Harvester Wheatsheaf.
Ewald, F. (1999). "Genetics, Insurance and Risk". In T. McGleenan, U. Wiesing, and F. Ewald (eds.) *Genetics and Insurance* (pp. 17-32). Oxford: BIOS Scientific Publishers Limited.
Ewald, F., and Moreau, J.P. (1994). "Génétique médicale, Confidentialité et Assurance". *Risques,* 18, 111-130.

Feurst, O. (1999). "One-to-One Marketing – a Way to Earn Loyalty in the Mature Consumer Markets?" Presented at Business Challenges in the 21st Century –

Japan and Sweden Business Relationships in the Wake of the Global Economic and Financial Crises. A conference at Nihon University together with Stockholm University, Friday 23 April and Saturday 24 April 1999 [Web Page]. URL http://www.fek.su.se/home/of/papers/121_japan.pdf [2004, January].

Foucault, M. (1995). *Discipline and Punish: The Birth of the Prison*. New York: Vintage Books.

Freriks, D. (1994). "De verzekeringswet van 25 juni 1992 en het medisch beroepsgeheim". In J. Van Steenberghe (ed.), *Medisch beroepsgeheim en verzekeringen* (pp. 13-34). Brugge: Die Keure.

Friedman, A.S. (1997). "ACLI airs concerns of future competitiveness". *National Underwriter*, 24/11/2001. [Web Page]. URL http://www.nunews.com/archives/Lh_archive/1997/L11-24/0047a4af.asp [2002, March 15].

Fromme, H., and Klager, F. (2001) "German insurers ponder genetics moratorium". *Insurance Day*, 12/06/2001. [Web Page]. URL http://www.insuranceday.com [2002, June 3].

Funtowitz, S., and Ravetz, J. (1993). "Science for the Post-normal Age". *Futures*, 25 (7), 739-755.

Garfinkel, H. (1967). *Studies in Ethnomethodology*. New Jersey: Prentice-Hall.

Genetic Deal. (2001). *Insurance Day*, 25/10/2001. URL http://www.insuranceday.com [2002, June 3].

Genetics & Insurance Committee (GAIC). (2000). "Decision of the Genetics and Insurance Committee (GAIC) concerning the application for approval to use genetic test results for life insurance risk assessment in Huntington's diseases" (GAIC/01.1) [Web Page]. URL http://www.doh.gov.uk/genetics/intro.htm [03/2003]

Giddens, A. (1990). *The Consequences of Modernity*. Cambridge: Polity Press.

Gifford, S.M. (1986). "The Meaning of Lumps: a Case Study of the Ambiguities of Risk". In C.R. James, R. Stall, and S.M. Gifford (eds.), *Anthropology and Epidemiology: Interdisciplinary Approaches to the Study of Health and Disease* (pp. 213-246). Dordrecht: D. Reidel Publishing Company.

Glenn, B.J. (2000). "The Shifting Rhetoric of Insurance Denial". *Law & Society Review*, 34 (3), 779-808.

Goetz, A.M., and Jenkins, R. (2001). "Voice, Accountability and Human Development: The Emergence of a New Agenda". Paper prepared for the Meeting of the UNDP HDR Advisory Panel, 5-7 November 2001, Greentree Estate, Manhasset, Long Island NY [Web Page]. URL http://www.bbk.ac.uk/polsoc/download/rob_jenkins/Voice_Accountability_Human_Development.pdf [2004, January].

Goffman, E. (1963). *Stigma: Notes on the Management of Spoiled Identity*. Englewood clifs: Prentice-hall.

Goford, J. (2002). "Thinking and Behaviour. Address by the President of the Institute of Actuaries". Delivered to the Institute of Actuaries, 1 July 2002 [Web Page]. URL http://www.actuaries.org.uk/files/pdf/library/inst_add_2002.pdf [2004, January].

Hacking, I. (1990). *The Taming of Chance*. Cambridge: Cambridge University Press.

Hall, M.A. (1996). "Insurers' Use of Genetic Information. " *Jurimetrics*, 7 (Fall), 13-22.
Hall, M.A. (1999). "Restricting Insurers' Use of genetic information: A Guide to Public Policy". *North American Actuarial Journal*, 3, 34-51.
Hank, G. (2000). "The New Epoch of Insurance: Lab Testing". *National Underwriter*, 20 November 2000, 22.
Hanney, B. (2001). "The DNA Dilemma". *Insurancetimes*, 15 November 2001, 18-19.
Haraway, D. (1997). *Modest_Witness@Second_Millennium. FemaleMan_Meets _Oncomouse*. New York: Routledge.
Hartnett-Barry, J. (1996). "Massachusetts weighs genetic testing safeguards". *National Underwriter*, 21 October 1996. [Web Page]. URL http//www.nunews.com/archives/Lh_archive/1996/L10-21/0043mass.asp [2002, March 15].
Heimer, C.A. (1985). *Reactive Risk and Rational Action: Managing Moral Hazard in Insurance Contracts*. Berkeley: University of California Press.
Heimer, C.A. (2002). "Insuring More, Ensuring Less: The costs and benefits of private regulation through insurance". In T. Baker, and J. Simon (eds.), *Embracing Risk: The Changing Culture of Insurance and Responsibility* (pp. 116-145). Chicago and London: University of Chicago Press.
Hennekens, C.H. (1998). "Increasing Burden of Cardiovascular Disease: current knowledge and future directions for research on relevant risk factors". *Circulation*, 97, 1095.
Hiatt, D. (1999). "Breaking the Code. *Money Management*, May, 65-68.
Higgs, P. (1998). "Risk, Governmentality and the Reconceptualisation of Citizenship". In G. Scambler and P. Higgs (eds.), *Modernity, Medicine and Health. Medical Sociology towards 2000* (pp. 177-197). London: Routledge.
Hirschman, A.O. (1970). *Exit, Voice, and Loyalty: Responses to Decline in Firms, Organizations, and States*. Cambridge and London: Harvard University Press.
Hirschman, A.O. (1981). *Essays in Trespassing: Economics to Politics and Beyond*. Cambridge: Cambridge University Press.
Holmes, B.J. (1999). "Discussion after Chambers". *North American Actuarial Journal*, 3, 29-31.
Horstman, K. (2001). *Public Bodies, Private Lives: The Historical Construction of Life Insurance, Health Risks, and Citizenship in the Netherlands. 1880-1920*. Rotterdam: Erasmus Publishing.
Horstman, K. (2004). "Leefstijl, genen en cholesterol. Een nieuwe arena voor strijd over verantwoordelijkheid en solidariteit". In G. de Vries, and K. Horstman (eds.), *Genetica van Laboratorium naar Samenleving. De Ongekende Praktijk van Voorspellende Genetische Testen*. (pp. 64-89) Amsterdam: Aksant. "Life-style, genes and cholesterol. A new arena for conflict over responsibilities and solidarity. In G. de Vries and K. Horstman (eds.) (2006). *Genetics from Laboratory to Society*. London: Palgrave Macmillan, forthcoming)
Horstman, K., de Vries, G.H., and Haveman, O. (1999). *Gezondheidspolitiek in een risicocultuur. Burgerschap in het tijdperk van de voorspellende geneeskunde*. Den Haag: Rathenau Instituut.
Horstman, K., van der Made, J., and Vos, R. (2004). "Exit en voice in de verzekeringswereld. Gebrekkige gezondheid, gebrekkig verweer?" *Beleid & Maatschappij*, 31, 1, 42-51.

Howard, L.S. (1996). "Genetic testing debate starts to bubble in the UK". *National Underwriter,* 5 August 1996. [Web Page]. URL http://www.nunews.com/archives/Lh_archive/1996/L08-05/0032u1lh.asp [2002, March 15].
Huebner, S.S., and Black, K. Jr. (1969). *Life Insurance.* New York: Appleton-Century-Crofts.
Hulbert, J.M., Pitt, L.F., and Ewing, M.T. (2000). "Defections, Discourse and Devotion: Some Propositions on Customer Desertion, Dialogue and Loyalty", Presented to ANZMAC 2000 Visionary Marketing for the 21st Century: Facing the Challenge [Web Page]. URL http://130.195.95.71:8081/www/ANZMAC2000/CDsite/papers/h/Hulbert1.PDF [2004, January].
Human Genetics Advisory Committee Sub-Group on Insurance (HGAC). (1997) "The implications of genetic testing for insurance", London [Web Page]. URL http://www.doh.gov.uk/hgac/papers/papers_b.htm [2001].
Human Genetics Commission (HGC). (2000). "Whose Hands on Your Genes?" Consultation paper [Web Page]. URL http://www.hgc.gov.uk [2002, March].
Human Genetics Commission (HGC). (2001a). "Human Genetics Commission: Comment to inform the government response to the House of Commons report on genetics and insurance of the use of genetic information in insurance: interim recommendations of the HGC" [Web Page]. URL www.hgc.gov.uk/business_publications_statement-01may.htm [2002, March].
Human Genetics Commission (HGC). (2001b). "Information-gathering meeting on genetics and insurance 09 February 2001 Royal commonwealth club, London WC1" [Web Page]. URL http://www.hgc.gov.uk/business_meetings_09-february.htm [2001, April].

Institute and Faculty of Actuaries. "Genetics Group of the Social Policy Board. (2001). "Genetics and Insurance Inquiry – Memorandum from the UK actuarial Profession 22 January 2001" [Web Page]. URL http://www.actuaries.org.uk/Display_Page.cgi?url=/genetics/memorandum.xml [2003, April 7].
Insurance Day News. (2000). "Under-insurance a big factor in the debate on genetic information". *Insurance Day,* 14/02/2000. [Web Page]. URL http://www.insuranceday.com [2002, June 3].
Ivanovic, B. (1999). "Making medical findings useful for insurance". *Reinsurance Reporter,* 1, 25-30.

Jasanoff, S. (2003). "Technologies of Humility: Citizen Participation in Governing Science". *Minerva,* 41 (3), 223-244.
Jefferey, R. (1979). "Normal Rubbish: Deviant Patients in Casualty Departments". *Sociology of Health & Illness,* 1 (1), 90-107.
Johansen, R.J. (1999). "Effective Underwriting in the Genetic Testing Era". *North American Actuarial Journal,* 3, 52-55.
Jones, C.S. (1999). "The current state of genetic testing: an insurance industry perspective on the rush to legislate", *North American Actuarial Journal,* 3, 1, 56-66.
Jureidini, R., and White, K. (2000). "Life Insurance, the Medical Examination and Cultural Values". *Journal of Historical Sociology,* 13 (2), 190-214.

Kaufert, P.A. (2000). "Health Policy and the New Genetics. *Social Science & Medicine,* 51, 821-829.

KBVA-ARAB. (2001). *Actuanews* [Web Page]. URL http://www.actuaweb.be/actuaweb/documents/ActuaNews [02/2002].

Kitcher, P. (1996). *The Lives to Come: The Genetic Revolution and Human Possibilities.* London: Penguin.

Knight, F. (1921). *Risk, Uncertainty and Profit.* Boston: Houghton Mifflin.

Kriegler, N. (1994). "Epidemiology and the Web of Causation: has anyone seen the spider?", *Social Science & Medicine*, 39, 7, 887-903.

Krinik, J.J. (1999). "Discussion after Lowden". *North American Actuarial Journal*, 3, 78-82.

Kumar, S., and Gantley, M. (1999). "Tensions between Policy Makers and General Practitioners in Implementing New Genetics: Grounded Theory Interview Study". *British Medical Journal*, 319 (7222), 1410-1413.

Latour, B. (1987). *Science in Action: How to Follow Scientists and Engineers through Society.* Cambridge: Harvard University Press.

Latour, B. (1988). *The Pasteurization of France.* London: Harvard University Press.

Latour, B. (2005). *Reassembling the Social: An introduction to Actor-Network-Theory*, Oxford: Oxford University Press.

Latour, B., and Woolgar, S. (1979). *Laboratory Life. The Construction of Scientific Facts.* Chichester: Princeton University Press.

Latour, B., and Woolgar, S. (1986). *Laboratory Life: The Construction of Scientific Facts.* (1979) Princeton: Princeton University Press.

Latour, B., and P. Weibel (2005). *Making Things Public: Atmospheres of Democracy.* Cambridge: MIT Press.

Law, J. (1991a). "Introduction". In J. Law (ed.), *A Sociology of Monsters: Essays on Power.* London: Routledge

Law, J. (1991b). "Power, Discretion and Strategy". In J. Law (ed.), *A Sociology of Monsters? Essays on Power, Technology, and Domination* (pp. 165-191). London: Routledge.

Law, J. (2000). "Networks, Relationships, Cyborgs: on the Social Study of Technology" [Web Page]. URL http://www.comp.lancs.ac.uk/sociology/soc042jl.html [2004, January].

Law, J. (2001). "Ordering and Obduracy". Published by the Centre for Science Studies, Lancaster University, Lancaster, UK, [Web Page]. URL http://www.lancs.ac.uk/fss/sociology/papers/law-ordering-and-obduracy.pdf [2004, January].

Law, J. (2003). "Making a Mess with Method". Published by the Centre for Science Studies, Lancaster University, Lancaster [Web Page] URL http://www.comp.lancs.ac.uk/sociology/papers/Law-Making-a-Mess-with-method.pdf [2004, January].

Law, J., and Urry, J. (2002). "Enacting the Social". Centre for Science Studies and Sociology Department, Lancaster [Web Page] URL. http://www.comp.lancs.ac.uk/sociology/soc099jlju.html [2004, January].

Leigh, S. (1999). "The Freedom to Underwrite". In T. Sorell (ed.), *Health care, ethics and insurance.* (pp. 11-53). London: Routledge.

Lemmens, T. (2000). "Selective Justice, Genetic Discrimination and Insurance: Should We Single out Genes in our Laws?" *McGill Law Journal*, 45, 347-412.

Ling, T. (2000). *The Nuffield Trust Genetics Scenario Project. A Literature Review.* Public Health Genetics Unit.

Lippman, A., (1993). "Prenatal Genetic Testing and Geneticization: Mothers Matter for All", *Fetal Diagnosis and Therapy*, 8, 1, 175-188.
Lockyer, J. (1997). *Genetics, a first draft of the report by the Working Party of the Institute of Actuaries and Faculty of Actuaries*. London: Institute of Actuaries.
Lowden, J.A. (1998a). "The Legislative Perspective: Federal, State, Insurers and Industry - Underwriting Genetic Disease Risks". Paper presented to the American Medical Association Conference 1998 American Medical Association. [Web Page]. URL http://www.ama-assn.org/ama/pub/article/1880-2377.html. [01/2001]
Lowden, J.A. (1998b). "Underwriting Lethal Genetic Diseases". *Journal of Insurance Medicine*, 30 (1), 5-11.
Lowden, J.A. (1999). "Where is Genetics Taking Us? In Geneva Association, *Selected Papers from the Seminar on Genetics and Life/Health Insurance held in Paris, February 11-12, 1999* (pp. 45-52). Paris: Geneva Association.
Lowden, J.A., and Roberts, N. (1998). "A Genetic Testing Code of Practice for Insurers". *Journal of Insurance Medicine, 30* (1), 39-42.
Luhmann, N. (1996). "Modern Society Shocked by its Risks". Social Sciences Research Centre Occasional Paper 17, Hong Kong.
Lupton, D. (1993). "Risk as Moral Danger: The Social and Political Functions of Risk Discourse in Public Health". *International Journal of Health Services*, 23 (3), 425-35.
Lupton, D. (1994). *Medicine as Culture: Illness, Disease and the Body in Western Societies*. London: Sage.
Lupton, D. (1995). *The Imperative of Health: Public Health and the Regulated Body.* London: Sage.
Lynch, M. (2000). "Against Reflexivity as an Academic Virtue and Source of Privileged Knowledge". *Theory, Culture and Society*, 17 (3), 26-54.

MacDonald, A.S. (1999a). *Human Genetics and Insurance Issues*. (Report no. 3). Edinburgh: The Genetics and Insurance Research Centre, 11p.
MacDonald, A.S. (1999b). "Modeling the Impact of Genetics on Insurance". *North American Actuarial Journal*, 3 (1), 83-101.
MacDonald, A.S. (2001). "The cost of genetic information: how much, and who pays? Presented at Consultation meeting for Geneticists and Insurers UK Forum for Genetics and Insurance" (UKFGI) Monday 2 July 2001 [Web Page]. URL http://www.ukfgi.org.uk/02%2007%202001/2%20July%202001%20Full%20Summary%20PD.htm [2001].
MacDonald, A.S. (2003a). "Genetics and health costs: some actuarial models" [Web Page]. URL http://www.ma.hw.ac.uk/_angus/papers/vienna2.pdf [January, 2004].
MacDonald, A.S. (2003b). "Moratoria on the Use of Genetic Tests and Family History for Mortgage-Related Life Insurance". *British Actuarial Journal*, 9, 217-237.
MacDonald, A.S., and Pritchard D.J. (2001). "Genetics, Alzheimer's Disease and Long-Term Care Insurance". *North American Actuarial Journal*, 5 (2), 54-78.
MacNamara, J. (2001). "The Road to the Code: a UK Insurer's Genetics Odyssey". *AMS Bulletin*, March, 3-7.
Mast, J.L., and Gaubatz, D.L. (2000). "There's no substitute for experience studies". *Reinsurance Reporter*, 164, 4. [Web Page]. URL http//www.lincolnre.

com/eprise/main/lrepublications/Reporter/Issues/164/164_03.htm. [2001, January].
McGleenan, T. (1999). "Insurance, Genetics and the Law". In T. McGleenan, U. Wiesing, and F. Ewald (eds.) *Insurance and Genetics* (pp. 75-95). Oxford: BIOS Scientific Publishers.
McGleenan, T. (2001). *Insurance and Genetic Information*. London: Association of British Insurers (ABI).
Metcalfe, A. (1993). "Living in a Clinic: the Power of Public Health Promotions". *Anthropological Journal of Australia*, 4 (1), 31-44.
Miller, P., and Rose, N. (1993). "Governing Economic Life". In M. Gane, and T. Johnson (eds.), *Foucault's New Domains*. London: Routledge.
Mol, A. (1999). Ontological Politics. A Word and Some Questions. In J. Law, and J. Hassard (eds.), *Actor Network Theory and After* (pp. 74-89). Oxford: Blackwell Publishers.
Mol., A. (2002). "Cutting Surgeons, Walking Patients: Some Complexities Involved in Comparing". In J. Law, and A. Mol (eds.), *Complexities: Social Studies of Knowledge Practices* (pp. 218-257). Durham and London: Duke University Press.
Moore, P. (2002). "Testing Times Ahead". *The Scientist*, 26th September 2002. [Web Page]. URL http://www.biomedcentral.com/news/20020926/06/ [2004, January].
Moseley, R., and Allen, B. (1999). "What Does Genetic Technology Have To Do with Ethics? *North American Actuarial Journal*, 3 (1), 106-115.
Moultrie, T.A., and Thomas, R.G. (1996). "The Right to Underwrite? An Actuarial Perspective with a Difference". Presented at The Actuarial Society of South Africa Convention [Web Page]. URL http://www.guythomas.org.uk/pdf/rtu.pdf. [2004, January].

Nelkin, D., and Tancredi, L. (1989). *Dangerous Diagnostics: The Social Power of Biological Information*. New York: Basic Books Publishers.
Nowlan, W. (2000). "Genetic Testing Debate May Be Entering a New Era". *National Underwriter*, 31 January 2000. [Web Page]. URL http://www.nunews.com/archives/Lh_archive/2000/L01-31/L200005genetic.asp [2002, March 15].
Nowotny, H. (2003). "Dilemma of Expertise: Democratising Expertise and Socially Robust Knowledge". *Science and Public Policy*, 30 (3 June), 151-156.
Nowotny, H., Scott, P., and Gibbons, M. (2001). *Re-Thinking Science: Knowledge and the Public in an Age of Uncertainty*. Cambridge: Polity Press.
Nowotny, H., Scott, P., and Gibbons, M. (2003). "Introduction: 'Mode 2' Revisited: The New Production of Knowledge". *Minerva*, 41 (3), 179-194.
Nys, H. (1992). "Van afkomst naar toekomst? Juridische grenzen van erfelijkheidsonderzoek bij verzekeringen", *Bulletin des Assurances – Tijdschrift voor verzekeringen*, 299, 209-219.
Nys, H., Dreezen, I., Vinck, I., and Dierickx, K. (2002). *Genetic Testing: Patient's rights, insurance and employment – A survey of regulations in the European Union*, Luxembourg: Office for the Official Publications of the European Communities, EUR 20446.

O'Leary, T. (1998). "Genetics: A UK Code of Practice". *On the Risk*, 14 (1), March, 23-26.

Petersen, A. (1998). "The New Genetics and the Politics of Public Health". *Critical Public Health*, 8 (1), 59-71.

Petersen, A., and Bunton, R. (1997). *Foucault, Health and Medicine*. London: Routledge.

Petersen, A., and Lupton, D. (1996). *The New Public Health: Health and Self in the Age of Risk*. London: Sage.

Pokorski, R.J. (1995). "Genetic Information and Life Insurance". *Nature*, (376), 13.

Pokorski, R.J. (1997). "Medical Underwriting in the Genetics Era. Selected transactions of the international underwriting congress 1997". *Journal of Insurance Medicine*, 29 (2), 107-119.

Polanyi, M. (1958). *Personal Knowledge*. London: Routledge and Kegan Paul.

Pope, C. (2002). "Contingency in everyday surgical work", *Sociology of Health & Illness*, 24, 4, 369-384.

Porter, T.M. (1995). *Trust in Numbers: The Pursuit of Objectivity in Science and Public Life*. Princeton: Princeton University Press.

Porter, T.M. (2000). "Life Insurance, Medical Testing, and the Management of Mortality". In L. Daston (ed.) *Biographies of Scientific Objects* (pp. 226-246). Chicago: University of Chicago Press.

Power, M. (1997). *The Audit Society: Rituals of Verification*. Oxford: Oxford University Press.

PricewaterhouseCoopers. (2002). "The trust challenge: How the management of financial institutions can lead the rebuilding of public confidence" [Web Page]. URL http://www.pwcglobal.com/images/gx/eng/fs/121602eiubrief.pdf [2004, January].

Prior, L. (2001). "Rationing through Risk Assessment in Clinical Genetics: All Categories Have Wheels". *Sociology of Health & Illness*, 23 (5), 570-593.

Prior, L., Wood, F., Gray, J., Pill, R., and Hughes, D. (2002). "Making Risk Visible: the Role of Images in the Assessment of (cancer) Genetic Risk". *Health, Risk & Society*, 4 (3), 241-259.

Raman, S. (2003). "From uncertainty to indeterminacy: Implications for the politics of risk". Paper for Political Studies Association (PSA) Conference 2003, April 15-17, Leicester, UK.

Regenauer, A. (1998). "Medical Underwriting on the Eve of the Millennium". *Journal of Insurance Medicine*, 30 (4), 255-264.

Rose, N. (2000). "Governing Liberty". In R. Ericson and R. Stehr (eds.) *Governing Modern Societies*. (pp. 141-176). Toronto: University of Toronto Press.

Rose, N. (2002a). "At Risk of Madness". In T. Baker, and J. Simon J. (eds.), *Embracing Risk: The Changing Culture of Insurance and Responsibility* (pp. 209-237). Chicago: University of Chicago Press.

Rose, N. (2002b). *Lecture presented at the Postgraduate Forum on Genetics and Society*, 10 September 2002, Sidney Sussex College, Cambridge, UK.

Rouvroy, A. (2000). "Informations Génétiques et Assurance. Discussion Critique autour de la Position 'Prohibitioniste' du Législateur Belge". *Journal Des Tribunaux*, 119 (5978), 585-602.

Sandberg, P. (1995). "Genetic Information and Life Insurance: A Proposal for an Ethical European Policy". *Social Science & Medicine*, 40 (11), 1549-1559.

Scott, S., and Williams, G. (1991). Introduction. In S. Scott, G. Williams, S. Platt, and H. Thomas (eds.), *Private Risks and Public Dangers*. Avebury: Aldershot.

Sen, A. (1999). "Democracy as a Universal Value". *Journal of Democracy*, 10 (3), 3-17.

Shklar, J.N. (1990). *The Faces of Injustice*. New Haven and London: Yale University Press.

Simon, J. (1988). "The Ideological Effects of Actuarial Practices". *Law & Society Review*, 22, 771-800.

Sklaroff, S. (2001). "Genetic testing and insurance. Presented to the Human Genetics Commission information-gathering day on genetics and insurance, 9th February 2001, Royal Commonwealth Club, London, UK" [Web Page]. URL http://www.hgc.gov.uk/stephen.pdf [2003, July 4].

Skrabanek, P. (1994). *The Death of Human Medicine and the Rise of Coercive Healthism*. Social Affairs Unit London.

Slesenger, J. (1997). "All in the genes". *Post Magazine*, 23 January 1997, 30-31.

Smith, C. (1998). *Huntington's Chorea: a Mathematical Model for Life Insurance*. Zurich: Swiss Re Publications.

Smith, R. (2002). "In Search of 'Non-Disease'". *British Medical Journal*, 324 (7342), 883-885.

Society of Actuaries. (1997). "Session 111SM Risky Business: The Collision of Genetics and the Life Insurance Industry". Palm Desert Spring Meeting, May 21-23, 1997. *Record*, 23, 1, [Web Page] http://www.soa.org/library/record/1990-99/rsa97v23n1111sm.pdf [03/2001].

Society of Actuaries. (1999). "Session 100PD Medical Underwriting – A Retroperspective". San Francisco Annual Meeting, October 17-22, 1999. *Record*, 25, 3. [Web Page]. URL http://www.soa.org/library/record/1990-99/rsa99v25n3100pd.pdf. [03/2001].

Stone, D. (1993). "The Struggle for the Soul of Health Insurance". *Journal of Health Politics, Policy and Law*, 18 (2), 287-317.

Straub, R.E., Sullivan, P.F., Ma, Y., Myakishev, M.V., et al. (1999). "Susceptibility genes for nicotine dependence: a genome scan and follow-up in an independent sample suggest that regions on chromosomes 2, 4, 10, 16, 17, 18 merit further study". *Molecular Psychiatry*, 4, 129-144.

Strauss, A. (1993). *Continual Permutations of Action*. New York: Aldine de Gruyter.

Subramanian, K., Lemaire, J., Hershey, J.C., and Pauly, M.V. (1999). "Estimating Adverse Selection Costs From Genetic Testing for Breast and Ovarian Cancer: the Case of Life Insurance". *The Journal of Risk and Insurance*, 66 (4), 531-550.

Swiss Re. (1991). *Mortality and Extra Mortality*. Zurich: Swiss Re.

Swiss Re. (2002). *Life Underwriting Experience Study 2000. Mortality investigation based on data from the medical statistics of Swiss Re Zurich 1965-1996*. Zurich: Swiss Re.

Swiss Re. (n.d.) "Life and health reinsurance" [Web Page]. URL http://www.swissre.com [2003, September].

Tabarrok, A. (1994). "Genetic Testing: An Economic and Contractarian Analysis", *Journal of Health Economics*, 13, 1, 75–91.

Thévenot, L. (2002). "Which Road to Follow? The Moral Complexity of an "Equipped" Humanity." In J. Law, & A. Mol (eds.), *Complexities. Social Studies of Knowledge Practices* (pp. 53-87). Durham and London: Duke University Press.

UK Actuarial Profession. (2001). "Whose hands on our genes? Response from the UK Actuarial Profession to the Consultation Document issues by the Human Genetics Commission" [Web Page]. URL http://www.hgc.gov.uk/whoyg-consultation_responses/actuarial_profession.htm [2003, July 4].

"UK insurers grapple with an expected genetic moratorium". (2001). *Insurance Day*, 26 April 2001 [Web Page]. URL http://www.insuranceday.com [2002, June 3].

"UK treads carefully on issue of genetic testing". (1998). *Insurance Day*, 12 November 1998. [Web Page]. URL http://www.insuranceday.com [2002, June 3].

Van Gunsteren, R.H. (1998). *A Theory of Citizenship: Organising Plurality in Contemporary Democracies*. Boulder: Westview Press.

Van Hoyweghen, I. (2004). "Verzekeringen en genetica. De effecten van wetgeving". In G. de Vries and K. Horstman (eds.) *Genetica van laboratorium naar samenleving. De ongekende praktijk van voorspellende genetische testen* (pp. 118-139). Amsterdam: Aksant. ("Genetics and Insurance. The Effects of Legislation. In G. de Vries and K. Horstman (eds.) (2007). *Genetics from Laboratory to Society*. London: Palgrave Macmillan, forthcoming)

Van Hoyweghen, I., Schepers, R. and Horstman, K. (2005). 'Genetics is not the issue'. Insurers about Genetics and Life Insurance. *New Genetics & Society*, 24, 1: 81-100.

Van Hoyweghen, I., Horstman, K., and Schepers, R. (2006). Making the Normal Deviant. The Introduction of Predictive Medicine in Private Insurance. *Social Science & Medicine*, 63, 5, 1225-1235.

Van Rossum, A. (2004). "Ethics, Governance, Trust and Customer Relations". *The Geneva Papers on Risk and Insurance*, 29 (1), 52-55.

Vaughan, D. (1996). *The Challenger Launch Decision: Risky Technology, Culture, and Deviance at NASA*. London: University of Chicago Press.

Webster, A. (2002). "Innovative Health Technologies and the Social: Redefining Health, Medicine and the Body". *Current Sociology*, 50 (3), 443–457.

West, D. (1997). "Agents can wait on genetic test debate". *National Underwriter*, 03 November 1997. [Web Page]. URL http://www.nunews.com/archives/Lh_archive/1997/L11-03/0044gene.asp [2002, March 15].

Wet van 9 juli 1975 betreffende de Controle der Verzekeringsondernemingen. *Belgisch Staatsblad*, 29 July 1975.

Wet van 25 juni op de Landverzekeringsovereenkomst (LVO). *Belgisch Staatsblad*, 20 August 1992, 18283-18333.

Wet van 22 augustus 2002 betreffende de Rechten van de Patiënt. *Belgisch Staatsblad online*, 26 September 2002. URL http://www.lachambre.be/documents/1642/15.pdf [DBase]. Brussel: Ministerie van Justitie. [2003, July]

Wet van 25 februari 2003 ter Bestrijding van Discriminatie en tot Wijziging van de Wet van 15 februari 1993 tot oprichting van een Centrum voor gelijkheid van kansen en voor racismebestrijding. *Belgisch Staatsblad online*, 17 March 2003. [Dbase] Brussel: Ministerie van Justitie.

White, S. (2002). "Accomplishing 'The Case' in Paediatrics and Child Health: Medicine and Morality in Inter-Professional Talk". *Sociology of Health & Illness*, 24 (4), 409-435.
Williams, G. (1993). "Chronic Illness and the Pursuit of Virtue in Everyday Life". In A. Radley (ed.), *Worlds of Illness, Biographical and Cultural Perspectives on Health and Disease* (pp. 92-108). London: Routledge.
Wils, W.P.J. (1994). "Insurance Risk Classifications in the EC: Regulatory Outlook. *Oxford Journal of Legal Studies*, 14 (3), 449-467.
Wynne, B. (1996). "May the Sheep Safely Graze? A Reflexive View of the Expert-Lay Knowledge Divide". In S. Lash, B. Szerszinski, and B. Wynne (eds.), *Risk, Environment and Modernity: Towards a New Ecology* (pp. 44-83). London: Sage.

Zimmerman, S.E., and Meyer, R.B. (1998). "Genetic Testing Legislation: a Review of the past two years". *Journal of Insurance Medicine*, 30 (4), 265-266.

Index